TRAC 2002

Proceedings of the Twelfth Annual

THEORETICAL ROMAN ARCHAEOLOGY CONFERENCE

which took place at

The University of Kent at Canterbury
5–6 April 2002

edited by

Gillian Carr, Ellen Swift and Jake Weekes

Oxbow Books

Published by
Oxbow Books, Park End Place, Oxford OX1 1HN

ISBN 1 84217 100 3

This book is available direct from
Oxbow Books, Park End Place, Oxford OX1 1HN
(Phone: 01865-241249; Fax: 01865-794449)

and

The David Brown Book Company
PO Box 511, Oakville, CT 06779, USA
(Phone: 860-945-9329; Fax: 860-945-9468)

or from our web site

www.oxbowbooks.com

Printed in Great Britain by
The Short Run Press, Exeter

Contents

Preface iv

Seeking a material turn: the artefactuality of the Roman Empire
Andrew Gardner 1

An Empire in Pieces: Roman Archaeology and the fragment
Iain Ferris 14

Restoring ontological security: Roman and native objects in Early Roman Gallaecia
Alfredo Gonzalez-Ruibal 29

Transformations in meaning: amber and glass beads across the Roman frontier
Ellen Swift... 48

The Realm of Janus: Doorways in the Roman World
Ardle Mac Mahon 58

Deconstructing the Frampton Pavements: gnostic dialectic in Roman Britain?
Dominic Perring.. 74

Becoming consumers: looking beyond wealth as an explanation for villa variability
Chris Martins 84

Late Roman economic systems: their implication in the interpretation of social organisation
Paul Johnson 101

Creolisation, pidginisation and the interpretation of unique artefacts in early Roman Britain
Gillian Carr 113

Breaking Ground or Treading Water? Roman archaeology and constructive implications of the critique of meta-narratives
Stephanie Koerner... 126

A brief comment on the TRAC session dedicated to interdisciplinary approaches to the study of Roman women
Patricia Baker.. 140

Sex and the city: a biocultural investigation into female health in Roman Britain
Rebecca Redfern 147

Preface

The papers included in this volume are a selection of those offered at TRAC 2002. They illustrate a range of different theoretical approaches; one trend, though, is apparent; a wider engagement with interdisciplinary research, drawing theoretical ideas from many diverse fields of study, including philosophy, psychology, history of art, and consumer theory. The subject matter of the papers is similarly wide.

Andrew Gardner re-examines the relationship between humans and material culture in the Roman context, considering issues raised within recent debates in archaeology (as well as other disciplines) concerning agency. The paper looks at the materiality and intersubjectivity of human interaction; assessing the validity of universalist models of agency. Testing theory against specific artefactual examples, Gardner goes on to suggest frameworks for future research.

Iain Ferris discusses fragments of human bodies, from fragmentary statues and Roman busts and portrait heads, to anatomical *ex-votos* of eyes, sexual and internal organs, to depictions of beheaded individuals. Ferris looks for a pattern or trend represented by the fragmented images in terms of illuminating aspects of belief or value within Roman or Romanised societies which created and consumed such images, arguing that the *context* within which the images were used was the key to understanding them.

Alfredo Gonzalez-Ruibal takes a phenomenological approach to the study of Roman identities. He applies the philosophical ideas of Heidegger, specifically the question of 'Being' and the relationship between humans and objects, to both ancient and modern case studies: Roman Gallaecia in northwest Iberia, and Benishangul in present day Ethiopia. He suggests a new way to think about 'Romanization': as a process of dealing with uncertainty, and restoring and maintaining ontological security.

Ellen Swift considers artefactuality and cultural interaction with reference to dress accessories (in particular beads), which can be shown to be of 'Germanic' influence, but 'imported' into Late Roman contexts. The variant meanings of such 'Germanic inspired' objects found in burial contexts within the Roman empire are explored in relation to concepts of value and consumption, concluding that connections between the cultural style of objects and the cultural identity of the consumer should not be simply assumed.

Ardle Mac Mahon looks at the symbolic, ritual and spiritual significance of doorways into dwellings of the élite of the Roman empire, as emphasised by architectural embellishments to doorways, discussed here with reference to Pompeii and Herculaneum. Mac Mahon explains the significance of the transition over the doorway, which took place under the watchful gaze and domain of the god Janus.

Dominic Perring focuses on the dependence of current theory on the Classical heritage of Western ideas, arguing from this for the validity of a Hegelian reading (thesis, anithesis, synthesis) of the Frampton pavements. His paper puts forward a dialectical, Gnostic interpretation of the mosaic scheme which is suggested to represent a particular sequence: quest, mystery, and finally, revelation.

Chris Martins applies consumer behaviour theory to the subject of villa aggrandizement with reference sites in the east of Roman Britain in particular. Through a series of case studies, assumptions based on the conspicuous consumption model are challenged and further insights into consumer behaviour are drawn from psychological approaches; finally, a close connection between villa variability and the rise of individualism is postulated.

Paul Johnson looks at the relationship between social organisation and economic activity. Following a brief study of previous scholarship on the Roman economy, he suggests a new approach to its study based on the relationship between social practices and modes of distribution of goods. The use of a social framework within which to contextualise economic activity is illustrated through a case study of Late Roman Ostia.

Gillian Carr investigates the usefulness of the concept of creolisation, putting forward another, related linguistic metaphor – that of 'pidginisation' – to understand aspects of early Roman Britain, specifically, unique or 'pidgin' artefacts. As a 'pidgin' is the equivalent of the first generation of those who used what later became a 'creole', this concept might allow us to understand the first use of 'creolised' artefacts. Carr illustrates the concept of pidginisation here with reference to artefacts in the 'doctor's grave' at Stanway, Colchester.

Stephanie Koerner places the study of Roman Archaeology against a historical and philosophical background: that of the dominant meta-narratives of Western civilization. She focuses on the importance of the role played by the Roman Empire in the construction of historical and philosophical meta-narratives, and the implications for Roman archaeology of subsequent critiques. She then considers Roman archaeology's relevance to the future development of a constructive critique of meta-narratives.

Patricia Baker, in response to the surprising lack of interest shown in the session on 'Interdisciplinary approaches to Roman Women' held at TRAC in 2002, traces the development and significance of gendered approaches to Roman Archaeology. The paper goes on to offer suggestions as to how such studies might be improved; in particular, it is argued that the historic 'segregation' of women's studies is counter productive.

Rebecca Redfern looks at the health of women in Roman towns who suffered from a range of conditions, including infectious diseases caused by living in dense communities and in closely packed houses. Until a full comparison of health statuses between women in urban and in rural settlements has been made, the cause of ill-health of women living in towns cannot be shown to have been caused by urbanism; however, the main differences between rural and urban areas are through the modes of transmission and frequencies of disease only, not the diseases themselves.

We would like to thank the speakers who gave papers at TRAC 2002 and those who attended the conference and participated as session discussants. Thanks go to the organisers of the sessions: Patricia Baker, Ken Dark, Hella Eckhardt, Andrew Gardner, Stephanie Koerner, John Pearce, and Jake Weekes. Thanks also to the conference organisers, Patricia Baker, Gillian Carr, Ellen Swift, and Jake Weekes. We would also like to thank the willing and helpful cohort of student volunteers, staff in the Classical and Archaeological Studies Department of the University of Kent and UKC secretarial & technical staff including Charles Young, John Harris, Maureen Nunn, and Susan McLaughlin. Thanks also to UKC hospitality, Ken Reedie of Canterbury Museum, the Kent Institute for Advanced Studies in the Humanities, and the Archaeology Committee of the Roman Society. Finally we would like to thank the referees, and Val Lamb and David Brown of Oxbow Books.

Gillian Carr, Ellen Swift and Jake Weekes

Seeking a Material Turn: the artefactuality of the Roman empire

Andrew Gardner

Introduction: material culture and language

In this paper, my aim is to get closer to an understanding of the unique relationship between human beings and material culture. In so doing, I hope to offer a way of making the most of the major variations and changes in material culture that we see in the Roman world, and of directing our interpretations of these towards very broad problems. Recent debates on the theme of agency have served to bring the wider community of archaeologists closer to these kinds of problems, which have significant ethical and political implications in the contemporary world. One of the key themes in such debates has become the issue of whether one model of agency – such as that put forward by Anthony Giddens (1979, 1984) – is a universal schema appropriate for all people in all times and all places, or whether there are context-specific ways of defining persons and their powers. There is, as will be shown below, a good case for supporting the latter suggestion, and in what follows I wish to pursue the argument that different kinds of materiality are a significant factor in generating this variation. The Roman world is an excellent arena in which to explore this kind of problem, and indeed one which demands new ways of dealing with the many and varied kinds of social interaction taking place within it. The kind of approach discussed here does of course beg a question regarding the relative reality of different classifications of personhood. This I will put to one side at the outset with the assertion that all such categories are real insofar as they are socially consequential (cf. Jenkins 1996: 111), having real effects on the lives of human beings.

Before going in to a detailed consideration of the links between persons and materiality, it is worth summarising some of the major trends in the interpretation of material culture in the social sciences, particularly in relation to language. Within post-processual archaeology, material culture has rightly been treated as meaningfully-constituted (e.g. Hodder 1993: xvii). Understandably, in attempts to interpret this meaning-content, language has proved to be an important analogy, with structuralist, post-structuralist and hermeneutic approaches all based in ways of comprehending spoken or written language. Indeed, it can be argued that the relationship between material and linguistic meanings is more than merely analogical; that because thought is structured by language, so must any kind of meaning be likewise (Crossley 1996: 38–9). This is indeed true in many cases, but precisely because material culture often confounds our ability to describe it in language, it becomes necessary to consider ways in which it has significance in a non-linguistic sense (Hodder 1999: 74–7), and beyond this to suggest that these may in fact be extremely important – through processes of objectification, mediation or hybridisation – to the *intersubjective* constitution of human agency.

I will expand upon what I mean by intersubjectivity in the next section, but the general importance of non-linguistic or practical aspects of material culture meaning has indeed begun to come across in recent criticisms of the linguistic turn in archaeology. The idea of a linguistic turn – a move towards a dominant interest in the role of language in the creation of meaning – describes the impact of the theoretical trends referred to above on many disciplines, not least including history (Munslow 2000: 151–3). In archaeology, to grossly over-simplify, the early 1980s saw individuals like Ian Hodder and Christopher Tilley interested in structuralist analyses of Neolithic pottery decoration in, respectively, the Netherlands (Hodder 1982) and Sweden (Tilley 1984). These studies attempted to elaborate the underlying symbolic grammar of the material concerned, and to explore its relationship to social and cognitive structures.

From the later 1980s, and into the 1990s, this trend bifurcated, with Tilley, among others, working through the impact of post-structuralism on the writing of archaeological texts (Tilley 1989, 1991a; cf. Bapty and Yates 1990), and Hodder turning to the more arcane art of textual interpretation embodied in the hermeneutic tradition (1991a, 1991b; cf. Johnsen and Olsen 1992). The former undermined the determinacy of meanings by exposing the arbitrariness of associations between words and things, while the latter sought more purchase on textual ambiguity by emphasising the contextual interconnections of specific readings. By the late 1990s, Tilley had moved back to considering much more generalised linguistic concepts like metaphor, but giving them particular material expressions (1999), while Hodder and a number of others, including Matthew Johnson and John Moreland, have argued for overlapping but distinctive realms of material and linguistic meaning (Hodder 1999: 73–9; Johnson 1999: 31–2; Moreland 2001; cf. Gardner 2001a). A growing body of work on the social choices involved in technological processes constitutes another, largely separate strand of recent archaeological and anthropological research on material culture [e.g. Lemonnier (ed.) 1993].

Meanwhile, and based more squarely in anthropology, a new field of 'material culture studies' has been carved out, with Danny Miller a leading figure in promoting the understanding of the distinctive role of material culture in social life, albeit largely within the context of modern consumer societies (e.g. 1998, although cf. 1994; see also Attfield 2000; Schiffer 1999). Recently, this kind of approach has been taken up and extended in a sociological setting in Tim Dant's book *Material Culture in the Social World* (1999), in an attempt to redress the marginal position of material culture within that discipline. Overall, we now have an emerging cross-disciplinary synthesis [exemplified also by Graves-Brown (ed.) 2000], which stresses the ways in which spoken, written and material forms of meaning-communication overlap – for instance in the importance of context-specific readings – and in which they differ – as in the greater temporal extension of writing versus speaking, or the more practical or biographically-evocative meanings of things. This is a promising situation, and one to which Roman archaeologists, with access to a broad range of material of both written and unwritten kinds, have a lot to contribute. In focusing on materiality, we can, however, go even further, and address questions not just of how different kinds of meaning are constructed by people, but at how people are themselves constructed by their meaningful relations with the material – as well as the social – world around them.

Materiality and intersubjectivity

Such questions have not been entirely ignored by archaeologists (e.g. Thomas 1989; Tilley 1991b), but it is only now, in the context of the inter-disciplinary developments described above, that substantive progress in developing them further is a real prospect (cf. Thomas 2000). In this section, I will make some general comments about the kinds of issues involved, before using a couple of specific objects to elaborate upon these in the context of the Roman empire. Here I want to argue that human agency is not an innate feature of an isolated subject, detached from an object world (cf. Gero 2000: 37–8; Elliott 2001: 41), but rather that it is constituted in intersubjective relationships between people, partly constructed and mediated by things, such that both people and things can take on some of the properties of each other. This position extends, by virtue of its greater emphasis on objects as *material culture* (i.e. as culturally-laden artefacts), a long-established tradition of thought on human subjectivity, exemplified by the work of George Herbert Mead (1934; cf. McCarthy 1984), Alfred Schutz (1967), and Maurice Merleau-Ponty (1962 [2002]), and effectively summarised in Nick Crossley's recent book, *Intersubjectivity* (1996).

This tradition, which encompasses a range of diverse perspectives and within which a number of other thinkers could be included, shares a common rejection of subject–object dualism, and indeed overcoming this is the core issue at the heart of this paper. Just as the mind cannot be separated from the body in the manner that Descartes once desired, as both are combined in the perceiving, dwelling human subject (Crossley 1996: 25–9; Merleau-Ponty 1962 [2002]: 235–9), neither can such a subject be detached from the world of other subjects and objects within which it dwells, and with which it interacts in a range of different, and sometimes overlapping, ways. The importance of the relationships which a human subject sustains with the social and material elements of its world is such that its constitution as an agent (i.e. a knowledgeable actor) is dependent upon, and defined by, these relationships – by 'between-spaces' (Crossley 1996: 29). While 'intersubjectivity' describes this connectivity between people, the purpose of this paper is to show that things are a critical part of such networks, not least because "intersubjective relations are conducted in and by way of a physical environment" (Crossley 1996: 97).

Indeed, these kinds of 'between-ness' are also critical to broader aspects of human social life: "culture exists neither in our minds, nor does it exist independently in the world around us, but rather is an emergent property of the relationship between people and things" (Graves-Brown 2000: 4). From this point, it follows – importantly for archaeologists – that such a relational approach to breaking down the subject/object dichotomy allows us to accommodate cultural variation in the way that social selves are constructed. This kind of variation is well attested. Marcel Mauss, for instance, has charted the development of the concept of the unitary, free, individual persona through Roman and Christian Europe (1979: 78–94), and there are numerous anthropological studies highlighting differential constructions of the 'normal person', from the pueblos of south-western North America to China, with varying aspects of social connection (e.g. role, kinship) being emphasised over individuality (Carrithers et al. 1985; Hirst and Woolley 1982: 93–130; Mauss 1979: 59–77). The theme of the changing social definition of personhood, in a western context, also figures strongly in the work of Foucault on sexuality, discipline and other forms of social exclusion (e.g. 1967), Elias on the process of the 'civilization' of the western self (1939 [2000]), and Goffman, on social stigma (1963). In short, different cultures can have different ideas of what a normal person is – and indeed of what a person is – and I am arguing that these differences will necessarily involve relationships between people and things.

Igor Kopytoff has suggested as much in the sense that categories of things often relate to categories of people – that social and material typologies may be based on the same principles of hierarchy or identity (1986: 89–90; cf. Foucault 1970 [2002]; Miller 1994). On a more abstract level, however, we can argue that things play a fundamental role in structuring our intersubjective relations with either specific or generalised others (i.e. individuals or groups; Crossley 1996: 56, 97; Mead 1934: 154). There are a number of facets to this role, and I am going to focus on three: objectification, mediation, and hybridisation. Objectification itself can be thought of in a number of ways. In one sense, artefacts literally objectify social relations, evoking in a physical and often routinely-utilised form the identities and power relationships which structure the human social world (Miller 1994: 402–8; Strum and Latour 1987). In doing so, they make such relationships more 'real'; it is for this reason that artefacts are so important in the construction of ideologies (see e.g. Leone 1984).

In another sense, though, things provide one model for the relationship between embodied consciousness and both itself and that which is other (McCarthy 1984: 107–10). Physical things help to draw the infant self 'out of itself', and are critical in the development of the capacity of human beings to regard both themselves and others objectively, from the 'outside' (Crossley 1996: 49–59). It is in these circumstances that a division between subject and object *is* (artificially) created, but importantly the object in this relationship can be another person treated as a thing. There are many examples of situations in the present day where particular ethnic, gender or class groups have been politically subordinated through such processes of objectification, and slavery is one which also applies in the Roman world. The general process of self-alienation, though, need not be negative and while it may, concomitant with variable material and social technologies of the self, develop culturally-specific trajectories, in its earliest phases it is likely to be a ubiquitous feature of human socialisation (Crossley 1996: 57–68; cf. Williams and Costall 2000).

The mediating role of material culture is easier to grasp, and more clearly subject to cultural variation. Objects mediate between people in a range of ways, and in so doing are, along with language, essential to the way that selves are constructed in relation to others – i.e. to intersubjectivity (Crossley 1996: 58–9; Dant 1999: 153–75; Latour 2000; Mead 1934: 124–5). It is in this sense that material cultures communicate, and variation between them can have profound implications. This is true in the context of face-to-face interactions, but more obviously so for the range and scale of interactions which different technologies permit with wider groups of contemporaries, predecessors and successors (Crossley 1996: 88–92). These are the three broad communities of 'others' which Alfred Schutz distinguishes (1967: 176–214), and they are particularly amenable to archaeological investigations which pay close attention to spatial and temporal patterns. Different kinds of material culture promote different kinds of concrete contact between people in different locations in space and time, an obvious example being writing (cf. Giddens 1984: 200–1). Furthermore, the physicality and relative longevity of material culture, compared to speech (Miller 1994: 409–15), plays an important and distinctive role in allowing the imaginative interaction between individuals and distant others within an individual lifetime, evoking memory and anticipation.

A third way in which materiality is fundamental to intersubjective relations, and therefore to human agency, is through hybridisation with a subject (Urry 2000: 77–9; cf. Dant 1999: 124–7). In a sense this is a synthesis of the previous two points, whereby the identity of a human subject in its intersubjective relations becomes partly defined by particular kinds of object. This again involves the blurring of the categories of subject and object, as each takes on attributes of the other. John Urry (2000: 78) encapsulates this idea well: "machines, objects and technologies are neither dominant of, nor subordinate to, human practice, but are jointly constituted with and alongside humans." Material practices are essential to the successful performance of particular identities, and objects and people thus become mutually associated in the construction of individuals and groups, and of their power to act in the world (Gardner 2002). Schutz also touches on this point by stressing the importance of typifications in intersubjective relations (1967: 181–201). Interactions are frequently based on the stereotyping of an 'other' according to assumptions about their identity (Jenkins 1996: 122–3). Very often, these will be based on material things forming a hybrid with the human, like the belt-soldier or the toga-citizen. This process thus combines elements of the objectifying (reifying) and mediating (communicating) roles of material culture, in a way which is quite distinct from language.

The artefactuality of the Roman empire

There are a range of other general approaches to materiality that could be discussed, such as Heidegger's important work on building, and on the distinction between objects (equipment) being ready-to-hand (practically engaged with) or present-at-hand (discursively engaged with; 1962: 95–122; 1954 [1993]). However, I will focus on the ideas presented above, and illustrate these points with some examples of Roman material culture. In the presentation upon which this paper is based, I used actual artefacts to accompany this section, in an attempt to emphasise the physicality of things. In this printed version, the reader will have to make do with two-dimensional illustrations (Figs. 1 and 2), but perhaps the tangibility of this book can also convey some of the same general points about the complexity of our social relationships with material things, such as their mediating role, or their embeddedness in the biographies and identities of authors, publishers and readers (Dant 1999: 196–201; cf. Johnson 1999: 31–2). However, returning to material from the Roman period, the first artefact on which I would like to focus is a fragment of a mortarium (Figure 1). Pottery, certainly in the context of Britain during this period, presents quite a good example for exploring some of the more routinized aspects of human-material interaction.

It is certainly possible to envisage pottery as objectifying specific sets of social relations, as between producers, distributors and users, or between different kinds of users according to the identities – perhaps age, gender, status or locality – associated with cooking in a particular context, whether this be a farmstead kitchen or a military barrack room. Insofar as these relations will entail differences of power, this may be tangible in the materiality of the pot, yet embedded in routine and scarcely conscious practices. Thus the pot helps to reify – to make real – those specific relations of inequality for the people concerned. At the same time, and because it serves to draw the self into the between-space of the intersubjective world, the pot can mediate these relations in a more consciously-negotiated way, being discursively accorded specific cultural value by different individuals or groups. In certain contexts, for example, the pot may communicate the adoption of a new regime of dietary practices, valued as culturally exclusive by some and perhaps resisted by others (cf. Hawkes 2002).

This is something that is clearly likely to vary over the course of the Roman period in Britain, and change at different tempos in different areas, with phases of routinized use being interspersed with phases of discursively-contested fluctuation. Patterns of variability are certainly discernible in the archaeological data (Going 1992, Tyers 1996), and their contextual analysis in terms of practices like cooking and eating does, I would argue (Gardner 2002 cf. Hawkes 2001; Stallibrass 2000), permit us to consider periods of stasis and transformation in terms of these different kinds of meaningful relationship with material culture. In turn, these open up much more sophisticated interpretations of cultural change than simple paradigms like 'Romanisation', by allowing for greater variation in the cultural choices (passive or active, free or constrained) that people make in the ongoing process of bringing a particular social formation into being through material practices (cf. Barrett 2001: 152–7).

The multi-layered connection between materiality and temporality (in the form of continuity and change, or tradition and mobility – see below) becomes even more apparent by thinking about the pot when it is *not* present. One of the main changes that archaeologists recognise as being a significant element in the 'end' of Roman Britain is the disappearance of pottery manufactured in the kind of fashion exemplified by the piece illustrated in Figure 1. In an important and interesting paper, Nick Cooper (1996) has suggested that this may have had relatively limited cultural impact, as pottery was primarily used with only convenience in mind. I would have to argue, though, based on the theoretical position developed above, that such a material transformation, though it may certainly be less sudden than it appears to us, is necessarily significant. Highly routinized material practices are more, not less likely to be an important element in the structuration of social relations in late Roman Britain. Disruptions to such practices will be correspondingly traumatic (cf. Giddens 1984: 64), at the very least entailing a drastic reduction in the spatial and temporal scale of those relations. This in turn has potentially serious implications for the connections between individual persons and different kinds of wider community.

Indeed, it is precisely because the Roman world encompasses such dramatic shifts and transformations of materiality that it is worth studying in pursuit of differential constitutions of agency, insofar as these will involve material culture in the ways described above. Many of these changes are generated by the dynamics of Roman imperialism, which seem to entail the adoption, emulation or denial of quite specific and overt 'technologies of the self' (Foucault 1988; this phrase conveniently encapsulates the combined material and social influences on the formation of selfhood). These include things like transformations in body appearance and comportment associated with bathing, grooming, or becoming a Roman soldier (e.g. DeLaine 1999: 12–14; James 1999: 16–21). They also include technologies like writing, and this brings me to my second artefact (Figure 2).

Inscriptions are an extremely important feature of Roman material culture. They materialise one of the key linguistic technologies of the self – the personal name – which in the Roman world was clearly a culturally-charged label which encapsulated an individual's relationship with his or her contemporary community, ancestors, and successors (Hope 2000: 131–2). In other situations, religious dedications to personifications of institutions, ideas, and most importantly places of all kinds (Huskinson 2000: 7–8) indicate the complex interplay between subject and object in Roman culture. This entails a different kind of hybridisation than that which might be envisaged for the pot, between buildings or other material symbols and an anthropomorphic deity. All of these different conceptual relationships, between human or divine subjects, are made more 'real' or 'objective' (outside the self) by being carved into a stone.

Again, though, we come back to the variation which the Roman world encompasses as a source of interpretative leverage on a series of fundamental problems to do with personhood and agency. It is well known, for instance, that the 'epigraphic habit' was quite uneven in social, geographical, and temporal distribution (MacMullen 1982). In Britain, for instance, inscriptions on stone are found relatively rarely outside of military contexts (Mann 1985). To interpret this in terms of a failure of Romanisation is to drastically underestimate the range of roles that inscriptions, both in material form and conceptual content, might have played through their making and reading (cf. Miles 2000).

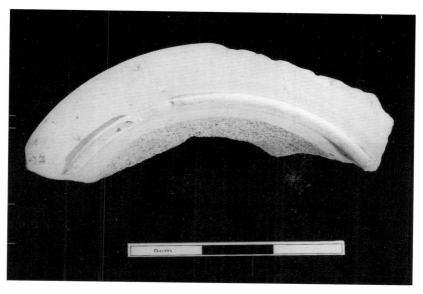

Figure 1. Fragment of a mortarium. Photograph taken by Stuart Laidlaw; published with the kind permission of Institute of Archaeology Collections (UCL).

Figure 2. Fragment of an inscription. Photograph taken by Stuart Laidlaw; published with the kind permission of Institute of Archaeology Collections (UCL).

At the very least, this difference in distribution speaks to the relations between insiders and outsiders in particular contexts, with soldiers from other parts of the empire perhaps driven to reinforce their identities more materially in unfamiliar environments; in a similar fashion, 'Britons' are commonly referred to as such primarily in *non*-insular contexts in later antiquity (Snyder 1998: 70–2).

I would argue, though, that we should explore even further, and consider whether the interaction between different social groups in the Roman world might have been structured by different technologies of the self. In considering the balance of factors defining agency, we should not just ask whether Roman soldiers, local elites or peasant farmers had different capabilities to affect the world based on their resources, but also on the extent to which they actually saw their place in the world in different ways. In the interpretation of slavery, to take a more extreme example, we need to try to explore how people who were conceived of as things responded to this categorisation, and how this response fits in with our ideas of agency. The modern western concept of the self may have its origins in the Roman period, as Mauss has argued (1979: 78–86), but in such a formative period, with competing models offered by slaves and free, or pagan and Christian, let alone those to be found in other cultural traditions across the empire, we must surely be ambitious in attempting to explore the relationships between self, agency, and materiality.

Conclusion: theoretical and ethical agendas for the 21ˢᵗ century

Materiality is, however, but one element in the constitution of agency. In this paper, I have tried to develop a theory of materiality which lays emphasis on three kinds of role – mediation, objectification, and hybridisation – that material culture plays in the formation of intersubjective relations, and to draw attention to the ways in which this might allow for cultural differences in the formation of the self. In order to capture more fully the complexity and variability of the constitution of agency, across the Roman world and beyond, two other dimensions have to be considered, with which materiality is intimately bound. These are temporality and sociality (Figure 3). Some reference has been made above to the first of these, and two key concepts which are of use in sensitising us to the social aspects of time are tradition (routine, reproduction, 'history') and mobility (movement, transformation; see Gardner 2001b).

These alternatives to the more abstract ideas of 'continuity' and 'change' reflect the importance of the temporal dimension in processes of structuration (Giddens 1984: 34–7), while emphasising the active ways in which humans engage with the ongoing flow of life as "repetition with variation" (Adam 1990: 53). Also considered in the foregoing paper have been some of the main aspects of social life ('sociality') which are central to the ongoing construction and reproduction of agency – not least the concept of intersubjectivity itself (cf. Barnes 2000: x). Beyond this, and as touched upon above, different social identities (negotiated in time through material practices) are a vital part of the relationship between agency and structure, allowing for the formation of collective agency ('community'; cf. Parker 2000: 106), and also for differentiation in power relations ('hierarchy'; see Gardner forthcoming). Taken together, these three concepts of materiality, temporality and sociality provide a powerful analytical framework for understanding the constitution of agency in different cultural contexts.

While this paper was originally presented as part of a session sub-titled 'theoretical agendas for the 21st century', the position developed here is not intended to be in any sense prescriptive. However, a couple of general points can be made which follow on from the discussion above that I would like to advocate more strongly. One of these is that Roman archaeologies, and specifically Roman archaeologies which are explicit about addressing theoretical concerns, need to be more adventurous.

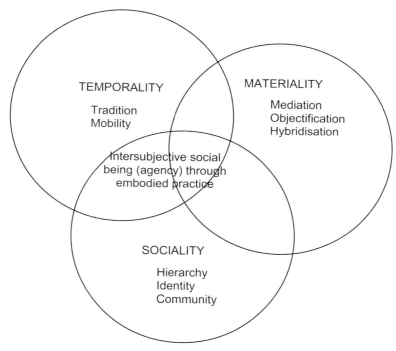

Figure 3. Multi-dimensional model of human agency, which allows for cultural variation in the construction of the constituent elements of materiality, temporality and sociality, through mechanisms like mediation, objectification and hybridisation.

To me, this means going beyond the 'add-social-theorist-and-stir' approach, which I have been as guilty of as anyone else in TRAC papers (e.g. Gardner 2001a). This is not to suggest that we stop reading outside the field – on the contrary, I believe in casting our nets as widely as possible to encourage the stimulation of new ideas. Rather, it is to advocate *writing* outside the field – considering to what debates the questions we ask are contributing. Understanding the Roman world is an important end, but it should not be an end in itself. As I hope to have demonstrated in this paper, there are a number of very fundamental debates in the human sciences to which archaeologies of this world can add a great deal.

This brings me to my second point. The potential of Roman studies lies not simply in what is perceived by Romanists and non-Romanists alike as a rich data-set, but also hinges upon more subtle relationships between past and present. In a range of scholarly and popular discourses about the Roman world, one frequently encounters the perception that the Romans were 'just like us' (e.g. Wilkinson 2000). This is often based on some of the more obvious technological elements of Roman life, like central heating, coined money, or the Latin alphabet. It is also possible, though, to discern formative stages in many of the social and philosophical ideas underpinning subsequent western culture within this period, particularly in the interaction between classical and Christian understandings of the world. As noted above, Mauss identifies this as precisely the context for the generation of the western 'self' (1979: 78–94), with Roman juridical practice bestowing rights and freedoms upon the individual, and Christian doctrine adding the rational moral conscience and the unitary soul. From these elements have been crafted the idea of a person as "a rational, indivisible, individual substance" (Mauss 1979: 86).

It is precisely these perceived and actual connections between Roman and later western culture that oblige us to look all the harder for the differences of the Roman world, for the alternative ways of thinking and ways of doing that speak to the complexity of the human condition, and which have since been subordinated to the dominant meta-narratives of the west. Such an agenda has significant ethical implications. Among the many contemporary debates surrounding issues of globalisation and multi-culturalism, one important question hangs over the validity of universalising models of humanity and agency, with their attendant universal morals, for dealing with the complex cultural encounters that are currently taking place. An understanding of human being which is believed to prevent discrimination can also flatten diversity. Such debates are complex, and ongoing (see e.g. Barnes 2000; Bauman 1993; Gero 2000). Archaeologists have much to contribute to them, and not only passively as the past is drawn upon by diverse identity groups with specific interests. In attempting to better understand the difference of the Roman past in terms of concepts like materiality and agency, we can adopt an actively critical – and therefore invigorating – stance on the present.

Institute of Archaeology, University College London.

Acknowledgements

The ideas presented in this paper are developments of work originally forming part of my doctoral thesis, and I owe a continuing debt to Mark Hassall, Richard Reece, Stephen Shennan, Jeremy Tanner, Simon James and Matthew Johnson for their roles in that project, which was funded by the AHRB. I am also grateful to Ian Carroll and Stuart Laidlaw for their assistance with the preparation of Figures 1 and 2, and have further benefitted from conversations with Stephanie Koerner, Bill Sillar and Steve Townend, and from the continued support of my other friends and colleagues at the Institute of Archaeology. Lastly, though by no means least, I would like to thank the editors and anonymous referee for their guidance in the preparation of this paper.

Bibliography

Adam, B. 1990. *Time and Social Theory*. Cambridge: Polity Press.

Attfield, J. 2000. *Wild Things: the material culture of everyday life*. Oxford: Berg.

Bapty, I. and Yates, T. 1990. *Archaeology After Structuralism: post-structuralism and the practice of archaeology*. London: Routledge.

Barnes, B. 2000. *Understanding Agency: social theory and responsible action*. London: Sage Publications.

Barrett, J. C. 2001. Agency, the duality of structure, and the problem of the archaeological record. In I. Hodder (ed.) *Archaeological Theory Today*. Cambridge: Polity Press. 141–164.

Bauman, Z. 1993. *Postmodern Ethics*. Oxford: Blackwell.

Carrithers, M., Collins, S. and Lukes, S. 1985. *The Category of the Person: anthropology, philosophy, history*. Cambridge: Cambridge University Press.

Cooper, N. J. 1996. Searching for the blank generation: consumer choice in Roman and post-Roman Britain. In J. Webster and N. J. Cooper (eds.) *Roman Imperialism: post-colonial perspectives*. Leicester: School of Archaeological Studies, University of Leicester. (Leicester Archaeology Monographs 3). 85–98.

Crossley, N. 1996. *Intersubjectivity: the fabric of social becoming*. London: Sage Publications.

Dant, T. 1999. *Material Culture in the Social World*. Buckingham: Open University Press.

DeLaine, J. 1999. Bathing and society. In J. DeLaine and D. E. Johnston (eds.) *Roman Baths and Bathing, Part I: Bathing and Society*. Portsmouth, RI: JRA Supplementary Series 37. 7–16.

Elias, N. 1939 [2000]. *The Civilizing Process*. Oxford: Blackwell. (Revised single volume edition, translated by E. Jephcott).

Elliott, A. 2001. *Concepts of the Self*. Cambridge: Polity Press.

Foucault, M. 1967. *Madness and Civilization: a history of insanity in the Age of Reason*. London: Tavistock Publications.

Foucault, M. 1970 [2002]. *The Order of Things: an archaeology of the human sciences*. London: Routledge.

Foucault, M. 1988. Technologies of the self. In L. H. Martin, H. Gutman and P. H. Hutton (eds.) *Technologies of the Self: a seminar with Michel Foucault*. London: Tavistock Publications. 16–49.

Gardner, A. 2001a. Identities in the late Roman army: material and textual perspectives. In G. Davies, A. Gardner and K. Lockyear (eds.) *TRAC 2000: Proceedings of the 10th Annual Theoretical Roman Archaeology Conference, London 2000*. Oxford: Oxbow Books. 35–47.

Gardner, A. 2001b. The times of archaeology and archaeologies of time. *Papers from the Institute of Archaeology*, 12: 35–47.

Gardner, A. 2002. Social identity and the duality of structure in late Roman-period Britain. *Journal of Social Archaeology*, 2.3: 323–351.

Gardner, A. forthcoming. Agency and community in 4th century Britain: developing the structurationist project. In A. Gardner (ed., in prep.) *Agency Uncovered: archaeological perspectives on social agency, power, and being human*. Accepted in principle for publication by Institute of Archaeology, UCL.

Gero, J. M. 2000. Troubled travels in agency and feminism. In M.-A. Dobres and J. Robb (eds.) *Agency in Archaeology*. London: Routledge. 34–39.

Giddens, A. 1979. *Central Problems in Social Theory: action, structure and contradiction in social* Press.

Giddens, A. 1984. *The Constitution of Society*. Cambridge: Polity Press.

Goffman, E. 1963. *Stigma: notes on the management of spoiled identity*. London: Penguin.

Going, C. J. 1992. Economic 'long waves' in the Roman period? A reconnaissance of the Romano-British ceramic evidence. *Oxford Journal of Archaeology*, 11.1: 93–117.

Graves-Brown, P. M. 2000. Introduction. In P. M. Graves-Brown (ed.) *Matter, Materiality and Modern Culture*. London: Routledge. 1–9.

Graves-Brown, P. M. (ed.) 2000. *Matter, Materiality and Modern Culture*. London: Routledge.

Hawkes, G. 2001. An archaeology of food: a case study from Roman Britain. In G. Davies, A. Gardner and K. Lockyear (eds.) *TRAC 2000: Proceedings of the 10th Annual Theoretical Roman Archaeology Conference, London 2000*. Oxford: Oxbow Books. 94–103.

Hawkes, G. 2002. Wolves' nipples and otters' noses? Rural foodways in Roman Britain. In M. Carruthers, C. van Driel-Murray, A. Gardner, J. Lucas, L. Revell and E. Swift (eds.) *TRAC 2001: Proceedings of the 11th Annual Theoretical Roman Archaeology Conference, Glasgow 2001*. Oxford: Oxbow Books. 45–50.

Heidegger, M. 1962. *Being and Time*. Oxford: Blackwell. (Translated by J. Macquarrie and E. Robinson).

Heidegger, M. 1954 [1993]. Building Dwelling Thinking. In D. F. Krell (ed.) *Martin Heidegger: Basic Writings*. San Francisco: Harper Collins. (Revised and expanded edition). 343–363.

Hirst, P. And Woolley, P. 1982. *Social Relations and Human Attributes*. London: Tavistock Publications.

Hodder, I. 1982. Sequences of structural change in the Dutch Neolithic. In I. Hodder, (ed.) *Symbolic and Structural Archaeology*. Cambridge: Cambridge University Press. 162–178.

Hodder, I. 1991a. *Reading the Past*. Cambridge: Cambridge University Press. (Second edition).

Hodder, I. 1991b. Interpretive archaeology and its role. *American Antiquity*, 56.1: 7–18.

Hodder, I. 1993. Bridging the divide: a commentary on Theoretical Roman Archaeology. In E. Scott (ed.) *Theoretical Roman Archaeology: first conference proceedings*. Aldershot: Avebury. (Worldwide Archaeology Series 4). xiii–xix.

Hodder, I. 1999. *The Archaeological Process: an introduction*. Oxford: Blackwell.

Hope, V. 2000. Status and identity in the Roman world. In J. Huskinson (ed.) *Experiencing Rome: culture, identity and power in the Roman empire*. London: Routledge/Open University. 125–152.

Huskinson, J. 2000. Looking for culture, identity and power. In J. Huskinson (ed.) *Experiencing Rome:culture, identity and power in the Roman empire*. London: Routledge/Open University. 3–27.

James, S. 1999. The community of the soldiers: a major identity and centre of power in the Roman empire. In P. Baker, C. Forcey, S. Jundi and R. Witcher (eds.) TRAC 98: *Proceedings of the 8th Annual Theoretical Roman Archaeology Conference, Leicester 1998*. Oxford: Oxbow Books. 14–25.

Jenkins, R. 1996. *Social Identity*. London: Routledge.

Johnsen, H. and Olsen, B. 1992. Hermeneutics and archaeology: on the philosophy of contextual archaeology. *American Antiquity*, 57.3: 419–436.

Johnson, M. 1999. Rethinking historical archaeology. In P. P. A. Funari, S. Jones and M. Hall (eds.) *Historical Archaeology: back from the edge*. London: Routledge. (One World Archaeology 31). 23–36.

Kopytoff, I. 1986. The cultural biography of things: commoditization as process. In A. Appadurai (ed.) *The Social Life of Things*. Cambridge: Cambridge University Press. 64–91.

Latour, B. 2000. The Berlin key or how to do words with things. In P. M. Graves-Brown (ed.) *Matter, Materiality and Modern Culture*. London: Routledge. 10–21.

Lemonnier, P. (ed.) 1993. *Technological Choices: transformation in material cultures since the Neolithic*. London: Routledge.

Leone, M. P. 1984. Interpreting ideology in historical archaeology: using the rules of perspective in the William Paca Garden in Annapolis, Maryland. In D. Miller and C. Tilley (eds.) *Ideology, Power and Prehistory*. Cambridge: Cambridge University Press. 25–35.

MacMullen, R. 1982. The epigraphic habit in the Roman empire. *American Journal of Philology*, 103: 233–246.

Mann, J. C. 1985. Epigraphic Consciousness. *Journal of Roman Studies*, 75: 204–206.

Mauss, M. 1979. *Sociology and Psychology: essays*. London: Routledge & Kegan Paul. (Translated by B. Brewster).

McCarthy, E. D. 1984. Toward a sociology of the physical world: George Herbert Mead on physical objects. *Studies in Symbolic Interaction*, 5: 105–121.

Mead, G. H. 1934. *Mind, Self, and Society, from the standpoint of a social behaviorist*. Chicago: University of Chicago Press. (Edited with an Introduction by C. W. Morris).

Merleau-Ponty, M. 1962 [2002]. *Phenomenology of Perception*. London: Routledge. (Translated by C. Smith; Routledge Classics edition).

Miles, R. 2000. Communicating culture, identity and power. In J. Huskinson (ed.) *Experiencing Rome: culture, identity and power in the Roman empire*. London: Routledge/Open University. 29–62.

Miller, D. 1994. Artefacts and the meaning of things. In T. Ingold (ed.) *Companion Encyclopedia of Anthropology: humanity, culture and social life*. London: Routledge. 396–419.

Miller, D. 1998. Why some things matter. In D. Miller (ed.) *Material Cultures: why some things matter*. London: UCL Press. 3–21.

Moreland, J. 2001. *Archaeology and Text*. London: Duckworth.

Munslow, A. 2000. *The Routledge Companion to Historical Studies*. London: Routledge.

Parker, J. 2000. *Structuration*. Buckingham: Open University Press.

Schiffer, M. B. (with A. R. Miller) 1999. *The Material Life of Human Beings: artifacts, behavior, and communication*. London: Routledge.

Schutz, A. 1967. *The Phenomenology of the Social World*. Evanston, IL: Northwestern University Press. (Translated by G. Walsh and F. Lehnert).

Snyder, C. A. 1998. *An Age of Tyrants: Britain and the Britons AD 400–600*. Stroud: Sutton Publishing.

Stallibrass, S. 2000. Cattle, culture, status and soldiers in northern England. In G. Fincham, G. Harrison, R. R. Holland and L. Revell (eds.) *TRAC 99: Proceedings of the 9th Annual Theoretical Roman Archaeology Conference, Durham 1999*. Oxford: Oxbow Books. 64–73.

Strum, S. S. and Latour, B. 1987. Redefining the social link: from baboons to humans. *Social Science Information*, 26: 783–802.

Thomas, J. 1989. Technologies of the self and the constitution of the subject. *Archaeological Review from Cambridge*, 8.1: 101–107.

Thomas, J. 2000. Reconfiguring the social, reconfiguring the material. In M. B. Schiffer (ed.) *Social Theory in Archaeology*. Salt Lake City: University of Utah Press. 143–155.

Tilley, C. 1984. Ideology and the legitimation of power in the middle Neolithic of southern Sweden. In D. Miller and C. Tilley (eds.) *Ideology, Power and Prehistory*. Cambridge: Cambridge University Press. 111–146.

Tilley, C. 1989. Interpreting material culture. In I. Hodder (ed.) *The Meanings of Things: material culture and symbolic expression*. London: Harper Collins Academic. 185–194.

Tilley, C. 1991a. *Material Culture and Text: the art of ambiguity*. London: Routledge.

Tilley, C. 1991b. Materialism and an archaeology of dissonance. *Scottish Archaeological Review*, 8: 14–22.

Tilley, C. 1999. *Metaphor and Material Culture*. Oxford: Blackwell.

Tyers, P. A. 1996. *Roman Pottery in Britain*. London: Batsford.

Urry, J. 2000. *Sociology Beyond Societies: mobilities for the 21st century*. London: Routledge.

Wilkinson, P. 2000. *What the Romans Did for Us*. London: Boxtree.

Williams, E. and Costall, A. 2000. Taking things more seriously: psychological theories of autism and the material-social divide. In P. M. Graves-Brown (ed.) *Matter, Materiality and Modern Culture*. London: Routledge. 97–111.

An Empire in Pieces. Roman Archaeology and the Fragment

Iain Ferris

Artemidorus of Daldis, writing in the second century AD, in a work concerned with the recording and interpretation of dreams, described how "a man dreamt that he went into a gymnasium in his home town, and saw his own portrait actually hanging up there. Then he dreamt that the whole frame surrounding the picture disintegrated. When another man asked him what had happened to his portrait, he seemed to say: 'There is nothing wrong with my portrait, but the frame is broken'. Unsurprisingly he went lame in both feet: for the gymnasium symbolised the good health of his entire body, while the portrait represented the area around his face, and the frame surrounding it meant the other parts of his body." (Artemidorus *Oneirocritica* 5.3).

Our evidence for the past is all too often fragmentary, broken, damaged, or incomplete. Archaeological practice dictates that we reconstruct the past from these fragments, that we study the parts in order to understand the whole. Sometimes, when fragments are seen to be out of place in the archaeological record or their presence is perhaps too awkward to explain, we argue away that presence with terms such as residuality or contamination. However, in the Roman world the fragment or partial object or image itself was on occasions considered to represent the whole. Busts and portrait heads represented the whole person (Barr-Sharrar 1987) (Figure 1). Anatomical *ex votos* at healing shrines and sanctuaries represented the diseased whole body, or sometimes the cured whole body, of visitors to these sites (van Straten 1981; Ferris 1999). Hollow cuirasses and arms and armour hung on trophies in Roman art represented the absent bodies of defeated enemies (Picard 1957; Ferris 2000: 19–21). The process of fragmentation itself, as well as the manipulation and use of the fragment, may also have been a significant act in some circumstances in this period. Any analysis of fragmentation and the use of the fragment will encompass ideas relating to the human body, as it does here specifically, but it could equally be extended and applied to the study of artefacts and their creation, consumption, manipulation and discard.

Lynda Nead in her ground-breaking reanalysis of the place of the female nude in the history of western art asked whether there had not been for many, mostly male, art historians an allure codified within the broken female images from classical antiquity, such as the Venus de Milo, that related specifically to their fragmented and incomplete state. This aestheticization of the fragment, as she termed it (Nead 1992: 79), may have been driven by a subconscious desire to reconstruct such partial images, almost perhaps to fetishise them. Whether this fulfilled a deep-seated need within these art historians, as she suggests, is open to question. Her equation of this need to that of a child wanting to recreate its mother as a whole person, having at first viewed her as being made up of disassembled individual body parts, is based on theories first proposed by Melanie Klein (for a Kleinian view of the Neolithic see Ellis 2001). Page Dubois (1966: 55) has written about the "desire, fear, pleasure we feel" in relation to studying fragments from the past, so this is not obviously a problematic stance relating simply to the male psyche.

Figure 1. Portrait bust of unknown Roman male. Museo del Palazzo dei Conservatori, Rome. (Photo: I.M. Ferris)

Of course, modern sensibilities with regard to accidentally broken ancient artworks or those damaged through iconoclasm are not principally the issues under discussion here, interesting though they undoubtedly are (Nylander 1998).

Rather, this paper will consider the conceptual principles behind the medium of the representation of the human body as fragments or as partial figures, and how these principles can perhaps be identified and isolated in Roman art and archaeology, with an apparent differential application or acceptance of these principles discernible in different parts of the Roman world at different times and in different contexts.

Theorising the fragmented body is an undertaking that must rely heavily on the work not only of archaeologists, but also of ancient historians and classical art historians who have for some years been concerned with exploring the idea of the body, much in the same way that studies of gender in the Roman world have benefited from a similar uniting of our fragmented discipline.

Figure 2. The so-called Barberini togatus statue, Museo del Palazzo dei Conservatori, Rome. Photo: Faraglia DAIR 37.378

Recently Mary Beard and John Henderson (Beard and Henderson 2001: 207) have noted in their volume on classical art in the Oxford History of Art series that "it was an emphatically Roman, rather than Greek, drive to surround available living-space with armies of abbreviated figures of prestige-heads or busts; and to leave the western world with a collective acceptance of the convention of representing persons from the neck up." Although this is not an original observation, it is interesting that this Roman innovation is still deemed worthy of comment in this way.

Beard and Henderson (2001: 230–232) go on to discuss the possible origins of this Roman predilection for portraits and suggest its positioning within a cultural milieu that encouraged this development into a wider social phenomenon than the funerary context in which it is thought to have first appeared. Does it really logically follow, though, as they suggest and had been earlier suggested by J.J. Pollitt (1993: 224), that the creation of the new medium of the Roman portrait bust naturally grew from a desire on the part of Roman aristocrats to have more durable representations of their ancestors' images than was represented by the *imagines* or wax ancestor masks attested by historical sources but absent in the archaeological record?

The use of such masks or ancestors' images (Rambaud 1978; Dupont 1987; Flower 1996) was described by the Greek historian Polybius in the second century BC, when he wrote that "they place a portrait of the deceased in the most prominent part of the house, enclosing it in a small aedicular shrine. The portrait is a mask which is wrought with the utmost attention being paid to preserving a likeness in regard to both its shape and its contour. Displaying these portraits at public sacrifices, they honour them in a spirit of emulation, and when a prominent member of the family dies, they carry them in the funeral procession, putting them on those who seem most like [the deceased] in size and build." (Polybius *Historiae* 6.53). Pliny in his Natural History of the mid-first century AD (Pliny *Naturalis Historia* 35.6–7) also made mention of such masks and their display in the *atria* of Roman houses (Dwyer 1982). As Harriet Flower has pointed out (Flower 1996), these wax images would all have been of male ancestors, given that they were allowed to be made only for those who had held the office of *aedile* or higher, roles reserved exclusively for men.

The so-called Barberini *togatus* statue represents one of the most significant and important pieces of evidence for the way in which fragmentary representations, in this case in the form of ancestral busts, may have been used (Figure 2). Though restored, with another ancient portrait head grafted onto the original statue's shoulders, the work is otherwise complete and portrays a togate male, his clothes marking him out as a member of the Roman elite, standing in an upright pose with a portrait bust of a man held in each hand. The busts face forward and the viewer's gaze is invited to move between the faces of the two busts and that of their owner in an almost triangular movement. There is a sense of anticipation in the piece, as if the man is about to join a procession or walk into a room. As has been pointed out by both Harriet Flower and Diana Kleiner (Flower 1996: 5–6 and 10; Kleiner 1992: 36) the male figure is holding portrait busts probably modelled in terracotta, and is not holding *imagines*, images in the form of wax masks of dead ancestors who had held magisterial office, as they have been incorrectly identified by a number of authorities in the past. Such busts could have been kept in the home, like the *imagines*, or have been placed in burial *columbaria*, like the three busts, two male and one female, found *in situ* in the *columbaria* of Vigna Codini in Rome (Della Portella 1999: 128). Flower stresses the point that the wax *imagines* were never intended to be placed in tombs in this way.

In the Greek world the representation of a head without a body was largely confined to the herm, with a head on top and a phallus at the front. Two-dimensional images of heads or busts appeared on coins after Alexander and on late Hellenistic gems. The Roman infatuation with the head or bust representing the whole body may have been a visual manifestation, as Janet Huskinson has suggested, of "the ancient study of physiognomics which related physical features to moral traits, making the body, and especially the face, an image of the whole person" (Huskinson 2000: 157), although this does not altogether tie in with the story about one individual's perception of the significance of his portrait recorded by Artemidorus of Daldis and alluded to above. More widely, the bodies of Roman statues sometimes acted simply as 'props' for the heads which were often carved separately (Kleiner 1992: 10).

Even within the field of the conception of whole bodies as portrait busts there were changes in Roman art in terms of what constituted a bust. Pollitt has noted (1993: 249) that while originally portrait busts had included just the head, neck and part of the shoulders, in the later first century AD more of the shoulders and the chest were included in some depictions. Of course, the portrait bust came to be copied in other media in two dimensions, on mosaics and gemstones for instance and on coins, though the cropping of other types of human image by framing or by the bleeding of images into the frames did not occur.

Interestingly, though, some of these new uses of portrait busts and heads were confined to funerary contexts. Roman freedmen reliefs with rows of portrait busts, including women and sometimes children, became fashionable in the Augustan period, based on Republican forerunners then reserved for the tombs of the aristocracy (Walker 1985: 45–46) (Figures 3–5). It was also relatively common on children's sarcophagi of the first to fourth centuries to have a portrait bust of the dead child framed and confined within a *clipeus* (see, for instance, Huskinson 1996, nos. 6.33, 8.15 and 9.36). Away from Rome and Italy, perhaps the most interesting group of material is the so-called Fayum encaustic portraits attached to the mummified bodies of those men and women depicted. The earliest of these date to the first half of the first century AD and mark a firm break with previous Egyptian burial rites (see, for instance, Doxiadis 1995). Local forms also appeared at Palmyra, in the shape of funerary reliefs of portrait busts (see, for instance, Vermeule 1981, nos. 329–333), and in Cyrenaica (Libya) where miniature bust portraits were set in niches in rock-cut tombs (Walker 1995: 82).

Links between the Roman funeral and the Roman triumph have been pointed out by John Bodel (1999), amongst others, who noted that such links were even thought worthy of comment in Roman times. At triumphs "missing persons were represented by realistic portraits" (Bodel 1999: 261), in the same way that the absent deceased ancestors were represented by the *imagines* in funeral processions or later by busts and other portraits at the burial place.

Highly symbolic in this context is the treatment meted out to the Dacian king Decebalus after his suicide, ahead of his imminent capture by Roman military forces. He was subsequently beheaded and his right hand was chopped off, these gruesome trophies then presumably being somehow preserved, to allow them to be taken to Rome to be paraded in Trajan's triumph to mark the end of the Dacian Wars, when Decebalus' head is recorded as being thrown onto the Gemonian Steps. This incident, together with other incidents of headhunting depicted on Trajan's Column, marks a perverse blurring of the boundaries between image and reality, between the whole and the fragment, between the living and the dead (Ferris 2000: 80–81).

But it is not only heads that were treated as separate parts in this way in Roman art, and indeed this treatment of the head may be part of a more complex phenomenon. Both Richard Brilliant and Diana Kleiner (Brilliant 1963: 26–31; Kleiner 1992: 10 and 34) have referred to the 'appendage aesthetic', a phrase used to describe a trend in first Etruscan sculpture, and then in Roman sculpture, towards the singling-out and overemphasising of a particular part of the body of a sculpture, the best examples of which are probably the orator or *Arringatore* statue of Aulus Metullus of c. 90–70 BC, with his exaggeratedly and unfeasibly oustretched arm (Figure 6), and the Prima Porta statue of Augustus, again with an outstretched arm that appears to have some independent existence away from the body to which it is attached (Nodelman 1975: 15–16).

Figure 3. Grave relief of unknown freedmen. Museo Romano di Brescia. (Photo: I.M. Ferris)

There may certainly be some links between Etruscan and Italian belief systems and later Roman practices (Gazda 1973; Damgaard Andersen 1993). Stefano Bruni (2000: 368–369) has discussed a specific link between death rites and artistic representation at Vulci in the seventh century BC when composite statues made up of assembled parts, often made in different materials, appeared. These "recompose the image of the deceased, which is 'de-structured' as a result of the particular treatment to which the body was submitted" (Bruni 2000: 369), in this instance cremation. "They give monumental expression to the same ideology as that expressed by the sealed cinerary urns with lids in the form of the human body, which were typical of this area from the last quarter of the eighth century to the middle of the seventh century BC".

The art historian Linda Nochlin, in her published lecture 'The Body in Pieces. The Fragment as a Metaphor of Modernity' (1994), has explored the way in which the conscious manipulation of the fragment or the fragmentary was a recurring trend in certain schools of painting from the end of the eighteenth century onwards. While she was careful not to claim that her isolated and discrete chosen case studies constituted a generalised situation or a regular trajectory of intent, she nevertheless felt that together they at least constituted a model of difference, and that two main trends could be differentiated, one in which the fragment played a ritualistic or psychosexual role, as sacrifice or fetish, and the other in which it maintained a rhetorical role as metonymy or synecdoche (Nochlin 1994: 56).

Figure 4. Grave relief of freedman and family members. Museo Nazionale, Ravenna. (Photo: I.M. Ferris)

Figure 5. Grave relief of Roman family group. Museo del Palazzo dei Conservatori, Rome. (Photo: I.M. Ferris)

Nochlin discussed occasions during the French Revolution in which "both outright vandalism" and a kind of "recycling of the vandalised fragments of the past for allegorical purposes" (Nochlin 1994: 8) took place. "The imagery-and the enactment-of destruction, dismemberment and fragmentation remained powerful elements of Revolutionary ideology at least until the fall of Robespierre in 1794 and even after" (Nochlin 1994: 10). Underlying what simply may be viewed as iconoclasm were several sets of deeply felt tensions – between the act and action, between image and reality, and between tradition and modernity.

Tellingly, towards the end of her lecture, Nochlin declared that "it is by no means possible to assert that modernity may only be associated with, or suggested by, a metaphoric or actual fragmentation. On the contrary, paradoxically, or dialectically, modern artists have moved towards its opposite, with a will to totalisation." (Nochlin 1994: 53). This struggle to attempt to bring forth order out of a perceived social, physical, or political chaos suggests that the fragment can be seen as both a positive and a negative trope. But is the "sense of social, psychological and even metaphysical fragmentation" merely a marker for modern experiences? – "a loss of wholeness, a shattering of connection, a destruction or disintegration of permanent value" (Nochlin 1994: 23–24) – (and for modern urban life in particular, with its concomitant desire for a return to the whole?) Or is it possible to pursue this question, though not perhaps to answer it, through examination of a number of archaeological contexts of the Roman period?

Turning away from the subject of busts and heads, consideration will now be given to other disassociated body parts in the form of what are known as anatomical *ex votos*, models or representations of body parts dedicated principally at healing shrines or sanctuaries throughout the Graeco-Roman world, though with perhaps significant chronological, geographical and representational variations. Creation and use of such *ex votos* possibly had independent origins in Greece and the Italian regions of Etruria and Latium in the fifth and fourth centuries BC (van Straten 1981). In Italy the dedication of anatomical *ex votos* had become a less common custom by the first century BC, though it does occur as a manifestation of Graeco-Roman practice at numerous sites elsewhere within the empire well beyond this date, of which the Gallo-Roman healing shrine of *Fontes Sequanae* at the Source of the Seine, near Dijon, represents one of the best published examples.

Simone Deyts, in one of her studies of the remarkable collection of dedicated *ex votos* and statuary from the site (Deyts 1994: 15), has tabulated and quantified the occurrence here of different kinds of representation in different types of material, that is stone, bronze, pipeclay and wood, and compared this assemblage with those from other healing sanctuaries.

At the Sources de la Seine there is a large number of representations of what might best be termed here, awkward though it is, whole people, a total of 97–102 men, women, unsexed representations and swaddled infants. There are 212 busts and heads, 172 torsos and pelvises, 57 internal organs, 149 legs and feet, 54 hands and arms, 119 eyes, a ratio of body parts to whole people of *c.* 7:1. At the other three sites quantified by Deyts, that is Alesia, Essarois and Halatte, ratios of body parts to whole people are respectively 200:1, *c.* 11:1 and *c.* 2:1.

Anatomical *ex votos*, along with other categories of *ex votos* dedicated at religious sites, signify the making of a contract between a man or woman and their gods, in this case related to petitions for the restoring of health to a sick individual through divine intervention. Every type of *ex voto,* anatomical or otherwise*,* through purchase or commissioning and by dedication relates to an individual person. Anatomical *ex votos* obviously and very specifically relate to that individual's body and in many cases to highly specific parts of that body. The sick in the Graeco-Roman world have been described by the medical historian H.E. Sigerist (1977: 390–391) as being viewed as temporarily or permanently stigmatised, depending on the nature or duration of their illness. Seeking a cure for the sick body was not only linked to issues of personal health, it was also a way of seeking reintegration back into society. The special tension inherent in many assemblages of *ex votos* between emotion and feeling on the one hand, representing self, and documentation on the other, mirroring their time of creation, is somewhat allayed by the overall sense of structural order in the way they were used.

In a paper delivered at a previous TRAC conference in 1993 I considered the use of anatomical *ex votos* in Roman Britain, and concluded that the number of these so far recovered by excavation at various religious sites was extremely small, compared to numbers recovered in other areas such as Gaul, though, of course, no strictly comparable sites to the Sources de la Seine have been identified or excavated in Britain (Ferris 1999). Indeed, I identified a trend towards the customisation of other artefacts to create anatomical *ex votos* rather than there being an industry making these items to order.

Perhaps such items were not particularly regarded by Romano-Britons as acceptable parts of the religious rites at healing shrines, and, indeed, it might be suggested that a reason for this could be a failure on their part to engage in mental strategies of disassembling bodies into body parts, as was required as part of the process. Following on from this, an examination of the published volumes of the *Corpus Signorum Imperii Romani* volumes for Britain suggests that busts and portrait heads, in other words representations of whole individuals by partial portrayals, are again not well represented among the art from Roman Britain. Does all of this imply that the fragmented image and the concepts behind it were anathema to most of the people of Roman Britain? If so, this would appear to represent a perhaps significant difference in perceptions of both the individual and the body, and the role of art in articulating such perceptions between Roman Britain and other parts of the empire.

Figure 6. Bronze statue of Aulus Metullus, the 'Arringatore'. Museo Archeologico, Florence. (Photo: Koppermann. DAIR 62.40)

Another artistic innovation of the Roman period was the use of what is called continuous narrative, but which might be better called simultaneity, which, by displacing time, fragmented human experiences and turned disparate events into actions all apparently happening simultaneously, though not in what would have appeared to the viewer as real time. The images of individuals replicated in adjacent scenes become fragments of the one, same body; they once more become something other than the corporeal body. While Trajan's Column in Rome is perhaps the best known example of this style of narrative, with multiple Trajans adorning the relief spiral scrolls around the column shaft, another interesting example is provided by the legionary distance slab from Bridgeness on the Antonine Wall in Scotland. I have discussed this scene at length elsewhere (Ferris 1994 and 2000) and here will only briefly draw attention to the appearance of what is intended to be an image of the same individual barbarian appearing four times in a single scene. His Roman opponent, a cavalryman in this case, appears only once. The barbarian is first knocked over by the charging horse, he then drops or throws away his shield and sword, he then sits in a mourning pose, lamenting his defeat and awaiting capture, and he then appears, quite literally, in fragments, beheaded, doubtless by his Roman captors.

In its ability to defy linear or sequential time, to allow a version of the past sometimes to coexist with the present, continuous narrative, often when used as a technique on imperial and military monuments, contradicted the concept of reality being defined by physical and visible phenomena alone, and dealt with a reality from which fragmentary elements could be selected and reorganised to form a new visible representation of the whole.

It is suggested that collage theory, as well as the study of modernist approaches to the use and definition of the significance of the fragment and of the partial image, as exemplified by the work of Nochlin discussed previously, has a considerable relevance to the study of the fragment and fragmentation both of images and of time. Underpinning the theoretical basis of the arts of collage and assembly as defined by Kurt Schwitters in the first quarter of the twentieth century, was the process he called, using a self-created word, *Entformung*, a process involving, through assembly, both the metamorphosis and the dissociation of fragmentary or fragmented objects and materials which he viewed as possessing what he called *Eigengift*, that is "their own special essence of poison" (Elderfield 1985: 51), which would be lost during, and as a result of, their *Entformung*. The intention was not that these materials would now function as if they were transformed into some other kind of material, rather that they now formed part of a new whole.

To conclude, theorising the fragment, real, imagined or metaphorical, in the Roman world might require the application of an interdisciplinary approach. This paper has argued that certain studies of the emergence of modernism, both in the visual and literary arts, particularly the writings of the artist Kurt Schwitters and the art historian Linda Nochlin, may be of great value in any such undertaking (as may indeed be studies by Elsen 1969 and 1969–1970 and Pingeot 1990). Page Dubois in her article 'Archaic Bodies in Pieces' (1996) and in her longer study 'Sowing the Body' (Dubois 1998) has considered the value of psychoanalytical schema for interpreting the fragmentary remains of the classical world, though she has cautioned against, as she puts it, "the ahistorical importation of psychoanalytical categories into our understanding of ancient culture" (Dubois 1996: 57). Another possible route might be in the kind of study carried out by Terry Wilfong who looked at the language of Coptic texts and how they suggested metaphorically "the disjoining and fragmenting of the human body along gender lines" (Wilfong 1998: 116) or of Caroline Bynum who has looked at the connection between fragmentation and redemption in medieval religion (Bynum 1992). Studies of the

French poetic form, the blason anatomique, literally a eulogy of the body fragment (see Pacteau 1994: 209, n3), could again provide useful frameworks for comparative analysis. Finally, in looking at the fragmented object, the work of the prehistorian John Chapman (Chapman 2000) will also prove of great value.

It can be asked whether the fragmented images of the human body discussed in this paper represent any kind of coherent pattern or trend in terms of elucidating aspects of belief or value within the Roman or Romanised societies which created and consumed such images. As ever in such studies, the key element would seem to be the context in which these fragmented images were used. Did context affect or dictate form, or are there other issues bearing upon these aspects still to be considered? Are there in fact any conceptual links between wax *imagines*, portrait busts and individual body parts dedicated as *ex votos* at healing shrines? While in Greek society and art the body remained an almost inviolable whole, in Roman art the fragmentation of the body when it occurred perhaps reflected the permeability of boundaries in Roman society and culture between life and death, sickness and health, Roman and barbarian, and class status and lineage.

Most studies of the classical body have dealt with the whole body, with issues of gender and representation, health and medical practice, or exclusion through disability or other perceived differences, but once we start to consider the concepts behind an empire in pieces perhaps other types of analysis may be required to be brought into play. In some of the situations presented in this paper the human body was not simply modified, it was transformed into a series of unrelated parts. The social body had in certain contexts approved the dismemberment of the corporeal body as images. There was an undoubted "tension between the belief in the body as an ideal form, and the body as dehumanised parts" (Pacteau 1994: 61).

In a number of the archaeological case studies presented it can perhaps be argued that the active manipulation of the fragment created a new whole and, in so doing, not only stressed the indivisibility of the present from the past, but acted as a metaphor for their conscious dissociation. Wax ancestor masks or *imagines* were used to keep the memory of notable ancestors alive in the present. They were also didactic devices for demonstrating to the young the moral qualities of earlier generations of Romans. Together these elements provided society with the experience and security of returning to the whole, a process of interpreting often ambiguous and contradictory phenomena and translating that interpretation into a new vision of reality. Partial representations in portraiture allowed the same process to be extended to other classes of Roman society and to other parts of the empire and for this to occur in other social and cultural situations, often linked to funerary commemoration. Anatomical *ex votos* were used in a process of both trying to seek a cure and reintegration back into society and in a way were props for seeking a return to the whole through re-incorporation within the social body.

No matter how much metamorphosis is reinforced by the dividing, deforming, and fragmenting of the body as an image in Roman art, the inherent tension between inner and outer reference always remains, as does the extension and even preservation of tradition in the face of what might be considered almost avant-garde technique. The metaphor of containment or inclusion frequently used was basically an image of possession, of things taken from the world, dematerialised and made to belong to society itself. In some instances the corporeal body was reduced to the status of an artefact (contra Merleau-Ponty as quoted by Meskell 2000: 16).

Field Archaeology Unit, University of Birmingham.

Acknowledgements

I would like to thank Lynne Bevan for reading a draft of this paper before its delivery at TRAC 2002. Thanks also to Giorgia Migatta of the Fototeca of the Deutsches Archaologisches Institut in Rome for providing copies of photographs reproduced here, and Graham Norrie, photographer in the Institute of Archaeology and Antiquity, University of Birmingham, for help in producing the other photographic plates from my slides.

Bibliography

Ancient Sources
Artemidorus *Oneirocritica.* (Translated by D. Montserrat in Doxiadis, E. 1995) *The Mysterious Fayum Portraits. Faces from Ancient Egypt.* London: Thames and Hudson. 87.
Polybius *Historiae.* (Translated by J.J. Pollitt 1983) in Pollitt, J.J. 1983 *The Art of Rome c.753 B.C.–A.D. 337: Sources and Documents.* Cambridge: Cambridge University Press. 53.

Modern Sources
Barr-Sharrar, B. 1987. *The Hellenistic and Early Imperial Decorative Bust.* Mainz: Verlag Philipp Von Zabern.
Barton, C. 1993. *The Sorrows of the Ancient Romans. The Gladiator and the Monster.* Princeton, New Jersey: Princeton University Press.
Beard, M. and Henderson, J. 2001. *Classical Art. From Greece to Rome.* Oxford: Oxford University Press.
Bevan, L. 1994. Powerful Pudenda: the Penis in Prehistory. *Journal of Theoretical Archaeology,* 3(4): 41–57.
Bodel, J. 1999. Death on Display: Looking at Roman Funerals. In B. Bergmann and C. Kondoleon (eds.) *The Art of Ancient Spectacle.* Studies in the History of Art 56. Washington: Center for Advanced Study in the Visual Arts Symposium Papers XXXIV. Washington: National Gallery of Art. 259–282.
Brilliant, R. 1963. *Gesture and Rank in Roman Art.* New Haven: ConnecticuAcademy of Arts and Sciences.
Bruni, S. 2000. Sculpture. In M. Torelli (ed.) *The Etruscans.* London: Thames and Hudson. 365–391.
Bynum, C. W. 1992. *Fragmentation and Redemption: Essays on Gender and the Human Body in Medieval Religion.* New York: Zone Books.
Chapman, J. 2000. Fragmentation in Archaeology. London: Routledge.
Damgaard Andersen, H. 1993. The Etruscan Ancestor Cult-Its Origin and Development and the Import-ance of Anthropomorphization. *Analecta Romana Instituti Danici,* 21: 7–66.
Della Portella, I. 1999. *Subterranean Rome.* Cologne: Konemann.
Deyts, S. 1994. *Un Peuple de Pelerins. Offrandes de Pierre et de Bronze des Sources de la Seine.* Dijon: Revue Archeologique de l'Est et du Centre-Est, Treizieme Supplement.
Doxiadis, E. 1995. *The Mysterious Fayum Portraits. Faces from Ancient Egypt.* London: Thames and Hudson.
Dubois, P. 1996. Archaic Bodies in Pieces. In N. B. Kampen (ed.) *Sexuality in Ancient Art.* Cambridge: Cambridge University Press. 55–64.
Dubois, P. 1998. *Sowing the Body: Psychoanalysis and Ancient Representations of Women.* Chicago:University of Chicago Press.
Dupont, F. 1987. Les Morts et la Mémoire: le Masque Funèbre. In F. Hinard (ed.) *La Mort, les Morts et l'Au-Delà Dans le Monde Romain.* Caen: Actes du Colloque de Caen 1985. 167–172.

Dwyer, E. 1982. *Pompeian Domestic Structures; a Study of Five Pompeian Houses and Their Contents.* Rome.

Elderfield, J. 1985. *Kurt Schwitters.* London: Thames and Hudson.

Ellis, P. 2001. Sexual Metaphors in the Neolithic. In L. Bevan (ed.) *Indecent Exposure. Sexuality, Society and the Archaeological Record.* Glasgow: Cruithne Press. 56–63.

Elsen, A. E. 1969. Notes on the Partial Figure. *Artforum,* 8: 58–63.

Elsen, A. E. 1969–1970. *The Partial Figure in Modern Sculpture: From Rodin to 1969.* Baltimore: Baltimore Museum of Art.

Ferris, I. M. 1994. Insignificant Others; Images of Barbarians on Military Art from Roman Britain. In S. Cottam, D. Dungworth, S. Scott and J. Taylor (eds.) *TRAC 94. Proceedings of the Fourth Annual Theoretical Roman Archaeology Conference, Durham 1994.* Oxford: Oxbow Books. 24–31.

Ferris, I. M. 1999. Alchemy of Suffering. Hope and Faith Beyond the Healing Arts in Roman Britain. In A. Leslie (ed.) *Theoretical Roman Archaeology and Architecture, The Third Conference Proceedings.* Glasgow: Cruithne Press. 1–13.

Ferris, I. M. 2000. *Enemies of Rome. Barbarians Through Roman Eyes.* Stroud: Sutton Publishing.

Flower, H. I. 1996. *Ancestor Masks and Aristocratic Power in Roman Culture.* Oxford: Clarendon Press.

Gazda, E. K. 1973. Etruscan Influence in the Funerary Reliefs of Late Republican Rome: a Study of Vernacular Portraiture. *Aufstieg und Niedergang der Römischen Welt,* 1(4): 855–870.

Huskinson, J. 1996. *Roman Children's Sarcophagi. Their Decoration and its Social Significance.* Oxford: Clarendon Press.

Huskinson, J. 2000. Portraits. In R. Ling (ed.) *Making Classical Art. Process and Practice.* Stroud: Tempus. 155–168.

Johns, C. 1982. *Sex or Symbol. Erotic Images of Greece and Rome.* London: British Museum Publications.

Kellum, B. 1996. The Phallus as Signifier: the Forum of Augustus and Rituals of Masculinity. In N. B. Kampen (ed.) *Sexuality in Ancient Art.* Cambridge: Cambridge University Press. 170–183.

Kleiner, D. E. E. 1992. *Roman Sculpture.* Yale: Yale University Press.

Meskell, L. M. 1998. The Irresistible Body and the Seduction of Archaeology. In D. Montserrat (ed.) *Changing Bodies, Changing Meanings. Studies on the Human Body in Antiquity.* London: Routledge. 139–161.

Meskell, L. M. 2000. Writing the Body in Archaeology. In A. E. Rautman (ed.) *Reading the Body. Representations and Remains in the Archaeological Record.* Philadelphia: University of Pennsylvania Press. 13–21.

Montserrat, D. 2000. Reading Gender in the Roman World. In J. Huskinson (ed.) *Experiencing Rome. Culture, Identity and Power in the Roman Empire.* London: Routledge. 153–181.

Nead, L. 1992. *The Female Nude. Art, Obscenity and Sexuality.* London: Routledge.

Nochlin, L. 1994. *The Body in Pieces. The Fragment as a Metaphor of Modernity.* London: Thames and Hudson.

Nodelman, S. 1975. How to Read a Roman Portrait. Art in America 63: 26–33. Reproduced with postscript in E. D'Ambra (ed.) 1993 *Roman Art in Context. An Anthology.* 10–26.

Nylander, C. 1998. The Mutilated Image. 'We' and 'They' in History and Prehistory? *Kungl. Vitterhets Historie och Antikvitets Akademien Konferenser,* 40: 235–251.

Pacteau, F. 1994. *The Symptom of Beauty.* London: Reaktion Books.

Picard, G. C. 1957. *Les Trophées Romain. Contribution à l'Histoire de la Religion et de l'Art Triomphal de Rome.* Paris: Bibliothèque des Écoles Francaises D'Athènes et de Rome, Fascicule Cent-Quatre-Vingt Septième.

Pingeot, A. (ed.) 1990. *Le Corps en Morceaux.* Paris: Musée d'Orsay.

Pollitt, J. J. 1993. Rome: the Republic and Early Empire. In J. Boardman (ed.) *The Oxford History of Classical Art.* Oxford: Oxford University Press. 217–295.

Potter, T. 1985. A Republican Healing Sanctuary at Ponte di Nona Near Rome and the Classical Tradition of Votive Medicine. *Journal of the British Archaeological Association,* 138: 23–47.

Rambaud, M. 1978. Masques et Imagines. Essai sur Certains Usages Funéraires de l'Afrique Noire et de la Rome Ancienne. *Les Études Classiques,* 46: 3–21.

Sigerist, H. E. 1977 [1960]. The Special Position of the Sick. Reprinted in D. Landy (ed.) *Culture, Disease and Healing. Studies in Medical Anthropology.* London: MacMillan. 388–394.

Van Straten, F. T. 1981. Gifts for the Gods, in H. S. Versnel (ed.) *Faith, Hope and Worship. Aspects of Religious Mentality in the Ancient World.* Leiden: Brill. 65–151.

Turnbull, P. 1978. The Phallus in the Art of Roman Britain. *Bulletin of the Institute of Archaeology,* 15: 199–206.

Vermeule, C. C. 1981. *Greek and Roman Sculpture in America. Masterpieces in Public Collections in the United States and Canada.* Berkeley: University of California Press.

Walker, S. 1985. *Memorials to the Roman Dead.* London: British Museum Press.

Walker, S. 1995. *Greek and Roman Portraits.* London: British Museum Press.

Wilfong, T. 1998. Reading the Disjointed Body in Coptic: From Physical Modification to Textual Fragmentation. In D. Montserrat (ed.) *Changing Bodies, Changing Meanings. Studies on the Human Body in Antiquity.* London: Routledge. 116–138.

Restoring ontological security: Roman and native objects in Early Roman Gallaecia (NW Iberia)

Alfredo González-Ruibal

In this paper, I would like to stress the importance of a phenomenological, specifically Heideggerian, approach to the study of identities in 'Romanisation'. I will draw upon Martin Heidegger for philosophical grounding and provide an anthropological case study. (For *Being and Time* the 1927 German edition is quoted but I usually resort to Dreyfus' commentary [1991] for the English translation of the concepts. For the concepts referring to aesthetics I quote also German editions but use English concepts as appear in Young [2000]).

The use of Heidegger for archaeological purposes is not new. Since the nineties some archaeologists have drawn attention to this philosopher, both for interpreting archaeological data (Tilley 1993, Thomas 1996) and for addressing epistemological issues (Dobres 2000, Karlsson 2000). However, no attention has been devoted to aesthetics, which are of the utmost importance because of their concern with material culture. Both ontological and aesthetic issues will be taken into account. Firstly, I will address the question of being amongst humans (which is really the question of 'being-there', and secondly, its relationship with material culture will be considered.

To explain in depth what 'Being-there' (*Dasein*) means in Heidegger's philosophy is well beyond the scope of this paper. Suffice it to say, at this point, that 'Being-there' is what characterises human beings as opposed to things; the essence in which a human being is rooted (Vycinas 1961: 68). For the purposes of this paper, I would stress a double possibility of being for 'being-there': the way of authenticity and the way of inauthenticity. This has significant implications for the analysis of identity, as I shall demonstrate.

The *way of inauthenticity* is that of the ambiguity of the common thought. It means 'being like the others', being simply 'one' and not 'oneself' (Heidegger 1927 § 37). The *Dasein* does not wish to go beyond appearances, it lives its ordinary life (*Alltäglichkeit*) as a life of full plenitude. For Heidegger, this way of being occurs as an irreflexive and acritical participation in a certain historical and social world, with all its prejudices. It is in this ambiguity in which the ontological security of beings and their permanence lies. As everything seems understood, people are not forced to ask about their being. In this way, the 'unsettledness' (*Unheimlichkeit*), of 'being-there', the sense of not being at home in the world, is concealed (Gaos 2000: 52). The inauthentic 'being-there' is characterised by the handling of tools (in a Heidiggerian sense) and a concern for people. The latter is named by Heidegger *Sorge*, 'worry', 'concern', 'care'. Nonetheless, this care, in the inauthentic way, leads to an absorption in the intra-mundane, whether things or human beings (Heidegger 1927 § 41). In anthropological terms: if we don't think that the word 'inauthentic' has any moral meaning, but we consider it just a philosophical label, we can say that preindustrial communities tend to live embedded in social relations and material relations, that is to say, they are involved in their relations with other people and with the material culture they ordinary handle in normal life (houses, pottery, ploughs). They don't care about their being, they simply take part in a "certain historical and social world"; the 'one', that is, the community, is more important than the 'oneself', the individual. As Giddens (1984) says, this embeddedness (feeling oneself part of a community, sharing a set of values and norms) acts as a 'protective cocoon', which protects us from any hint of ontological insecurity or social conflict. Social order in premodern societies is then based on 'inauthenticity', on accepting a given being and not reflecting about it. Individual freedom is sacrificed to the benefit of the community's ontological security.

This inauthentic way of being is not irremediable: the *way of authenticity* might be reached. Inauthenticity is redeemed by ways of considering Being, which implies some kind of becoming aware of 'being-there' through Fear and Anxiety (*Angst*, Heidegger 1927, § 30). Although change is a possibility rooted within 'being-there', what frightens, what brings anxiety, is always something external, an extra-mundane and menacing being. The opening of a world of possibilities is something lived by one 'being-there' as a dreadful menace: "Anxiety makes manifest in Dasein its Being towards its own most potentiality-for-Being – that is, its Being-free for the freedom of choosing itself and taking hold of itself" (Heidegger 1927 § 41, quoted in Moran 2000: 241). Let us talk in sociological terms again: in an embedded, ontologically secure society, where possibilities of being are restricted and identities are well defined, the appearance of choices of being puts collective, commonly accepted values in danger. Every human being has the possibility to think about him/herself and his/her place in the world. That is obvious. But premodern societies tend to inhibit this possibility. They are afraid of individuality, future, changes, the unknown, as opposed to our culture, where personal decisions, future and changes are regarded as something positive (Hernando 2002). But, in a cohesive premodern society changes may occur, leading to disembeddedness: war, invasions, famine, illness may alter the social order (they are all intra-mundane, menacing beings) and thus cause a whole rethinking of society: this is what happened in America when Europeans arrived (Wachtel 1977), and also in 19th century Africa. The tales and songs that have been recorded from different ethnic groups subjected to European or Muslim rule reflect confusion about their identity, the fear and existential anxiety before an uncertain future, in which their identity (their being) is in great risk. A Nuer song from 19th century says: "This land is invaded by foreigners / that throw our adornments to the river / and take the water from the bank. / Black Hair, my sister, / I am confused, / Black Hair, my sister, I am confused. / We are bewildered; we stare at God's stars" (quoted in Mathiessen 1998: 24).

The worry raised by the question of being leads to a situation of bewilderment or confusion; a state of not knowing what to do. Everything loses its meaning and our personal concerns are brought into sharp relief. Anxiety first causes the need to flee. However the ontical and existential fleeing unveils that from which one is fleeing, since this very act means that one is already aware of the fundamental ontological question: what is the being of "being-there"? The *Dasein*'s possibility of not-being (the contingency of being) is what leads the being-there to the way of authenticity. This way of authentic being is the state of resoluteness (*Entschlossenheit*) in which the not-being appears as another possibility of its being. Resoluteness means *Dasein* waking up from its embeddedness in common thought and ordinary life (Heidegger 1927 § 54). The first reaction to a situation of contact between groups of different cultural backgrounds (such as Incas and Spaniards: Wachtel 1977) is confusion, rejection and fear. Foreigners and invaders are regarded as a danger for the identity of the group. But once the contact is unavoidable (such as after a conquest or the installation of a colonial factory), the acceptance of the Other arrives. This acceptance of the contingency of being is what allows creole identities to be created. Creolisation means accepting the Other, but it is also accepting the loss of a part of one's identity. And this implies not being any longer embedded in the 'one', i.e., in previous community values, but being to some degree free to negotiate a new identity.

In the world there are beings other than human beings (that is, those who live in the way of 'being-there'). Those beings which are not human, are things. *Things* have been given great relevance in Heidegger's ontology. To be, for Heidegger, means belonging to an instrumental totality that is the world (Vattimo 1998). And even that is not being in the middle of a totality of instruments, but being acquainted with a totality of meanings (cf. the metaphorical character of things in Tilley 1999). As Lemonnier (1990: 27–28) puts it, speaking about a hammer: "but we also share, by virtue of being members of a given human group, representations of other kinds; regarding, for example, the supposed clumsiness of women with such a tool, or associations of hammers with anvils, with pianos, sharks and so on... Of course, we also know how to distinguish a hammer from a crucifix or a sickle". There are also two modes of being for things, tools and works of art. These Heideggerian concepts are crucial to an understanding of material culture from an ontological point of view. They have become blurred, especially with Modernity. In *The Question of Things* Heidegger (1962) says that, with the development of modern science, a conception of 'thing' was developed that ignores "the difference between a thing and a poem" [although even the poem has the character of thing (Heidegger 1950: 9)]. In fact, *work-of-art* and *tool* are akin, since they are both something created by a human being, to the point that it can be said that a tool is "half a work of art" (Heidegger 1950: 20). However, the thing-instrument, or tool, is characterized by its utility. With the famous example of the peasant boots in a Van Gogh picture, Heidegger defines the concept of tool: "the boots are more boots the less the peasant thinks of her boots during her work, when she even does not look at them or feels them. It is in the process of use of the tool when we have to meet truly with the character of tool" (Heidegger 1950: 22). Thus, what Heidegger means by tool is anything that is of use to be secure in the world, anything that gives confidence and with which one is acquainted: for example, houses, in which one lives, or a plough, which one uses, or dresses, which one wears. We do not need to think of our house to know what it is. And, of course, we do not usually reflect on a hammer (to use a Heideggerian example), we just use it to drive in nails – regardless of the social meanings to which it is attached, as Lemonnier (1990) points out.

We can easily find a relationship between the inauthentic way of 'being-there' and tools as defined by Heidegger. The 'Being-there' in the inauthentic way lives in a state of security, and the tools in their 'being-tool' transmit this reliability (*Dienlichkeit*) (Heidegger 1950: 23), ontological security. On the other hand, 'being-there' lives in the inauthentic way because it does not consider its 'being-there'. It is embedded in the ambiguity of the 'one' (*man*), of thoughtlessness. Material culture, then, is part and parcel of being embedded in community values: being acquainted with material things is directly related to an inauthentic way of being.

However, it is possible to move beyond this embeddedness; to reflect, for example, with Heidegger, on the peasant boots; in this instance this becomes possible through the work of art. The picture by Van Gogh "is the opening through which it is discerned what the tool really *is*. This being comes to light in the unconcealing of its being" (Heidegger 1950: 22). The *work of art*, then, unveils Being and opens it to the truth (Heidegger 1951): not really *the Truth*, but *a truth* (Heidegger 1943). Moreover, in the work of art, truth is materialized not only as revelation, but also as obscurity and concealment; this is called by Heidegger "conflict between the World and the Earth". The work of art is presented as a stock of meanings that have to be discovered, what the philosopher named 'Earth' (*Erde*). It simultaneously shows a World (*Welt*), and places in front the Earth. The fight (*Kampf*) between these dimensions, that cannot get rid of each other, is the very basis of the work of art (Heidegger 1950: 44). Work of art and tool live in a different manner in the world: the art-work is irreducible to the world, in opposition to tools, that are pure mundanity. The art-work takes with it its own world: it is a *radical novelty* (Heidegger 1950: 62). There lies precisely the *Stoss* ('shock') of the work of art: when I meet it, as Gianni Vattimo says, "the world as I was accustomed to see it becomes strange for me, it is put into crisis as a whole, since the work proposed is a new general systematization, a new epoch in history" (Vattimo 1993: 167). All which was until then ordinary and normal becomes non-existent by virtue of the work of art, and thus loses its capacity to impose and maintain Being as a measure. A tool becomes a work of art when it is not (or not only) regarded as something useful, but as something that can transform our being-in-the-world.

The work of art, anthropologically speaking, is anything capable of causing a great shock in 'being-there', a shock of such great magnitude that it leads one to rethink fundamental issues such as, for example, power, gender or identity. A work of art, in this sense, is not necessarily a Greek temple or a Gothic sculpture (on the contrary, those things might be mere tools, transmiting reliability and ontological security). A work of art may be a simple earthenware dish or a pin. The key lies in the social meanings which have become attached to the objects, that can be revolutionarily new (a radical novelty). Deetz (1996), for example, shows the relevance of the change from communal pots to individual dishes in rethinking social relations in 18th century North America, and Johnson (1989) points to the revolutionary character of chairs for manifesting hierarchy in 15th and 16th century Britain. Perhaps we should start looking at Roman objects in native environments as works of art – in a Heideggerian sense– leading to a renegotiation of social identities and the self. This will be attempted in the following case studies.

Restoring ontological security in past and present: Gallaecia (northwest Iberia) and Benishangul (Ethiopia)

At this point, I would like to adumbrate two parallel stories: that of the Roman-native interactions in NW Iberia and that of the fight between Modernity and tradition amongst Pre-Nilotes.

From the time of Augustus onwards the Northwest of Iberia (Figure 1) was effectively conquered by the Romans (for a comprehensive account of the process and its aftermath see Tranoy 1981). It was one of the latest territories to be conquered in Iberia and one in which in the Roman period native traditions seemed to remain very strong. Parallel to the study of the Iron Age Society in NW Iberia and its transformations under Roman rule, I am carrying out ethnoarchaeological research in Benishangul, a region in West Ethiopia (Figure 2), inhabited by Pre-Nilotic peoples (Grottanelli 1948), who, although maintaining a traditional way of life and a premodern material culture, have begun to enter Modernity, especially the younger generations in the 'urban' areas (González-Ruibal and Fernández Martínez forthcoming).

We cannot make direct comparisons between modern Ethiopian Pre-Nilotes and natives from NW Iberia. Historical circumstances are very different. We cannot forget, for example, that the cultural distance between the Western world and the Prenilotes is greater than that between Romans and Gallaecians and the fact that it was not Europe that conquered the land of the Berta and Gumuz, but an African State: the Abyssinian Empire.

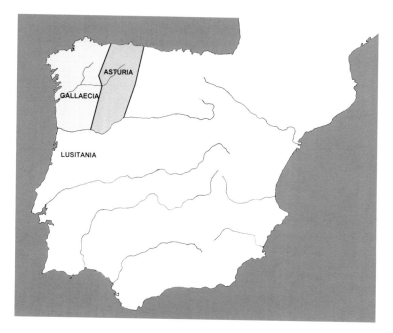

Figure 1. NW Iberia in the 1st century AD.

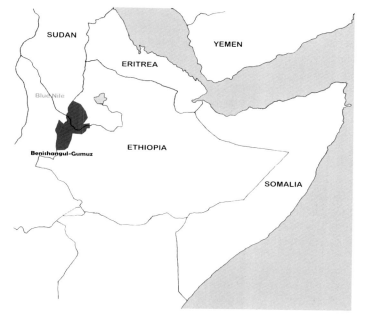

Figure 2. Benishangul in East Africa.

However, what I propose is to use the ethnographic data as "food for the archaeological imagination" (David and Kramer 2001: 195) not as a direct analogy. Some coincidences are worth considering: Post-conquest, it is no longer possible, for example, for Pre-Nilotes or Gallaecians to live in the way of inauthenticity, in the secure place of the ambiguous one. Their worlds are suffering an existential crisis, because of a dreadful menace: Rome or Modernity. Identity has to be negotiated on different grounds. In both cases, the appeal to past material elements and their stock of meanings (the Earth) is a way of maintaining oneself historically rooted in the past, that is to say, of preserving ontological security, while resorting to certain modern objects (the World) exemplifies the acceptance of the world newly founded. Romans and local populations have to deal with the Other, and build identities in which the Other (which is the same as saying novelty) can have a place. For Pre-Nilotes, also, the cohabitation with Otherness, as represented by Modernity, is necessary.

I think that it is possible to see the symbolic fight between Earth and World in the material record, whether archaeological or anthropological. The mechanisms involved for maintaining ontological security in convulsed times are very similar in both cases. In short: people resort to domestic items for constructing new identities, for re-understanding themselves in the changing order. But they do so in the security of the old architectural landscape.

The persistence of the pre-Roman house model in *Gallaecia* is greater than that of any other native item. Even in the 2nd century AD the presence of round huts is not uncommon. This survival may be explained by the very ontological character of homes. The house is where one is safe, the place of ontological security by definition. The construction of homes, as Parker Pearson and Richards (1994: 3) remind us, is an attempt to materialize an eternal and imperishable social order, a way of negating the changes that frighten a society. We must remember the term *Unheimlichkeit* (not-being-at-*home*) used by Heidegger to express the situation into which Being is thrown by Anxiety. The philosopher resorts to the metaphor of 'being at home' for expressing 'being located', 'being ontologically secure'. To the contrary, 'not-being-at-home' expresses the idea of confusion and fear in inauthentic beings, when they start to ask themselves about their Being (about their social identity). If homes can give us so good an idea of ontological security, this is due to the cosmological meaning of houses and their implication for the reproduction of the social order.

The transformations taking place throughout the Augustan period and later on are essentially discussed inside households. Webster (2001: 223) points out that the experiencing of Roman culture by natives should be understood "through the materiality of domestic life". In the case we are dealing with this is especially true – at least in the early period after the conquest– because change is centred on the domestic world (the world of the house), more than on any other thing (such as politics, law or administration, for example, the focus of much historical work), except probably the religious arena, an issue that merits further attention. Sanctuaries inside hill-forts and ritual baths are indigenous phenomena that characterize the Late Iron Age in NW Iberia. They suffer important transformations under the early period of Roman rule (up to the end of the 1st century AD) and disappear from the beginning of the 2nd century AD, if not before. In fact, changes associated with ritual are very similar to those occurring in the domestic sphere: in both cases many native elements are kept (external, structural features, such as kind of building, monumental shape, masonry), while important changes are taking place (as reflected by inscriptions, Roman deities, imported materials). The friezes showing people in togae at the ritual bath at Monte da Saia (Calo Lourido 1994: 433–434) or the inscriptions to Jupiter engraved on a rock inside the upper ritual enclosure at San Cibrán de Las (Rodríguez, Xusto y Fariña 1992: 50–51) are good examples of those changes.

Since a detailed account of these matters would merit another paper, I will focus here on the domestic space, defined as architecture, settlement organization and indoor activities.

While most of the material culture used by the inhabitants of Santa Trega (Peña Santos 1985–86, Peña Santos 2001), one of the greatest oppida in NW Iberia, was Roman (brooches, pins, pottery, containers, etc.) and most of the traditional material culture (mainly friezes and sculptured decoration) had been discarded or destroyed by the Claudian period, the shape and appearance of compounds is basically pre-Roman (Mergelina Luna 1944–45; Peña Santos 1998). Almost all the houses are round and virtually no *tegulae* have been discovered (Figure 3). The 'Being-there' has first to deal with the World through bodily actions, the physical appearance and the preparation and consumption of food, in a manner not dissimilar to that observed in Roman Britain (Hill 1997, Meadows 1997).

In the oppidum of Santa Trega, about 49% of the total amount of pottery (including containers) is of Roman pattern (Carballo Arceo 1989: 118), which is rather surprising for such an early period (Augustus to Claudius). (In fact, the percentage of Roman pottery in the Julio-Claudian period must be greater, since Santa Trega was occupied before the Augustan era. Lower layers have been much destroyed by later building activity, therefore earlier materials are expected to appear mixed in the foundation of Augustan or later structures.) High-quality vessels, such as *millefiori* glasses are not rare, and Samian ware, Campanian and Pompeian red slip ware are very common (Figure 4, Peña Santos 2001). The same can be said for other big oppida, such as Sanfins (Silva 1999) or Monte Mozinho (Almeida 1977), in NW. Portugal, although the Augustan layers are less well preserved here and most of the remains belong to the mid–1st century AD – early 2nd century AD. At least for Monte Mozinho it can be asserted that the settlement preserved round huts and compounds up to the mid–1st century AD and even in the early 2nd century AD pre- Roman compounds still existed. Foreign pottery is conspicuously displayed inside houses, showing a desire for assimilation with the Roman world, but ostentation is mainly restricted to the domestic sphere. In the same way in the Shamau Al-Hakim compound, in Asosa (Benishangul), up to 63% of the vessels are industrial: plastic, glass, porcelain and metal usually outnumber the wooden and pottery containers (Figure 5).

Nonetheless, the majority of the buildings are traditional Pre-Nilotic houses, round in plan and with thatched roof. Here it is also inside where modern identities are negotiated (Figure 6). Young people build their own houses, away from their parents, following an old tradition. These houses are absolutely identical to their parents. But the interior is completely different: paintings, posters, photos, dresses, everything reveals the impact of the Western world and the eagerness to adopt a Modern identity (Figure 7). The same changes noticed in cooking customs and the presentation of food can be observed in physical appearance. While during the 1st century BC the ideal model for men in NW Iberia was that of the warrior represented in big granite sculptures, with traditional weapons, jewels and decorated dress (Queiroga 1992) (Figure 8), during the 1st century AD the image is that of people in *toga* (Figure 9). As regards males, the warrior has given way to the citizen. This can be seen in sculptures and friezes as well as in the rapid and complete replacement of brooches: traditional fibulae disappear during the first decades of the 1st century AD, being replaced wholesale by omega brooches and Aucissa-type fibulae.

Alfredo González-Ruibal

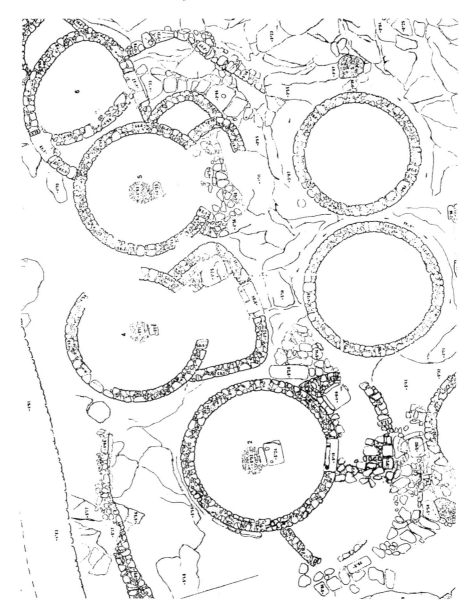

Figure 3. Plan of pre-Roman style huts in Santa Trega (Galizia, Spain) belonging to the Julio-Claudian period. After Peña Santos (2001).

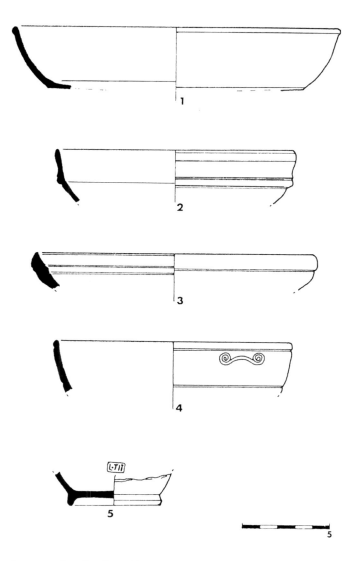

Figure 4. Roman fine ware found at Santa Trega in the houses of Figure 5 (After Peña Santos 1985–86).

As seen in Britain (Hill 1997), in NW Iberia tweezers, pins and other items related to personal appearance become common after the arrival of Rome. Traditional jewellery, such as torcs, also disappear to be replaced by Roman necklaces, earrings and rings, and the context of the consumption of jewels changes from the male to the female sphere. Symptomatically, many friezes representing *togati/-ae* appeared in native environments such as ritual saunas (Almagro-Gorbea and Álvarez Sanchís 1993), like those mentioned in Monte da Saia (NW Portugal), and sanctuaries (Fonte do Ídolo, Braga, NW Portugal). The body acts as a privileged arena for the negotiation of identity, as well as power. Meaningfully, colonial authorities controlled bodily practices during 19th and 20th century as a means of "civilizing the savages"(Farnell 1999: 349). For the Pre-Nilotes, the agents of Modernity, mainly western missionaries, and Islamisation, induced people to change their bodily habits by dressing them, and in so doing destroyed part of their identity reflected by scarifications and body art (Figure 10 and 11). Dress and appearance, then, are no longer a tool, in the Heideggerian sense, but a field for theorizing about new social relations and Being.

The conservative architectural ambience in both Benishangul and NW Iberia, that conceals the widespread changes in personal appearance and customs, at the same time, reinforces the World that is being founded, by radically expressing the contrast with the old (that is, showing the Earth), and makes the changes licit and comprehensible through the historicity of the being-there. Native architecture serves to diminish the importance of a social change, metaphorically represented by the small items mentioned. The building environment (not only indoor areas but the whole settlement) conceals these objects which are full of creative force, because of their novelty and because they are not linked to any previous meaning (Willis 1994). Nonetheless the work of art is already working here: the work can show us the place where we dwell (Heidegger 1950: 25), or make possible another dwelling (Biemel 1994).

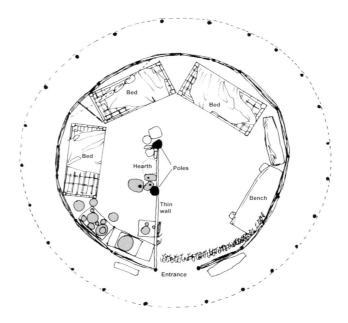

Figure 5. Distribution of industrial items inside a traditional Pre-Nilotic house (Asosa, Benishangul).

Figure 6. Traditional Pre-Nilotic hut (Asosa, Benishangul) (photo by Luis Luque).

Figure 7. The son of the magician in Kebele 03 (Asosa, Benishgangul): The shock of Modernity concealed by a traditional Pre-Nilotic house.

In fact, both things occur in Santa Trega and the Shamau Al-Hakim compound: the new World founded manifests the Being of the traditional space (its social and ideological meanings), and at the same time enables its reconstruction, which will finally lead to a Roman or Modern space. And if 'building' (*bauen*) is related to 'thinking' (Heidegger 1972), 'rebuilding' wiederbauen, must mean 're-thinking'.

From this point of view, domestic space and Roman items fail to be a tool, a place or things for living that go unnoticed, but become works of art, places and things for (re)thinking society. We see the use of objects as an attempt at *conversation* between radically different languages, as a means to survive the novelty, the World opened. In fact, this conversation is an ideological product aiming to conceal the battle (*Kampf*), that is being fought. Domestic space allows the Anxiety of not knowing who one is to be scared away, reinstating the possibility of being 'one' instead of 'oneself', embedded in community values, and, in so doing, reinforces the links with the past *Dasein*, making the new language acceptable through its domestication: in the sense of domination, making it familiar, and, in the most literal sense, inserting it into the household. However the work affects the totality of the being among which it is inserted. Samian ware or amphorae inside traditional buildings are reshaping vernacular space through display and consumption.

It must be acknowledged that both the anthropological and archaeological records are more complex than has been demonstrated here. In today's Benishangul, as well as in Gallaecia in

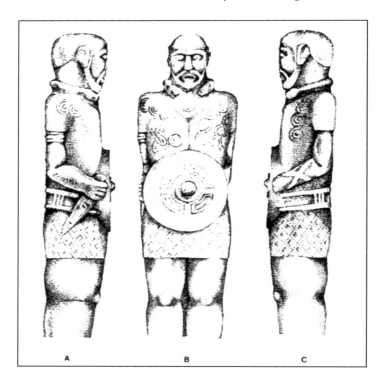

Figure 8. Gallaecian warrior from Lezenho, NW Portugal (after Silva 1986: CXX, 2).

the first half of the 1st century AD, square houses do exist. I cannot explain in detail why these exceptions appear; I will just mention a few motives for the archaeological instances:

1) square houses may belong to immigrants, probably merchants (ethnohistorical parallels in Botswana: Reid et al. 1997) from Italy or from other areas of the Iberian Peninsula, where square-angled houses are the norm –unfortunately, the lack of modern excavations makes this assumption untested.

2) Angled structures may belong to building types not previously known and therefore not constrained by social norms: this is the case with the Mozinho temple (Almeida 1980), but it must be borne in mind that this is a later example (Flavian era), when rectangular structures are already common.

3) Complex structures incorporating angles are known in a religious context, e.g. ritual saunas (Almagro-Gorbea and Álvarez Sanchís 1993) probably before Roman influences arrived on the area.

4) Rectangular buildings but with rounded angles are known from the IV century BC, at least (Carballo Arceo 1996) and in the eastern area (which has not been considered here) they are the norm from the pre-Roman times. The fact that many buildings maintain rounded angles while having a rectangular plan has been explained in functional terms –lack of architectural skill–, but it might be also explained as a way of showing respect to the ancestral habit of building round huts (square huts with round angles and round roof can be observed in Benishangul), i.e. a technical decision motivated by social constraints (Lemonnier 1986).

5).When rectangular huts first appear, they are probably used as stockyards or warehouses, not as the main living house: in Romariz, N. Portugal, traditional round houses articulate the space inside compounds where all huts are already square and still bear the most important social functions (Silva 1986: 51–53).

6) Besides, it is not only the shape, round or angled, but also the way structures are arranged, that counts, and most of the compounds inside oppida in the second half of the 1st century AD still show a native organisation, square and round houses being disposed around a central, enclosed yard.

Finally, personal building of identities (the decision of raising a square hut inside a compound) in earlier times may apparently contradict what I have defended here. But they are a minority before the mid 1st century AD and this complexity fits well within the theory that has been discussed. The diversity of solutions developed in order to face the Anxiety provoked by the foundation of a new World must come as no surprise. "Anxiety, said Heidegger, makes manifest in *Dasein* its Being towards its own most potentiality for Being, that is, its Being-free for the freedom of choosing" (Heidegger 1927 § 41, quoted in Moran 2000: 241). It represents a widening in the limits of social agency. This is why 'Romanisation' appears nowhere as a gradual, homogeneous imposition of Roman culture (Jones 1997: 129–135), uniformly accepted or resisted by natives, but as a permanent fight between Earth and World, between old and new *Dasein*, which generates diversity. We can describe trends, but we cannot offer recipes: individual agency is, post-conquest, far more complex and active than in pre-Roman times.

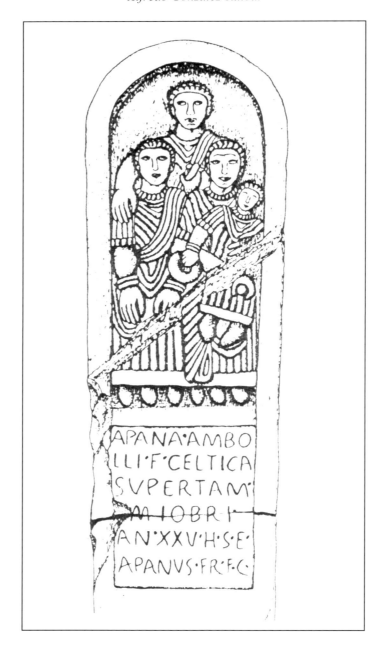

Figure 9. Natives in Roman dresses in the 1ˢᵗ century AD monumental stela from Crecente, Galiza, Spain (after Rodríguez Colmenero and Carreño Gascón 1996).

Figure 10. Berta woman in Islamic style dress (photo by Luis Luque).

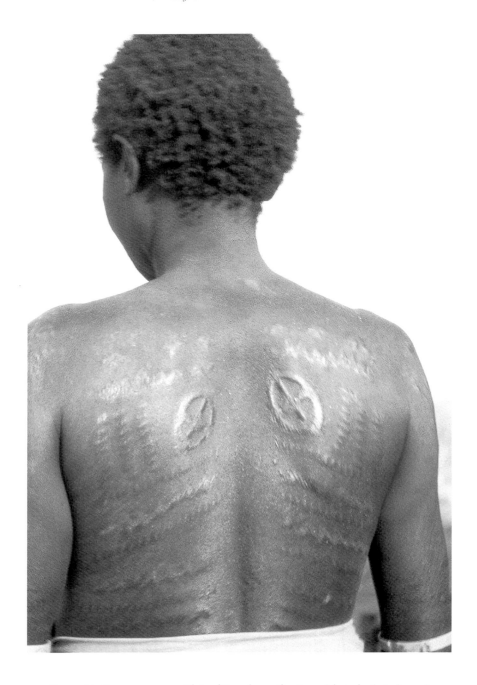

Figure 11. Gumuz woman with traditional scarifications (photo by Luis Luque).

Conclusion

'Romanisation', finally, is not a process of adopting an alien culture, whether by political or economical interests or constraints. 'Romanisation' is a manner of coming to terms with a new *Dasein*, it is first and foremost a change of being (Barrett 1994), both for Romans and for natives, since both have attended the creation of a new world. It is not only about understanding oneself, but also about making the new self comprehensible to others, trying to affect the least the ontological security in which society is grounded. This is especially true for élites (but not only élites), who have to negotiate the basis of their power with the rest of the population: this is what Kus (1988) has ironically called the 'social contract'. 'Romanisation', in Heideggerian terms, is therefore a change in the way one deals with things (*besorgen*) and people (*fürsorgen*). Things that passed unthought are now objects of reflection: tools have become works of art. The necessity of restoring the state of ambiguity (or embeddedness) leads to to the formation of Imperial identities (Woolf 1998), which means returning once more to a state of inauthenticity, embedded and ontologically secure. Being-Roman, by the beginning of the 2nd century AD, is having ordinary life (*Alltäglichkeit*) restored: pottery or brooches or houses are now simply tools, good for living, but also for maintaining, structuring and reproducing social reality. The fact that by the 3rd century AD Roman customs, material culture (including not only small items but also architecture) and language have been adopted all over NW Iberia without any apparent clash or major social disorder corroborates the importance of maintaining ontological security by inserting changes in a collective, historically sanctioned space.

Universidad Computense de Madrid

Acknowledgements

I want to thank TRAC editors and an anonymous referee for their valuable comments on this paper. The ethnoarchaeological research in Ethiopia is being carried out under the direction of Prof. Víctor M. Fernández Martínez (Department of Prehistory and Ethnology, Universidad Complutense de Madrid). The project is financed by the Dirección General de Bellas Artes – Ministry of Culture and Education of Spain–. The archaeological work in NW Iberia is possible through a F.P.U. (Training of Academic Staff) grant from the Ministry of Culture and Education of Spain, under the direction of Prof. Gonzalo Ruiz Zapatero. I would like to thank Dr. Luis Luque for kindly allowing the publication of figs. 6, 10 and 11 and Carmina Aguado for improving my English.

Bibliography

Almagro-Gorbea, M. and Álvarez Sanchís, J. 1993. La "Sauna" de Ulaca: saunas y baños iniciáticos en el mundo céltico. *Cuadernos de Arqueología de la Universidad de Navarra*, 1:177–253.
Almeida, C. A. F. 1977. *Escavaçôes no Monte Mozinho II*. Penafiel: Centro Cultural Penafidelis.
Almeida, C. A. F. 1980. O templo de Mozinho e o seu conjunto. *Portugália* 1:51–56.
Barrett, J. 1994. *Fragments from Antiquity*. Oxford: Blackwell.
Biemel, W. 1994. *La Interpretación del Arte en Heidegger*. València: Centro de Semiótica y Teoría del espectáculo. Universitat de València.

Calo Lourido, F. 1994. *A Plástica da Cultura Castrexa Galego-portuguesa*. 2 vols. A Coruña: Fundación Pedro Barrié de la Maza, Conde de Fenosa, Catalogación Arqueológica y Artística del Museo de Pontevedra.

Carballo Arceo, L. X. 1989. *Catálogo dos Materiais Arqueolóxicos do Museu do Castro de Santa Trega: Idade do Ferro*. Pontevedra: Deputación Provincial de Pontevedra.

Carballo Arceo, L. X. 1996. Os castros galegos: espácio e arquitectura. *Gallaecia* 14–15:309–357.

David, N. and Kramer, C. 2001. *Ethnoarchaeology in Action*. Cambridge: Cambridge University Press.

Deetz, J. 1996. *In Small Things Forgotten*. New York: Anchor Press.

Dobres, M.A. 2000. *Technology and Social Agency*. London: Blackwell.

Dreyfus, H. L. 1991. *Being-in-the-World. A commentary on Heidegger's Being and Time, Division I*. Cambridge (MA) and London: Massachussets Institute of Technology Press.

Farnell, B. 1999. Moving bodies, Acting Selves. *Annual reviews of Anthropology*, 28:342–373.

Gaos, J. 2000 [1951]. *Introducción a El Ser y el Tiempo*. Madrid: Fondo de Cultura Económica.

Giddens, A. 1984. *The Constitution of Society*. Cambridge: Polity Press.

González-Ruibal, A. and Fernández Martínez, V. (forthcoming). House ethnoarchaeology in Ethiopia. d M. Borrazás *Archaeotecture. Archaeology of architecture*. OElements for the study of domestic space in Benishangul (West Ethiopia). In X. Ayán, P. Mañana anxford: British Archaeological Reports / International Series.

Grottanelli, V. 1948. I Preniloti: un'arcaica provincia culturale in Africa. *Annali Lateranensi*, 12:280–326.

Heidegger, M. 1927. *Sein und Zeit*. Halle: Max Niemeyer.

Heidegger, M. 1943. *Vom Wesen der Wahrheit*. Frankfurt: Klostermann.

Heidegger, M. 1950. Der Sprung des Kunstwerkes. In *Holzwege*. Frankfurt: Klostermann.

Heidegger, M. 1951. *Erläuterungen zu Hölderlins Dichtung*. Frankfurt: Klostermann. [2nd ed.]

Heidegger, M. 1962. *Die Frage nach dem Ding. Zu Kant Lehre von den Transzendentalen Grundsätzen*. Tübingen: Max Niemeyer. [1935–36 lecture].

Heidegger, M. 1972. Building, dwelling, thinking. In D. Krell (ed.) *Basic writings*. London: Routledge.

Hernando, A. 2002. *Arqueología de la Identidad*. Madrid: Akal.

Hill, J.D. 1997. The End of one kind of Body and the Beginning of another kind of Body? Toilet Instruments and "Romanization". In A. Gwilt and C. Haselgrove (eds.) *Reconstructing Iron Age societies*. Oxford: Oxbow. 96–107.

Johnson, M. 1989. Conceptions of Agency in Archaeological Interpretation. *Journal of Anthropological Archaeology*, 8:189–211.

Jones, S. 1997. *The Archaeology of ethnicity*. London: Routledge.

Karlsson, K. 2000. Why is there material culture rather than nothing? Heideggerian thoughts and archaeology. C. Holtorf and H. Karlsson (eds.) *Philosophy and archaeological practice. Perspectives for the 21th century*. Goteborg: Goteborg University Press. 69–86.

Kus, S. 1988. Sensuous Human activity and the State: towards an archaeology of bread and circuses. In Ch. Tilley, M. Rowlands and D. Miller (eds.) *Domination and resistance*. Cambridge: Cambridge University Press. 140–154.

Lemonnier, P. 1986. The study of material culture today: toward an anthropology of technical systems. *Journal of Anthropological Archaeology*, 5:147–186.

Lemonnier, P. 1990. Topsy turvy techniques. Remarks on the social representations of techniques. *Archaeological Review from Cambridge*, 9(1):26–37.

Mathiessen, P. 1998 [1972]. *El Árbol en que Nació el Hombre*. Barcelona: Olañeta.

Meadows, K. 1997. Much Ado about Nothing: the social context of eating and drinking in early Roman Britain. In C. G. Cumberpatch and P. W. Blinkhorn (eds.) *Not so much a pot, more a way of life*. Oxford: Oxbow. 21–35.

Mergelina Luna, C. de 1944–45. La citania de Santa Tecla. *Boletín del Seminario de Estudios de Arte y Arqueología*, 37–39:14–54.

Moran, D. 2000. *An Introduction to Phenomenology*. Routledge, London and New York.

Parker Pearson, M. and Richards, C. 1994: Ordering the World: perceptions of architecture, space and time. In M. Parker Pearson and C. Richards (eds.) *Architecture and Order*. London: Routledge. 1–37.

Peña Santos, A. de la 1985–86. Tres años de excavaciones en el yacimiento galaico-romano de Santa Tecla. *Pontevedra Arqueológica*, 2:157–190.

Peña Santos, A. de la 1998. Santa Tegra (A Guarda, Pontevedra): Un ejemplo del urbanismo castrexo-romano del convento bracarense. *Actas del Congreso Internacional sobre los Orígenes de la Ciudad en el Noroeste Hispánico. Lugo, 15–18 de Mayo de 1996*. Vol. I. Lugo: Deputación Provincial de Lugo. 693–714.

Peña Santos, A. de la 2001. *Santa Trega. Un Poblado* Castrexo-romano. Ourense: Abano.

Queiroga, F. M. V. R. (1992). *War and Castros. New approaches to the northwestern Portuguese Iron Age*. Unpublished PhD Thesis, Oxford.

Reid, A., Lane, P., Segobye, A., Borjeson, L., Mathibidi, N. and Sekgarametso, P. 1997. Tswana architecture and responses to colonialism. *World Archaeology*, 28(3):370–392.

Rodríguez, C., Xusto, M. and Fariña, F. 1992. *A Cidade. San Cibrán de Lás*. Vigo: Fundación Caixa Galicia.

Rodríguez Colmenero, A. and Carreño Gascón, Mª. C. 1996. Estela romana, monumental, de Crecente (Lugo). *Larouco*, 2:283–288.

Silva, A. C. F. da 1986. *A Cultura Castreja do Noroeste de Portugal*. Paços de Ferreira: Museu Arqueológico da Citânia de Sanfins.

Silva, A. C. F. da 1999. *Citânia de Sanfins*. Paços de Ferreira: Câmara Municipal de Paços de Ferreira.

Tilley, Ch. 1993. *A Phenomenology of Landscape*. New York: Berg.

Tilley, Ch. 1999. *Metaphor and Material Culture*. Oxford: Blackwell.

Thomas, J. 1996. *Time, Culture and Identity. An interpretive archaeology*. London: Routledge.

Tranoy, A. 1982. *La Galice Romaine*. Paris: De Boccard.

Vattimo, G. 1993 [1967]. *Poesía y Ontología*. València: Universitat de València.

Vattimo, G. 1998 [1985]. *Introducción a Heidegger*. Barcelona: Gedisa.

Vycinas, V. 1961. *Earth and Gods: an introduction to the philosophy of M. Heidegger*. The Hague: Martinus Nijhoff.

Wachtel, N. 1977. *The Vision of the Vanquished: the Spanish conquest of Peru through Indian eyes, 1520–1570*. New York: Haper and Row.

Webster, J. 2001. Creolizing the Roman provinces. *American Journal of Archaeology*, 105: 209–225.

Willis, S. 1994. Roman imports into late Iron Age British societies: towards a critique of existing models. In S. Cottam, D. Dungworth, S. Scott, J. Taylor (eds.) *Proceedings of the Fourth Annual Theoretical Roman Archaeology Conference, Durham 1994*. Oxford: Oxbow Books. 141–150.

Woolf, G. 1998. *Becoming Roman*. Cambridge: Cambridge University Press.

Young, J. 2000. *Heidegger's Philosophy of Art*. Cambridge: Cambridge University Press.

Transformations in meaning: amber and glass beads across the Roman frontier

Ellen Swift

Introduction

Roman studies often focus on cultural interaction, frequently the relationship between Roman culture and the indigenous culture of an area under Roman occupation. The late Roman period, however, is a period in which we begin to be concerned not so much with indigenous use of Roman culture as Roman use of 'Germanic' culture. There is a significant repertoire of objects, many of them in the category of dress, which can be demonstrated to be 'Germanic' in inspiration. Evidence for this lies in their date and distribution beyond the Roman frontier in the Germanic homelands. There are problems in dating material from beyond the frontier, as it lacks the secure and narrow chronological context provided by coins and other artefacts within the Empire. However, as far as it can be established, a fairly well defined array of 'Germanic' objects are found widely in the Germanic homelands at a date preceding their appearance within the Roman Empire. One example would be the bracelets with thickened terminals known as 'Kolbenarmringe' studied extensively by Werner (1980). There are also some raw materials which can be sourced with some accuracy to the Germanic homelands, such as amber, which was used extensively for beads and which comes from the Baltic coast.

This paper will concentrate on two types of beads which have associations with the Germanic homelands, amber beads and opaque beads with trail decoration. As well as the Baltic origin of the amber itself, some of the shapes in which amber beads occur in fourth century Roman contexts can be demonstrated to be Germanic in style. Similarly, both the shape (annular, jug shaped, cone shaped etc.) and the decorative patterns and colours of opaque trail beads have a long history beyond the frontiers before their appearance within the Roman Empire. This material has in the past been interpreted in several different ways, for example, as 'obvious' or 'evidently'– Germanic material – representing the presence of Germanic people– or as material which has an intrinsic meaning, derived sometimes from the raw materials used. For example, amber and opaque beads with coloured trail, particularly those of unusual shapes, have both been regarded as 'amuletic'.

I would stress here that I am deliberately referring to these objects as 'Germanic inspired' rather than 'originating in', in the sense of produced, in the Germanic homelands. Some of course probably were produced there. For amber beads the raw material at least will have come from beyond the frontier. However, when these objects are found within the Roman Empire, we may not be able to give a definitive answer as to where they were produced. In fact, there is evidence, in the form of a known production centre with manufacturing evidence at Trier, that opaque beads with coloured trail decoration were produced within the frontier by the end of the fourth century. Some probably came from beyond the frontier as well. (Production within the frontiers itself could be regarded as a kind of 'consumption' of the idea of the object, of the style of the object)

Variability in consumption of objects by different groups or in different places can be viewed as as the 'biography' or life history of an individual object, moving in and out of the pool of consumption and being used and re-used in different ways (Kopytoff 1986). It is also possible, though, to consider the different uses to which the same **type** of object, rather than the same individual item, can be put. For example, a particular type of object, such as a pin, may be produced in the same style for many years, and widely used as a dress accessory used to pin clothing for the first decade of production. It may then continue in production for the next ten years, during which its habitual use might be as a hair adornment. Examining and comparing the contexts in which objects are found at the end of their 'life histories' (for example, when they are deposited as grave goods), might be a useful way to investigate such changes. Varied use of a particular type of object may also occur spatially, across different geographical regions. This type of approach might help us to question interpretations which give a single meaning to items wherever they are found. It should not, though, be confused with the variation in meaning which individual objects may have undergone during their lifespan, which may be related to individual circumstances rather than to wider social trends.

In this paper I will investigate whether Germanic-inspired material within the Empire was consumed in a different way to the way in which it was consumed beyond the frontiers, and examine how this relates to its 'meaning' where we find this material in grave contexts. Much of the data comes from an analysis of 276 bead strings from excavated contexts within the north-western provinces of the Roman Empire, which forms part of a wider study on the appearance and symbolism of bead necklaces in the Roman period (Swift forthcoming). This paper develops the analysis of material from beyond the frontier in more detail, however, and considers the material from a different perspective.

Amber beads within the frontier

Amber beads occur in graves together with glass beads quite widely within the Western Roman Empire, and are more commonly found in the Danube provinces than further to the north and west. Graves which contain amber beads generally have a typical range of late Roman goods; such as bracelets, earrings, finger-rings, pins, etc. in typical provincial Roman style, together with other grave goods such as glass and pottery vessels. A few graves contain more unusual finds. For example, at the cemetery of Tokod in Pannonia, grave 5 contained a string of beads including both amber and an animal tooth (Mocsy 1981: Abb.2); and the grave that included amber at Lankhills (Clarke 1979: SF 436) contained a headband. A grave from Cortrat containing amber also had Germanic-inspired items, in the form of a pair of tutulus brooches (France-Lanord 1963). It is clear, though, that the graves containing amber examined as a group in this study largely include typical provincial Roman material, and the above examples are very much the exception.

Considering the evidence from the physical anthropology of the skeleton, where known, overall proportions in the data sample of material from within the Empire were 55% children (including infant and juvenile) and 38% adult female. There were no examples in the data sample of beads in adult male graves. The graves containing a string of beads including amber, which could be defined individually as either adult females or children, were examined as a group. 87% were children's graves and 13% were adult female graves (figure 1). A slight bias towards children might be expected given the overall data profile, but the result is sufficiently pronounced to suggest that, independently of this, there is a strong correlation between glass bead strings containing amber and children's graves.

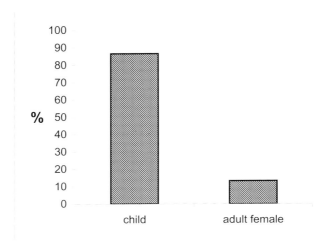

Figure 1. Bead strings including amber beads in graves with known age/sex

Amber beads are especially frequent in graves in 'barbarian' Europe, due to its origin on the Baltic coast. Can the same trend be established in graves beyond the frontier? A bias to amber in children's graves within *and* beyond the frontier, or the absence of such a bias in the Germanic homelands, would be of significance in any debate about the cultural identity of burials containing amber found within the Roman Empire.

Amber beads beyond the frontier

Tempelmann-Maczynska (1985) published a study of bead types occurring beyond the frontiers of the Roman Empire between the early Roman and Migration periods which can be used to compare trends within the empire with those beyond the frontier. Though she is working in many cases from incomplete and poorly recorded data, especially with regard to the large proportion of cremation burials, 242 graves include sufficiently detailed information relating to age, sex, or both to be useful for the purposes of this study (Tempelmann-Maczynzka 1985 Liste 5, 156–162). In addition, the vast majority of the grave contexts she uses can be dated to between AD 250 and 500 (Stufe C2, C3 and D, Tempelmann-Maczynzka 1985: 93–6). Her data is therefore roughly comparable with the material studied from within the frontier. Considering just the individual graves which contained adult females or children, 36% were adult females and 64% children (the disproportionate quantity of children stems from the way in which the data was recorded). Cross-referencing this with data available from the catalogue, of those adult female and child graves which contained amber, 44% were child graves and 57% adult female graves. It can be seen that amber beads are in fact more likely to occur in adult female graves than in children's graves, especially when the large proportion of children in the data sample as a whole is taken into account.

Of course, there may be regional patterns which are obscured by looking at a compilation of material from a wide geographical area. Indeed, these might be expected, as there was no unifying political or cultural sphere, as there was within the frontier. The number of graves with amber beads for which the physical anthropology is known is quite small at each site. However, the sites can be grouped into two larger areas: that between the Rhine and the Elbe, and that along the North Sea coast (see figure 2). Detailed information by site is given in the following tables.

Table 1: Rhine-Elbe area, graves with known age/sex containing amber beads (compiled from grave catalogues and appendices in Tempelmann-Maczynska 1985)

Site	Child	Adult female	Adult male	Adult other/ sex not known	Adult total
Salem	1	0	0	0	0
Mannheim	0	1	0	0	1
Gundelsheim	1	0	0	0	0
Gerlachsheim	0	2	0	0	2
Werbach	0	0	0	M+F 1	1
Guthmann-hausen	0	1	0	0	1
Gostau	0	1	0	0	1
Grobwirschleben	0	1	0	0	1
Zauschwitz	1	0	0	0	0
TOTAL	3	6	0	1	7

Table 2: North sea coast, graves with known age/sex containing amber beads (compiled from grave catalogues and appendices in Tempelmann-Maczynska 1985)

Site	Child	Adult female	Adult male	Adult other/ sex not known	Adult total
Stuchowo	0	0	1	0	1
Debczyno	2	1	0	2	3
Odry	2	0	0	0	0
Wesieg	0	1	0	0	1
Cielpe	1	0	0	0	0
Elblag	0	1	1	0	2
Lubowitz	6	1	0	3	4
Prucz Gdanski	1	4	3	0	7
Scherben	1	0	0	0	0
Rubokaj	1	0	0	0	0
Lumponen	1	0	0	0	0
Korkliny	1	0	1	0	1
Osawa	0	8	1	0	9
Haven	0	1	0	0	1
Heiligens-hafen	0	1	0	0	1
Szwajcara	2	1	0	0	1
TOTAL	18	19	7	5	31

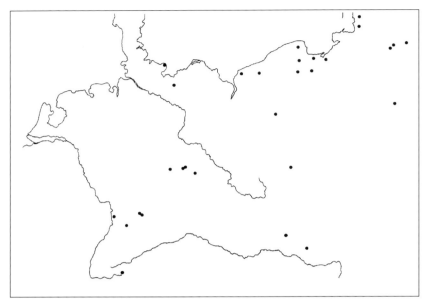

Figure 2. Sites with amber beads in graves with known age/sex (data compiled from Tempelmann-Maczynska 1985).

Naturally caution must be exercised as the graves with information on physical anthropology sometimes form a very small fraction of the total number of known graves. However, there seem to be some noticeable trends when the two main geographical areas are considered. Roughly speaking, in the area between the Rhine and the Elbe, it is twice as likely that amber beads will occur in adult female graves as in child graves. They are not found in male graves. This contrasts with the area of the north sea coast, in which it is equally likely that amber beads will be found in either adult female graves or child graves, and a significant minority also appear in male graves. In neither case, quite obviously, is there any tendency for amber beads to be restricted to children's graves. Nor are there any examples of single sites where this can be suggested, though in part data problems hinder the analysis here.

Opaque beads with coloured trail within the frontier

This type of bead occurs across large areas of the Western Empire in the late Roman period (Swift 2000), though in relatively small quantities. Numerous examples could be cited of bead strings containing a combination of opaque trail beads and provincial Roman style translucent beads in geometric shapes, and as with the amber beads, the accompanying grave goods fall into the normal provincial Roman repertoire. It has been established that there was a production centre for this type of bead at Trier (Schulze 1978: 53) though given its wide distribution spatially and chronologically beyond the Roman frontier (Tempelmann-Maczynscka 1985) it must also have been produced outside the Empire.

Martin (1976: 30) and Burger (1966: 145) both observe that, at the sites of Augst and Sagvar respectively, opaque beads with a coloured trail appear to be associated with the graves

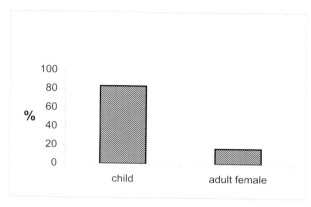

Figure 3. Bead strings including trail beads in graves with known age/sex

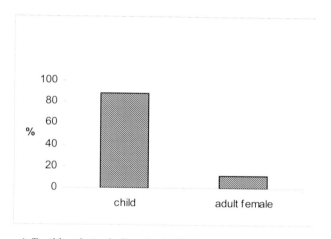

Figure 4. Trail beads (including single finds) in graves with known age/sex

of children. This trend can also be demonstrated more widely. Of the graves in the current study which could be defined as adult females and children, 83% of the trail beads were found in childrens graves and 17% in adult female graves (figure 3). Against a background of 55% child graves and 38% female graves in the data sample as a whole, beads with coloured trail appear to be strongly associated with child burials. This data can also be compared with data drawn from Swift (2000), which lists the occurence of trail beads as single finds in graves (Swift 2000: 297–9). Broadening the data sample to include single finds in graves as well as strings of beads in graves, of the graves with trail beads which could be defined as adult females or children (27 graves), 88% were child graves and 12% were adult female graves (figure 4).

Opaque beads with coloured trail beyond the frontier

Comparing this with the distribution of this type of bead in graves of known age and sex beyond the frontier (using data drawn from Tempelmann-Maczynska 1985) there is a notable contrast. Beyond the frontiers, trail beads do not appear to be associated with children's graves. Showing similar trends to those for the amber beads, in the Rhine-Elbe area they appear most often in adult female's graves, whereas on the north-sea coast they occur more or less equally in adult and child graves. Site distributions are given in figure 5 and details of the individual sites below:

Table 3: Rhine-Elbe area, graves with known age/sex containing opaque trail beads (compiled from grave catalogues and appendices in Tempelmann-Maczynska 1985)

Site	Child	Adult female	Adult male	Adult other/ sex not known	Adult total
Gerlachsheim	0	2	0	0	2
Gostau	0	2	0	0	2
Grobwirschleben	0	1	0	0	1
Niemberg	1	2	0	0	2
Zauschwitz	0	0	1	0	1
Zedau	0	1	0	0	1
TOTAL	1	8	1	0	9

Table 4: North sea coast, graves with known age/sex containing opaque trail beads (compiled from grave catalogues and appendices in Tempelmann-Maczynska 1985)

Site	Child	Adult female	Adult male	Adult other/ sex not known	Adult total
Hamfelde	0	0	1	0	1
Debczyno	3	3	0	0	3
Dingen	1	1	0	0	1
Preetz	0	2	0	1	3
Pritzier	3	0	0	0	0
Cielpe	1	0	0	0	0
Elblag	1	0	0	0	0
Lassahn	1	0	1	0	1
Lubowitz	3	1	0	0	1
Prucz Gdanski	0	2	0	0	2
Schernen	1	0	0	0	0
Wesiory	0	1	0	0	1
Haven	0	1	0	0	1
Heiligenshafen	1	0	0	0	0
Szwajcara	0	2	0	0	2
TOTAL	15	13	2	1	16

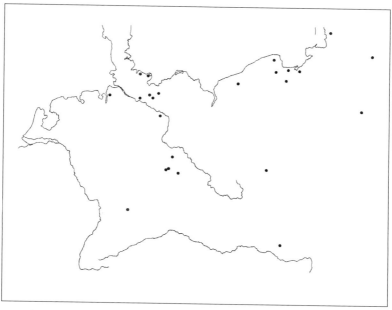

Figure 5. Sites with opaque trail beads in graves with known age/sex (data compiled from Tempelmann-Maczynska 1985).

The majority of the trail beads types listed by Tempelmann-Maczynska are not types which occur within the Empire. The remainder are those which are found on both sides of the frontier, but even among graves which contain these types of beads, there does not seem to be a bias to child graves. At Debczyno in Poland, for example, many of the beads are of types which are found within the Empire, but there is no bias towards child graves (see Tempelmann-Maczynska 1985: 275 for catalogue details of the exact types, listed by her typology numbers).

Conclusion

There are some similarities in the pattern of consumption of amber beads and opaque beads with coloured trail as grave goods across the Roman and non-Roman areas. For example, in all areas they are more strongly associated with female than with male, and therefore have some role in gendered display at death. However, from the data under consideration here, a strong correlation between these types of beads and child graves apparently exists only within the frontier, despite the fact that the bead types themselves are Germanic. This is a useful example of the fluidity of meaning attached to material culture, in which the same types of objects may possess different 'meanings' which are context-dependent; the objects being 'consumed' in different ways in different areas.

Consumption of an object depends inevitably on its **value**. This value is not an intrinsic quality, but something given to the object. Isherwood and Douglas (1996) discuss the relationship between the value of goods and a particular society. Values given to objects tend to be largely comparable within a society. We could say that a particular 'culture' is constituted of, among other things, a body of material culture which is broadly valued in the same way, in that it can be used in the construction of meanings which are commmunicable. (Objects may also, of course, have other 'layers' of private meanings or meanings which may be subversive or perceived only by a sector of a society, but this is beyond the scope of this paper).

Material culture patterning in which particular types of object tend to occur in a particular type of context, i.e., the use of some types of beads in childrens burials at sites across a wide area of the north-western provinces, implies that these objects have a well-defined and specific meaning which is widely recognised. The coincidence of object type and the practice carried out, namely deposition in a child's grave, is more likely to evidence a shared culture than the simple presence or absence of an object type in itself.

Possible cultural meanings for beads beyond the frontier, beyond that of gender signifiers, are harder to establish. This may result from a poorer data set beyond the frontiers. It could also be argued that objects are less likely to have specific meanings which are the same across broad geographical areas in the Germanic homelands because these areas were politically and perhaps culturally fragmented.

However, the status of amber as a 'found' material which has one particular source perhaps suggests another factor which may be significant, namely, rarity value. It could be suggested that the differing rarity value of amber beads in different areas may contribute to their consumption in divergent ways. Where amber is a relatively common material, on the north sea coast, there appear to be fewer constraints on its use and its role as a gender marker is less secure. Where it is less common, between the Rhine and the Elbe, it seems to become a material more strongly associated with gender-specific identity. Within the frontier, where its value is now possibly that of an exotic rarity, the pattern of consumption at burial becomes even more strongly constrained; the 'meaning' of the object is narrower and more securely defined. Roughly similar factors may be operating in the case of opaque beads with trail decoration, though for these we know less about the source area and the patterning beyond the frontier is less well defined.

The exact relationship between children and beads of these types remains unclear. It may be the case that these beads were deposited in childrens graves as amulets, or they may merely have been objects which were associated with children for other reasons. They may have been worn by children in life, or only deposited with them at death. However, explanations which assume that the presence of these beads indicates that the occupants of the graves in which they are found were Germanic can now be questioned. These objects were inspired by Germanic culture and some of them may have been made beyond the frontier. However, it is apparent that they cannot universally be taken to be signifiers of 'Germanic' identity. Their usage within the frontier, which appears to diverge from usage in the Germanic homelands, suggests quite a different meaning. It is evident that the continuity of an object type through space is not matched by exact continuity in meaning, and differences in perception of or value given to the object at burial, which may be related in this case partly to their rarity value, overrides what have often been considered to be 'intrinsic' qualities and/or uses and meanings.

School of European Culture and Languages,
University of Kent at Canterbury

Bibliography

Burger, A. 1966. The Late Roman Cemetery at Sagvar. *Acta Archaeologica Academiae Scientiarum Hungaricae* 18: 99–234.

Clarke, G. 1979. *The Roman Cemetery at Lankhills*. Winchester Studies 3. Oxford: Clarendon Press.

France-Lanord, A. 1963. Une cimetière de Létès à Cortrat. *Revue Archéologique* 1963 1: 15–35.

Isherwood, M. & Douglas, B. 1996. *The World of Goods: towards an anthropology of consumption*. London /New York: Routledge.

Kopytoff, I. 1986. The cultural biography of things: commoditization as process. In A. Appadurai (ed.) *The Social Life of Things. Commodities in Cultural Perspective*. Cambridge: Cambridge University Press. 64–91

Martin, M. 1976. *Das Spätromische-Fruhmittelalterliche Graberfeld von KaiserAugst, Kt. Aargau*. Derendingen: Basler Beitrage zur Ur-und-Fruhgeschichte 5B.

Mócsy, A. 1981. *Die spätrömische Festung und das Gräberfeld von Tokod*. Budapest: Akadémiai Kiadó.

Schulze, M. 1978. Zur Interpretation spätkaiserzeitlicher Glasperlen. *Archäologisches Korrespondenz-blatt* 8: 51–68.

Swift, E. 2000. *Regionality in Dress Accessories in the Late Roman West*. Monographies Instrumentum 11. Montagnac: Monique Mergoil.

Swift forthcoming. Roman glass bead necklaces and bracelets. *Journal of Roman Archaeology*.

Tempelmann-Maczynska, M. 1985. *Perlen in Mitteleuropäischen Barbaricum*.Römische-Germanische Forschungen Band 43, Mainz: Philipp Von Zabern.

Werner, J. 1980. Der goldene Armring des Frankenkönigs Childerich und die germanischen Handgelenkringe der jüngeren Kaiserzeit. *Fruhmittelalterliche Studien* 14: 1–49.

The Realm of Janus: Doorways in the Roman World

Ardle Mac Mahon

For the Romans, the doorways into their dwellings had tremendous symbolic and spiritual significance and this aspect was enshrined around the uniquely Latin god Janus. The importance of principal entrance doorways was made obvious by the architectural embellishments used to decorate doors and door surrounds that helped to create an atmosphere of sacred and ritual eminence. The threshold was not only an area of physical transition but also of symbolic change intimately connected to the lives of the inhabitants of the dwelling. This paper will explore the meaning of the architectural symbolism of the portal and the role of doorways in ritual within the Roman empire by an examination of the architectural remains and the literary sources. The exceptional assemblage of physical remains in Pompeii and Herculaneum offer the best evidence for an examination of the main portals of the houses of the élite in terms of height and preservation. A study of these towns may limit the implications that can be drawn concerning the social and ritual significance of doorways to the region of Campania, but by drawing upon the literary evidence and other sources inferences can be made for the importance of doorways in other regions of Italy, and perhaps the empire as a whole.

Janus and his realm

The characteristic feature of Roman religious conviction was the belief that different deities had charge over specific functions and fields of activity and that all-important events were divinely activated (Ogilvie 1969: 10). All that was seen as significant for the interests of the Romans and their society was presided over by a god (Kerenyi 1962: 222). The principal doorway into a dwelling had an important role in protecting the physical, and also the spiritual, well-being of those that dwelt within and it is understandable that the Romans believed that a deity watched over and safeguarded it.

Janus was a very ancient Italian deity and there was no Greek equivalent (Orr 1978: 1561; Hornblower and Spawforth 1996: 793). The few depictions of him show him as having two heads but he is more commonly shown as a two faced deity. One of these faces is that of a youth who was symbolic of beginnings and the other is of an old man emblematic of the end of things. He is sometimes shown holding a key to indicate that he opens at the beginning and shuts at the end (St. Augustine 7.7–8). To him the Romans ascribed all things, the ups and downs of fortune, and civilisation of the human race by means of agriculture, industry, art and religion. Janus was also connected to crossing-places, boundaries and more especially doorways. When the Sabines attacked Rome the entrance to the forum was barred by miraculous jets of boiling water emitted by the god preventing its capture (Morford and Lenardon 1999: 505), thus emphasising Janus' role as a protective deity.

He was a deity of considerable importance and this significance is emphasised by the fact that he was the first deity mentioned during the incantation of prayers. His eminence and the emblematic role of the doorway are emphasised in the opening book of Ovid's *Fasti* when Janus is made to say:

Every door has two fronts, one on either side, of which the one looks out upon the people, but the other looks inward upon the household shrine; and as the gate-keeper among you mortals, sitting near the threshold of the front of the building, sees both the goings out and the comings in, so do I, the door-keeper (1.135–140).

Ianua is the term normally applied to a house door (Holland 1961: 293, fn 32) or gate and his image is reputed to be found on town gates (Scullard 1981: 61). Cicero explains in his *De Natura Deorum* that the name Janus came from the root of the word 'to go' and this was why passages that opened onto the street were called *Jani* and the doors of secular buildings were called *Januae* (2.27.67). This would seem to be an etymology that is accepted by most linguists (Bonnefoy 1991: 619; Cotterell 2000: 128). Janus' charge at the doorway was the only place that the god played a domestic role (Orr 1978: 1562). More importantly, *ianua* was the noun that was used to describe the principal door of the house. There were other exits from the house but they did not open out from the front façade (Holland 1961: 304) and were known as the *posticum* or back door. Sometimes the owner of the house utilised this exit to escape the attention of importunate clients (Horace, *Ep.* 1.5.31).

Ovid states that "the month of Janus comes first because the door comes first" (*Fasti* 2.51). Janus was not only associated with doorways but also the beginning or the very threshold of events by which one embarked on every enterprise (St Augustine 7.7–9). Furthermore, the Romans saw places as sacred and every space was defined by a boundary. These boundaries were not hypothetical divisions that had the function of clearly defining territories but were intermediary zones at which people had to perform certain rites of passage (Dupont 1998: 83). As such, Janus was a god of separation and at the same time of proximity. Janus was seen as the guardian of the boundary between the homeland and the uncivilised lands beyond (Holland 1961: 305). In the first canton of Ovid's *Fasti* Janus is identified with the boundary between order and chaos (1.103). To leave the house meant withdrawing from the psychological safety of the known to the insecurity of the lesser known. The passage through a doorway, whether going inwards or outwards, is to begin something, and beginnings are heavily charged with magical significance. A house was only as secure as its door and these actions exposed the privacy of the home to the chaos of the outside world. Whether the opening and closing resulted in good or evil for the person concerned depended on the favour of Janus (Ogilvie 1969: 11; Scullard 1981: 61). The doorway was seen as a weak point in the defences of the *domus* through which evil (whether spiritual or material) could most easily enter. Therefore, it is not surprising that the doorway that let the Romans into or out of their home had special significance that took to itself a god of doorways.

Despite the many images of the Graeco-Roman deities that are known there are very few representations of Janus. There is barely any trace of him in the domestic cult and his image is not found in the *lararium*. However, it must be remembered that the Romans had a long religious history and like Vesta, another very ancient Italian deity, Janus was never entirely anthropomorphized. The concept of Janus worship was inherited by the Romans from their distant past, by ideas shaped by the nature of land and with elements of magic that had not entirely been discarded (Holland 1961: 265). The earliest reference to a monument to Janus is the Tigillum Sororium (Livy 1. 26). This consisted of a crude gate-monument in the shape of an *iugum*, that is, two upright wooden posts supporting a horizontal lintel (Holland 1961: 26 and 66). There were other monuments to the god and a later more ornate example is the Janus Quadrifrons which is located in the Forum Boarium and is dated to the early fourth century (Claridge 1998: 258–259). It was the very nature of Janus to be *pervius*, or passable, and the function of the *iugum* was to mark the entrance to the passage over which the god presided. The door or gateway became the object in which his power was manifest and was seen as his image rather than his symbol (Holland 1961: 70–71). The closest association of Janus to the private house was that the main entrance resembled a Janus and as such was an *ianua foris* (Holland 1961: 304). Thus, the main portal into the Roman house was a descendent of the isolated portals of Janus.

Roman doorways

The wall surfaces of Roman streets appear to have been quite plain and are frequently described as being 'blank' (Beard and Henderson 2001: 18; Thorpe 1995: 63). The occurrence of stark façades creates the problem of disorientation for any individual and this circulation predicament can be considerable and most acute for a stranger trying to find their way to a particular dwelling amongst a complex of buildings (Alexander 1977: 489). However, the façade of a building can be transformed by variations in the treatment of their openings onto the street. Doorways played a particular role in this environment and the principal entrances into the homes of the Roman élite were given particular attention. The size of a doorway, its position and decoration transmits information on the role of a building and the status of those that dwelt within. In their functional, visual and symbolic roles, doorways communicated the fundamental language by which a building was read and understood by those that entered or passed by the residences of the élite.

As pointed out by the modern architectural theorist Christopher Alexander, if a doorway is to be seen as significant it must appear large, solid, and bold, and be visible from the main avenues of approach (1977: 544). This will differentiate the portal from its immediate surrounds and emphasise its importance to those passing-by or approaching the door in the streetscape; and it will also emphasise the feeling of transition for those passing through (Alexander 1977: 279). Entrances should be wide but not so wide that they appear, according to Wallace-Hadrill, symbolically 'sordid' as in the case of *tabernae* openings that exposed their entire frontages for all to see (1994: 118). Buildings that create a graceful transition between the street and inner compartments are seen as more tranquil than those that opened directly onto the street. The Roman house was not entered directly from the street but was separated from it by the *vestibule* and *fauces* (Paoli 1975: 59). It is the creation of this transitional zone that helped to give the doorway an aura of spiritual significance. It is the whole experience upon entering a building, created by the doorway, which influences the behaviour and the attitude someone has towards the structure. Again, as Alexander points out, if the entry into a building is felt too abrupt, a feeling of arrival will not be created and the building fails to have a contrast between the exterior and interior which should be an inner sanctum (1977: 549). This transition zone must have the effect of transforming the behaviour that is seen as appropriate to the outside world, to one that is fitting to domestic life before an individual can feel relaxed (Alexander 1977: 550). This transformation takes place as an individual passes through the *vestibule* and *fauces* into the *domus*. As such, the main doorway is a natural form of monument to mark the boundary between the contrasting environments of the interior and exterior.

The doorway was a point that marked the terminus of one type of activity or place and the inauguration of another. If this boundary between actions and zones is to be significant in the minds to those passing through this transitional space then the line of demarcation must be present and obvious in the physical world. In a dwelling this function is performed by the principal doorway, and the significance of this feeling of transition over the boundary from the outside to the inside, and vice versa, is made more important by the architectural embellishment of the main doorway (Alexander 1977: 277). As such the doorway transcends its practical function and creates an atmosphere charged with spiritual and ritual significance.

The doorways of élite dwellings became a focal point in the façade and were used as elaborate architectural centrepieces to define the house as belonging to nobility. In some cases, the façade of a building was finished in fine drafted ashlar (Richardson 1988: 387), but this was not done to detract from the pre-eminence of the door. The decorative elements of the door and surrounds were designed to impress, and during the day the doorway stood open to allow a view of the interior. Its purpose was to draw the eye, stress the importance of the doorway, and invite entrance. The embellishments of the portal and environs were enhanced even more during ceremonial occasions and this further enticed the gaze of passers-by to examine the entrance, the building beyond and the activities within.

The Doorways of Pompeii and Herculaneum

The surviving remains that can be found in Pompeii and Herculaneum indicate the significance of doorways and can be seen by a casual glance along the sides of the streets. Town houses are easily recognisable by their façades and their entrances are impressive in their height and breath. The size of the entrance into the Casa del Menandro, I.x.4, was 1.6m wide and 4.15m in height (Ling 1997: 264) and that of the Casa del Fabbro, I.x.7, 1.69m wide and 2.82m in height (Ling 1997: 283). The doorway was not just imposing but often elegantly framed with pilasters or semi-columns of stone or stucco-covered brickwork (Brothers 1996: 41) and even of elegant woodwork (Guhl and Koner 1994: 465). This architectural treatment would enhance the importance of the portal in the façade. This can range from quite simple decoration of the door surround to quite considerable architectural magnificence (Figure 1).

The pilasters that flanked the portals of the Casa del Menandro, I.x.4, (Ling 1997: 49, plate 23, 265 and 336), and the Casa dei Capitelli Figurati, VII.iv.57, were plain and square (Maiuri 1966: 47). This arrangement is typified by the Casa di Pansa, VI.vi.1, and Casa del Fauno, VI.xii.2, where the pilasters were of stone without cement (Englemann 1929: 62 and 82). The Casa del Tramezzo di Legno, III.11–12, in Herculaneum and I.x.8 had square stucco pilasters (Ling 1997: 289–90). The entrance into the Casa della Vestali, VI.i.7, (Leach 1997: 55, fig 6.3) and the Casa del Gran Portale, V.8, in Herculaneum (Maiuri 1959: 50) were flanked by brick recessed columns and these would originally have been stuccoed. It is very probable that the pilasters and recessed columns would have been painted. The lower portions of the pilasters that flanked the entrance of the Domus of Lucius Caius Secundus, I.vi.15, were painted red and the rest was in white plaster (de Franciscis 1978: fig 47), and the recessed columns of the Casa del Gran Portale were also originally painted red (Maiuri 1959:50).

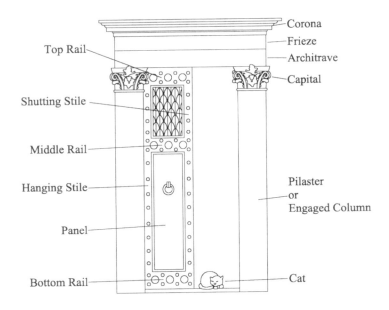

Figure 1. Reconstruction of Roman door (Drawn by author).

These pilasters and recessed columns were often capped by capitals. These could be very simple as in the case of the block tufa capitals of the Casa della Vestali, VI.xv.1 (Richardson 1988: 324), Domus of L Caius Secundus (Maiuri 1966: 47) (Figure 2). These cubical or square capitals appear visually very heavy when compared to the more stylistic Doric and Corinthian capitals. Of the more elaborate capitals, those of the Corinthian style seem to be the most common. The pilasters of the Casa di Pansa, VI.vi.1 (Richardson 1988: 121), Casa del Fauno, VI.xii.2 (Richardson 1988: 116), and the Casa del Menandro, I.x.4, (Ling 1997: 49, 264, 336) were surmounted by capitals in a fine Corinthian type (Figure 3). In other cases, these capitals were very ornate with figurative depictions. The impressive tufa capitals of the Casa dei Capitelli Figurati, VII.iv.57, which give the house its name, appear to be devoted to scenes connected to Dionysus (Zanker 2000: 37–39). The brick pilasters of the Casa del Gran Portale, V.35, in Herculaneum are surmounted by composite Corinthian capitals adorned with winged victories (Maiuri 1959: 50) (Figure 4).

The doorways that survive to a sufficient height show that the portal was often crowned with an entablature with an architrave, frieze and cornice. The entrance into the Casa del Tramezzo di Legno, III.11–12, (Figure 5) (Maiuri 1959: plate XII) and the Casa Samnitica, V.1, (Clarke 1991: 88, fig 24) in Herculaneum had entablatures decorated with dentals. The upper portion of the House of Julia Felix in Pompeii (Fagan 1999: fig 19) has an architrave decorated with *guttae* and *mutules* in terracotta as in the Casa del Gran Portale, V.35 (Maiuri 1959: 50). The entrance into the Casa di Julia Felix, II.iv.6, survived to a sufficient height to preserve a triangular pediment above the entablature.

Figure 2. Domus of Lucius Caius Secundus, I.vi.15, Pompeii (photo by author)

Figure 3. Casa del Fauno, VI.xii., Pompeii (photo by author)

Figure 4. Casa del Gran Portale, V.8 Herculaneum (photo by author)

Figure 5. Casa del Tramezzo di Legno, III.11–12, Herculaneum (photo by author)

A great deal of decorative detail may have been lost due to destruction and the rigors of time, but some indication of the embellishment of house doors can be surmised by a study of doorways depicted in wall paintings that were a frequent feature of First and Second-style interiors (Clarke 1991: 113).

The difficulty with this evidence is that it is often not clear whether the doorways shown are meant to be internal or exterior portals but in most cases the latter seems to have been the most common. In the painting of a doorway in the Villa of Publius Fannius Sinistor at Boscareale, the frieze above the door had been decorated with a depiction of the hunt for the Calydonian boar. In addition, the tympanum of the scrolled pediment had been embellished (Picard 1970: 48; Caro 2001: 148).

The actual doors that covered over the portal have not been preserved but there is sufficient evidence to reconstruct their probable appearance. The indentations in these sills show that the doors that covered these portals were single- or double-leafed and the overall impression is of the latter (Liversidge 1968: 80; Paoli 1975: 60; Guhl and Koner 1994: 465). House doors were composed of solid wood and none have survived but plaster moulds of several doors have been taken to recover their form. In these cases the volcanic dust hardened around the door, making it possible to make a cast of it by pouring Plaster of Paris into the cavity left by the wood in a technique known as the 'Fiorelli process' (Englemann 1929: 146; Connolly 1990: 12). The house doors of the Casa di Loreio Tiburtino, II.ii.2, is an example of doors that have been preserved in this fashion (Richardson 1988: 337). Ordinarily the leaf of the door is composed of a frame that has a horizontal top rail, middle rail, bottom rail, vertical hanging and shutting stile, and panels were set within this frame. Based upon the forms that have been preserved in plaster, these panels seem to be sunken and flush with the door. Sometimes the panels had mouldings set against the frame as can be seen on a wall-painting of a door in the Villa of Publius Fannius Sinistor at Boscareale (King 1982: 140; Caro 2001: 148) and in the Villa dei Misteri (Figure 6).

Although the actual doors have never been recovered, their fittings are familiar. The frame was often adorned with large gilt-headed nails with long shanks (MacKenzie 1910: 53; Richardson 1988: 337). In the plaster cast of the door in the Casa di Loreio Tiburtino, II.ii.2, these nails were placed in rows on the upper and middle bar (Englemann 1929: 136; Maiuri 1966: 75). This arrangement can also be found in the Domus of Octavius Quartio, II.ii.2, (Adam 1994: 296, plate 677) and the Domus of Popidius Montanus, IX.vii.9, which stood open during the time of the eruption (Englemann 1929: 146). Doors had knockers and handles and those that have been found are now preserved in the museum at Naples (Connolly 1990: 31).

It would seem that the doors that covered the portals into the houses of the élite were similar to doors illustrated on wall decoration. In the decorative alcove of *cubiculum* (6) in the Villa dei Misteri there is a painted depiction of a house door. This shows a double door with two panels in each leaf. In the lower panels, there are doorknockers or handles and the upper panels appear to be filled with some form of ornate latticework. The decorative nails that were used to decorate the Casa di Loreio Tiburtino, II.ii.2, can also be seen embellishing the upper, middle and lower rails of the doors (Englemann 1929: fig 14; de Franciscis 1978: fig 82).

Figure 6. Wall painting from the Villa dei Misteri (Photograph taken by author).

Doors and doorways are a common motif found on sepulchral sculpture in many parts of the empire from Italy (Lawrence 1928: 433; Lawrence 1958: 273–274), France (Toynbee 1971: 247) to the so-called Asiatic sarcophagi (Lawrence 1928: 421). These representations presumable have a symbolic value connected with death (Haarløv 1977) but they are still characteristic of doorways in a functional sense as they are similar in form and decoration to portals found on wall paintings. The remains and embellishments that survive in Pompeii and Herculaneum show that house doors may have been similarly decorated but were less ornate. If this is the case, then the preserved examples of doorways found in Pompeii and Herculaneum are not unique to the region of Campania, but similar forms, taking into account regional variations, would have existed in other parts of the empire.

The form of the doorway had a lot to say about identity and it is clear that the entrance into the houses of the élite was a symbol of the owner's ambitions and was the focus of much artistic attention (Thébert 1987: 354). The entrance and the various architectural elements used to decorate the door surround combined to create a monumental impression. The doorway and the *domus* beyond was based upon the principal of display and was organised in the belief that prestige and power went hand in hand with a presentation of discerning opulence. This display became essential in determining an individual's public status (Beard and Henderson 2001: 18).

Furthermore, the architectural features linked the doorways of the dwellings of the élite with the public role of municipal and religious buildings. As such, not only did the decorative elements help to create and display personal identity, they also reflected and echoed the architecture of public and, in particular, temple architecture. Similar design features were also used to decorate *lararia* found within the houses of Pompeii and Herculaneum. The simple niche shrine often had pilasters or applied columns and a pediment. Sometimes there was a low step against the shrine to further create the illusion of a small temple. This effect is made most complete in the *aedicula* type *lararium* (Boyce 1937: 10–14; Orr 1978: 1577 and 1585). Thus, the intimate connection between the house and temple was made most obvious and the doorway provided a basis for characterising the form of relationship between the gods and man.

The decorative details and many of the features that characterised doors and doorways had practical origins. Despite the functional and utilitarian purpose of a portal and its elements, it cannot be denied that the elaboration of a doorway gave special significance to the threshold as a symbol of transition. Doors were opened to communicate and even embrace the activities that took place in the world outside and closed to hide and protect those inside who no longer wished to be part of the wider community. It was in this manner that doorways transcended their utilitarian role as an entrance or exit but became an opening into the very sanctum of the family and a metaphor of vigilance and inner knowledge (Miers 2000: 11).

The gods in the realm of Janus

Not only was there a divinity associated with doorways, but the portal also had an important role in domestic custom and ritual. However, the difficulty with any discussion of family festivals or beliefs, regardless of how superficial, is attempting to ascertain what was carried out from the random details that have been preserved in the ancient sources. This evidence is derived from a small group of articulate and highly educated Romans who are only representative of a very small segment of that society. The sources do not provide details of how frequently rituals were carried out or by which stratum of society (Harmon 1978: 1592). Furthermore, as Fowler points out, it is impossible to recover the religious psychology of that age and no excavation will ever reveal it (1914: 158). Customs and beliefs must have varied enormously from region to region, in time, and with economic and social standing but there must have been some consistent pattern underlying them. Nonetheless, it would seem that concern for domestic religion went deep into the Roman psyche. Veneration of the household cult continued to be worshipped from the every earliest period until the fourth century when it was thought necessary in the interests of Christianity to forbid its worship by the emperor Throdosius (Fowler 1914: 15; Nilsson 1960: 285). What can be stated is, the people that partook in these rites believed in the efficacy of the household deities that had, for most of the Roman period, been resolute and general. It may not necessarily have been a strong one, as they may not have been able to explain or justify why they uttered certain prayers or performed certain ceremonies (Ogilvie 1969: 5).

While the particularities of the religious belief of the ordinary population are unknown, evidence of its existence is widespread. The numerous household shrines, of whatever form, show that the inhabitants of Pompeii and Herculaneum remained basically religious. Studies of domestic religion have naturally tended to focus upon its more obvious physical remains, such as *lararia* and their contents, contained within dwellings, and the role of the doorways within this activity have seldom been investigated and discussed. However, the entrance into the home was a region of religious belief and ceremony as is evident from shrines and religious representations found in the vicinity of the doorway (Waites 1920: 253, fn 4).

On the walls of the *fauces* into the Casa del Fauno, VI.xii.2, there are two ornate *lararia* with very fine stucco decoration (Maiuri 1966: 45; Ling 1999: 16). A shallow arched niche, the back of which is painted with a *Lar*, can be seen in the east wall of *fauces* into I.x.3 (Boyce 1937: 27). In the east wall of the *fauces* into I.ii.17 is a rectangular niche with an *aedicula* façade (Boyce 1937: 22). A similar niche surrounded by an *aedicula* façade was also located in the north wall of the *fauces* of the Domus of M Tofelani Valentis, V.i.28 (Boyce 1937: 12 and 33). Other examples have been found in the *fauces* of the Casa del Cenacolo, V.ii.N (Boyce 1937: 36), and VI.xv.9 (Boyce 1937: 55).

On a less ornate level, the belief in the presence of the gods or a divine element in the area of the doorway was shown by a depiction of deities. In the *fauces* of VI.ix.2 on the wall is a panel containing Melenger and Atlanta, and another panel including Mercury and probably Ceres. The figures of six deities can be found on the walls of the *vestibule* of I.ix.1. On the eastern side is Mercury, Hercules and possibly Bacchus and these are faced on the western wall by Minerva, Juno and possibly Venus Pompeiana. On the pilaster to the right of the entrance of I.iii.24 was a depiction of Mercury and, on the left pilaster, Hercules (Boyce 1937: 110). The entrance pilasters of VI.xiv.43 show depictions of Mercury and Fortuna (Boyce 1937: 111). Perhaps the best known illustration of a deity found in the region of the *vestibule* is that of Priapus in the House of the Vettii, VI.xv.1 (Caro 1999: 61; Beard and Henderson 2001: 33).

It is significant that many of the deities that are associated with doorways are protective gods. The *Lares* themselves were associated with boundaries and protected the *domus* of the family (Holland 1937: 436; Nilsson 1960: 278; Tybout 1996: 359). According to a farmer's prayer recorded in Cato's *de Agri Cultura* (142), Mars was seen as a protector of crops, house and land and was not simply a god of war (Scullard 1981: 84). Priapus protected the boundary from intruders by promising to assault them (Beard and Henderson 2001: 35, fig 30). He also had an apotropaic function (Caro 1999: 61), an attribute also recognised in Hercules (Nilsson 1960: 275; Scullard 1981: 171). It is quite possible that the aggressive posture adopted by snakes depicted in many of the *lararia* may have had the power of averting evil influence or spiritual threats to the household (Tybout 1996: 362). The *Lares* received particular veneration during the most important events in the life of the family, such as at weddings, births, deaths and at the leaving on a journey and return of a member of the family (Nilsson 1960: 278). These were also occasions in which the principal portal into the dwelling received ritual attention and it can be no accident of chance that shrines and representations of divine beings were located in the region of the doorway. The general purpose of these altars or depictions of deities must have been to protect the *domus* and purify the passer-by and purge them from the evil of the outside world. Certainly, these paintings and shrines in the area of the doorways illustrate a level of religious deference.

Ritual activity in the region of the portal

Given that there was a god of doorways, other deities associated with the postal and shrines located in the region of the doorway, it is understandable that the portal was a locale associated with many of the most important ritual and social activities of the household, such as the celebration of marriages, births and deaths. Inasmuch as they took place at the front door of the dwelling, they inevitably took on a wider social significance to the community. These activities involved purification rituals, not only for the benefit of an individual (or individuals) involved but, just as importantly, for the well being of the general community. Thresholds are liminal zones that can be both spatial and temporal and as people pass from one state to another, they are exposed to hazards that must be controlled through rituals that protect against corruption (Pearson and Richards 1994: 25). As such, they fulfil van Gennep's definition of 'rites of passage' or 'transitions' as they consisted of a sequence of rituals performed at a special time, in a particular order and in a designated place (Gennep 1960; Turner 1969: 14 and 95). However, they are by no means only rites of passage as many single rites can be interpreted in several ways and have individual purposes. The significance of these rituals to the wider community meant that it was necessary to carry them out in a public manner and forum, and the doorway provided such a location. It is the physical transition during a rite of passage that is important, such as the actual crossing over a threshold accomplished during the rite by walking through a doorway. Furthermore, ritual activities help "to enforce the usual rules of normal life" (Muir 1997: 19–20). Rituals and practices should not be seen, as Turner points out, as "grotesque' reflections or expressions of economic, political and social relationships" (Turner 1969: 6). They are decisive keys that enhance our understanding of how the Romans thought and felt about these relationships, and about the natural and social environment in which they lived and operated. Thus, the portal reflected both the symbolic use of architecture and the social implications attached to such activities.

According to Binski, the historian or archaeologist assessing rituals must make a distinction between what can, and cannot, be excavated; generally in considering ritual the historian or archaeologist is speculating not so much on belief, but on behaviour; not what people thought but what they did (Binski 1996: 51). The rituals of the household are imperfectly known but they nevertheless played an important role in Roman dwellings. However, evidence from the literary sources can help to reconstruct some of the ritual activities that took place in the area of the doorway. With the information provided by the physical remains and the ancient sources it is possible to study how the ancient Romans, in the anthropological words of Pearson and Richards, "categorise space and associated meanings in given social situations" (1994: 1). The doorway was perhaps seen as a 'pivotal point' or 'focus' as ritual activities became associated and attached to the portal, making it resonate with custom, tradition and experience. These culturally constructed ritual actions are thus transformed into a material and permanent marker and the physical place in turn gives credibility, stability and validity to the activity.

There were several important occasions in the life of the family in which the doorway became the focus of attention and decoration. Marriage was an event of such magnitude to the Romans that divine co-operation was essential for its success and this led to the evolution of an elaborate ritual to seek the assistance and favour of the gods (Ogilvie 1969: 103). During a wedding the door and doorposts of both the bride's and bridegroom's houses were hung with wreaths of flowers and branches of beeches, bay-trees and cypress (Cato 64.293) and evergreens such as ivy, myrtle and laurel, and these were decorated with coloured ribbons (Juvenal 6.51–2; Apuleius 4.26). The bride's physical entry into her new home was an important part of the marriage ceremony. When she reached the house, she further decorated the doorway with woollen fillets (Pliny 29.30). The use of wool in ritual was important for its lucky or apotropaic powers (Holland 1937: 435). Then the bride ritually anointed the doorposts with oil and fat to conciliate the spirits that operated them, to keep out evil (Pliny, *Historia*

Naturalis 28.135; 28.142) and as a sign of her domesticity (Harmon 1978: 1600). Her husband who stood at the threshold then greeted her and those that had accompanied her from her home lifted her over the threshold (Cato 61.160–3; Paoli 1975: 59; Dixon 1992: 135). This was to prevent the bride from stumbling, as this would have been an ill omen for her first entry into the house and a bad indication of how the marriage would fare in the future. Every precaution was taken to ensure that all went well from the very outset of the marriage (Ogilvie 1969: 104). Still at the entrance, her husband offered her a torch and a vessel containing water to welcome her into the partnership of fire and water (Varro 5.61). These were symbolic of the essential elements of domestic life and worship (Seyffert 1891: 378; Fowler 1963: 142) and the new bride was thereby admitted to share the domestic and religious life of the household (Kiefer 1934: 20). The entry of a bride, of one whom was not part of the household, could cause tension in the relationship between the spiritual and mortal members of the dwelling. Therefore, the entry of the bride was a matter of grave seriousness and difficulty and not to be done without the intervention and acceptance of the gods and any household deities (Fowler 1963: 135–7).

At the time of a birth to the household, the door was also wreathed (Statius 4.8.40). The decoration to the doorway would have had, as with a marriage, the useful purpose of publicising the important event to the rest of the community. There was also a rite, which is mentioned by St Augustine, in which three men impersonating three guardian deities at night went about the house striking the thresholds with an axe, then with a pestle and finally sweeping them with a broom (6.9.2). The purpose of this was to prevent Silvanus from entering the dwelling to attack the mother and newborn child. Childbirth was difficult and dangerous and took a heavy toll on mothers and infants (Balsdon 1962: 195; Balsdon 2002: 87–88). As a consequence the co-operation and the protection of the gods were sought and every effort was made to expel evil from the dwelling and set up barriers at the threshold against malevolent spirits that might harm the mother and infant (Ogilvie 1969: 102–103). Presumably, the main doorway into the household received particular attention. Silvanus was a god of nature and the woodland and in the words of Bonnefoy "is characterised by a clear allergy to women" who were not allowed to be present at his ceremonies (1991: 636). The use of agricultural implements, which brought civilisation and order to the land, was in order to set up a magical barrier against the threats of the wilderness that were embodied in Silvanus (Ogilvie 1969: 103; Harmon 1978: 1597). There is, perhaps, an interesting link to Janus here, who was reputed to have brought civilisation by the introduction of agriculture. On both the occasions of a marriage and birth, the doorway was the stage for the celebration of new beginnings and new life.

In contrast to this, the portal was also the setting for rituals connected with the ending of life. Death was taken very seriously by the Romans (Kerenyi 1962: 261) and was perceived as a major blemish striking the family of the deceased, with the risk of it affecting all with whom the family had contact. Furthermore, the failure to carry out appropriate funerary rites could have dire consequences for the departed soul (Toynbee 1971: 43). For nine days after the death, the household observed a time of purification known as the *feriae denicales* (Balsdon 2002: 127). Cyprus branches decorated the door, which remained shut for the period of official mourning, and announced the bereaved house to those outside (Hornblower and Spawforth 1996: 433).

If the family was wealthy, the body of the deceased was laid in state on a bed in the *atrium* with the feet of the corpus always pointed towards the house door (Persius 3.103–5). The exposition of a woman can be seen on the late-Flavian or early-Trajanic tomb of the Haterii family. Garlands of flowers and fruit are depicted decorating the walls of the *atrium,* which are presumably symbols of afterlife fertility. The great acanthus branch that can be seen on the far left of the funeral scene may represent the foliage that would have been hung from the front door to indicate that the household has suffered a loss (Toynbee 1971: 44–45). Great care was taken over funerals, as the powers of the underworld were mysterious and sinister (Ogilvie 1969: 104). The dead were seen as powerful spirits who expected reverence from the living and resented neglect. Furthermore, the departed were close to the living, and could help or injure their descendants, and were not distant like the gods. During the three-day festival of the *Lemuria* in May the dead were believed to revisit their early homes (Scullard 1981: 118). Apart from the expected visitations to the living, the dead could return to demand restitution for some ill deed or to haunt a malefactor, and Valerius Flaccus mentions this as a privilege of the dead (3.386). Certain rites needed to be carried out to prevent the dead from returning to the house and this is reflected in the custom of carrying a corpse feet first out through the doorways for fear that the departed spirits might find their way back through them (Scullard 1981: 18). The people that were involved in these ceremonies became part of, and lived in, the realm of Janus.

Exactly what was seen as magic and superstition for the Romans is perhaps less sharply defined than it is today. However, a simple distinction was made between what was seen as acceptable and what was inappropriate. Ritual that was done for some benefit or to heal was seen as acceptable while that which was intended to do harm was not (Liebeschuetz 1979: 126–127). Magic and superstition were very close to the everyday life of some Romans and the realm of the doorway was the object of superstitious belief. Although our knowledge of magic and superstition during the Roman period is limited it was probably based on very personal and individual belief. To stumble on the threshold whilst leaving the house was considered a bad omen and the superstitious believed it better to go back and spend the rest of the day safely in the house (Cicero, *De Div.* I.40.84; Ovid, *Meta.* 10.452; Paoli 1975: 281). The threshold was an object of reverence and to enter a doorway or tread on the threshold with the left foot first was considered to be a bad omen and on special occasions a boy was given the charge to caution visitors to put the right foot forward (Petronius 30; Dyer 1867: 267). It was for this reason that Vitruvius in his *On Architecture* states that the steps leading into a temple should be of an uneven number, because the worshipper, after placing their right foot upon the bottom step, would then place the same foot on the threshold (3.4). By writing the word *Arseverse* on the door of a house it was believed the risk of a fire could be avoided (Paoli 1975: 281). There was a great fear of witches gaining entry into the household (Apuleius 2.21; Petronius 63 and 134). To protect themselves against the power of sorceresses, some people nailed the beard of a wolf onto their door, as a wolf's beard had great potency in spells and could both render and dispel incantations (Pliny 28.157; Horace *Sat.* 1.8.42).

Conclusion

The vivid physical remains of Pompeii and Herculaneum offer the greatest opportunity for the study of the main doorways into the domiciles of the élite. Parallels with wall paintings and sepulchral monuments from around the empire indicate that the form of doorways found in Pompeii and Herculaneum was not unique to Campania. However, the material remains are limited in that they cannot explain the purpose and motivations behind their form and the activities that took place in the area of the portal. The evidence of structures and other material culture associated with doorways can be interpreted but these can only remain as hypotheses if they are not supported by other forms of evidence. The surviving written sources can create the opportunity to reconstruct some of the human activities and events that occurred within the excavated remains. Archaeological and literary sources have their biases and limitations, but they are both primary sources for the past, and should where possible compliment each other, as each present information about matters on which the other is silent. Neither should be neglected, as there is no common measure of the past and where feasible interdisciplinary approaches are important to present a more holistic and accurate picture of Roman society. Ultimately, the aim is to reconstruct and explain the physical and social milieu of the past in which life was lived.

It seems clear that the doorway into the homes of the Roman élite was an area of great socio-religious significance. Roman doorways were loaded with social and symbolic meanings that were inextricably linked to their function. The principal doorway offered a choice between exposure and observation from the outside world and shelter from unwanted extraneous scrutiny. The deities and rituals at the portal served to keep what belonged within the dwelling safe inside and to ward off intrusion from the outside. The shrines to the domestic cult and the ceremonies framed by the portal were part of the mental furniture, as definitely fixed in the minds of the Romans as the doorway itself, and the relationship between humans and the gods was characterised by the doorway. The main doorways into the domiciles of the élite performed an important ritualistic and symbolic purpose as well as a reference function in the construction and dissemination of culture and identity. Many and varied ritual activities took within the region of the doorway and the knowledge of most of these have probably been lost. In a perverse way, the rituals carried out at the doorway tell us more of the social units that practised the ritual than about the ritual they practised. On a superficial level the rituals that took place, and the shrines and depictions of deities found in the locale of the doorway, seemed to have had little connection to Janus. However, further study demonstrates the inextricable link between the ceremonial activity and the deities found at the doorway to Janus because they all took place under the watchful gaze and domain of the god and his image, the doorway. It can be seen that the Romans used vernacular detail to innovative effect to decorate their doorways and the embellishment of the doorway reinforced and provided a dignified setting for the ritual activities that took place in the realm of Janus.

Department of Archaeology, University of Durham.

Acknowledgements

I would like to thank all those who were involved in the organisation of TRAC at Canterbury, for organising a very enjoyable and stimulating conference, and those concerned with editing this TRAC volume. I am very grateful to all those to whom I spoke after my paper for their comments and suggestions which all helped to develop this article. I would also like to thank Mark Douglas from the Department of Archaeology in Durham, with whom I have often discussed (no pun intended) the ins and outs of doorways, and Dr Derek Craig for reading through this paper. Finally, I would like to thank Professor Rosemary Cramp, whose comments after I gave a paper on doorways in the Department of Archaeology at Durham, helped to formulate this paper.

Bibliography

Ancient sources

Apuleius (translated by R. Graves 1972). *Golden Ass.* London: Penguin.
Cato (translated by A. Dalby 1998). *De Agri Cultura.* Devon: Prospect.
Cicero (translated by W. A. Falconer 1952). *De Divinatione.* London: Loeb Classical Library.
Cicero (translated by H. Rackham 1933). *De Natura Deorum.* London: Loeb Classical Library.
Horace (translated by H. Rushton Fairclough 1970). *Satires, Epistles and Ars Poetica.* London: Loeb Classical Library.
Juvenal (translated by G. G. Ramsay 1979). *Satirae.* London: Loeb Classical Library.
Ovid (translated by J. G. Frazer 1989). *Fasti.* London: Loeb Classical Library.
Ovid (translated by F. J. Miller 1974). *Metamorphoses.* London: Loeb Classical Library.
Persius (translated by G. G. Ramsay 1979). *Satirae.* London: Loeb Classical Library.
Petronius (translated by J. Sullivan 1968). *Satyricon.* London: Faber and Faber.
Pliny (translated by H. Rackham 1940). *Historia Naturalis.* London: Loeb Classical Library.
Statius (translated by A. Hardie 1983). *Silvae.* Liverpool: Cairns.
St Augustine (translated by W. M. Green 1963). *De Civitate Dei.* London: Loeb Classical Library.
Valerius Flaccus (translated by H. J. W. Wijsman 1996). *Argonautica.* Leiden: Brill.
Varro (translated by R. G. Kent 1968). *De lingua Latina.* London: Loeb Classical Library.
Vitruvius (translated by F. Granger 1961). *On architecture.* London: Loeb Classical Library.

Modern sources

Adam, J-P. 1994. *Roman Building: materials and techniques.* London: Batsford.
Alexander, C. 1977. *A Pattern Language: towns, buildings, construction.* New York: Oxford University Press.
Balsdon, J. P. V. D. 1962. *Roman Women: their history and habits.* London: Bodley Head.
Balsdon, J. P. V. D. 2002. *Life and Leisure in Ancient Rome.* London: Phoenix Press.
Beard, M. and Henderson, J. 2001. *Classical Art: from Greece to Rome.* Oxford: Oxford University Press.
Binski, P. 1996. *Medieval Death: ritual and representation.* London: British Museum.
Bonnefoy, Y. 1991. *Mythologies.* London: University of Chicago.
Boyce, G. K. 1937. *Corpus of the Lararia of Pompeii.* Memoirs of the American Academy of Rome 14.
Brothers, A. J. 1996. 'Urban Housing'. In I. M. Barton. (ed.) *Roman domestic buildings.* Exeter: University of Exeter Press. 33–64.
de Caro, S. 1999. *Still Lifes from Pompeii.* Napoli: Electra.
de Caro, S. 2001. *The National Archaeological Museum of Naples.* Napoli: Electra.
Claridge, A. 1998. *Rome: an Oxford archaeological guide.* Oxford: Oxford University Press.
Clarke, J. R. 1991. *The Houses of Roman Italy 100 BC–AD 250.* London: University of California.
Connolly, P. 1990. *Pompeii.* Oxford: Oxford University Press.
Cotterell, A. 2000. *The Pimlico Dictionary of Classical Mythologies.* London: Pimlico.
Dixon, S. 1992. *The Roman Family.* Baltimore: Johns Hopkins University Press.
Dupont, F. 1998. *Daily Life in Rome.* Oxford: Blackwell.
Dyer, T. H. 1867. *Pompeii: its history, buildings and antiquities.* London: Bell and Daldy.
Engelmann, W. 1929. *New Guide to Pompeii.* Leipzig: Englemann.
Fagan, G. G. 1999. *Bathing in Public in the Roman World.* Michigan: University of Michigan.
Franciscis, A. de 1978. *The Buried Cities: Pompeii and Herculaneum.* London: Book Club Association.
Fowler, W. W. 1914. *Roman Ideas of Deity in the Last Century before the Christian Era.* London: Macmillan.
Fowler, W. W. 1963. *Social Life at Rome in the Age of Cicero.* London: Macmillan.
van Gennep, A. 1960. *The Rites of Passage.* London: Routledge.
Guhl, E. and Koner, W. 1994. *The Romans: their life and customs.* Middlesex: Senate Press.

Haarløv, B. 1977. *The Half-open Door: a common symbolic motif within Roman sepulchral sculpture.* Odense: Odense University Press.

Harmon, D. P. 1978. 'The family festival at Rome'. *Aufstieg und Niedergang der Römischen Welt,* 16.2: 1592–1603.

Holland, L. A. 1961. *Janus and the Bridge.* Rome: American Academy at Rome.

Hornblower, S. and Spawforth, A. 1996. *The Oxford Classical Dictionary.* Oxford: Oxford University Press.

Kerenyi, C. 1962. *The Religions of the Greeks and Romans.* London: Thames and Hudson.

Kiefer, O. 1934. *Sexual Life in Ancient Rome.* London: Routledge.

King, A. 1982. *Archaeology of the Roman Empire.* London: Hamlyn.

Lawrence, M. 1928. 'A sarcophagus at Lanuvius'. *American Journal of Archaeology* 32: 421–443.

Lawrence, M. 1958. 'Season sarcophagi of architectural type'. *American Journal of Archaeology* 62: 273–295.

Leach, E. W. 1997. 'Oecus on Ibycus: investigating the vocabulary of the Roman house'. In S. E. Bon and R. Jones (eds.) *Sequence and space in Pompeii.* Oxford: Oxbow Monograph 77. 50–72.

Liebeschuetz, J. H. W. G. 1979. *Continuity and Change in Roman Religion.* Oxford: Clarendon Press.

Ling, R. 1997. *The Insula of the Menander at Pompeii.* Oxford: Clarendon Press.

Ling, R. 1999. *Stuccowork and Painting in Roman Italy.* Aldershot: Ashgate.

Liversidge, J. 1968. *Britain in the Roman Empire.* London: Routledge and Kegan Paul.

MacKenzie, W. M. 1910. *Pompeii.* London: A and C Black.

Maiuri, A. 1959. *Herculaneum.* Roma: Instituto Poligrafico Dello Stato.

Maiuri, A. 1966. *Pompeii.* Novara: Istituto Geografico de Agrstini.

Miers, M. 2000. *Doors and Windows: 100 period details from the archives of country life.* London: Aurum.

Morford, M. P. O. and Lenardon, R. J. 1999. *Classical Mythology.* London: Longman.

Muir, E. 1997. *Ritual in early Modern Europe.* Cambridge, Cambridge University Press.

Nilsson, M. P. 1960. *Opuscula Selecta, Linguis Anglica, Francoggalica, Germanica Conscripta.* Lund: Skänska Centraltryckeriet.

Ogilvie, R. M. 1969. *The Romans and their Gods: in the Age of Augustus.* London: Chatto and Windus.

Orr, D.G. 1978. 'Roman domestic religion: the evidence of the household shrine'. *Aufstieg und Niedergang der Römischen Welt,* 16.2: 1559–91.

Paoli, U. E. 1975. *Rome: its people, life and customs.* London: Longman.

Pearson, M. P. and Richards, C. 1994. *Archaeology and Order: approaches to social space.* London: Routledge.

Picard, G. 1970. *Roman Painting.* London: Elek Books.

Richardson, L. 1988. *Pompeii: an architectural history.* Baltimore: Johns Hopkins University Press.

Scullard, H. H. 1981. *Festivals and Ceremonies of the Roman Republic.* London: Thames and Hudson.

Seyffert, O. 1891. *Dictionary of Classical Antiquities.* New York: MacMillian.

Thébert, Y. 1987. 'Private life and domestic architecture in Roman Africa'. In P. Veyne (ed.) *A History of Private Life: From pagan Rome to Byzantium.* London: Harvard University Press. 313–409.

Thorpe, M. 1995. *Roman Architecture.* London: Bristol Classical Press.

Toynbee, J. M. C. 1971. *Death and Burial in the Roman World.* New York: Cornell University Press.

Turner, V. W. 1969. *The Ritual Process: structure and anti-structure.* London: Routledge.

Tybout, R. A. 1996. 'Domestic shrines and 'popular painting': style and social context'. *Journal of Roman Archaeology,* 9: 358–374

Waites, M. C. 1920. 'The nature of the Lares and their representation in Roman art'. *American Journal of Archaeology,* 24: 241–63.

Wallace-Hadrill, A. 1994. *Houses and Society in Pompeii and Herculaneum.* Princeton: Princeton University Press.

Zanker, P. 2000. *Pompeii: public and private life.* London: Harvard University Press.

Deconstructing the Frampton pavements: gnostic dialectic in Roman Britain?

Dominic Perring

The quest

This paper explores some possible connections between the systems of understanding that inspired the design of a Romano-British mosaic pavement and those that can be brought to bear in its contemporary interpretation.

The point that I wish to illustrate is that some of the theoretical constructs employed in our explanation of the Roman past are embedded within the same intellectual discourse that engaged the attention of élite society in late antiquity. The philosophies of the ancient world provide a rich and stimulating theoretical environment that remain central to many areas of modern thinking, but have been little exploited in giving academic direction to Romano-British studies.

I base my argument on an individual and speculative reading of a single artefact: a mid-fourth century mosaic pavement found over two hundred years ago at a site near Frampton in Dorset (Lysons 1817; Henig 1984). In preparing the results of a doctoral thesis for publication I decided that this mosaic would make an attractive illustration to a technical chapter on the different types of floor used in Roman houses (Perring 2002, fig. 52). I therefore came to the evidence with no immediate interest in the meaning of the images deployed, beyond the need to provide a caption that did justice to a complicated and confusing array of images (Figure 1).

I was, however, predisposed to believe that the pavement had been structured with meaning in mind. Shortly before engaging with the detail of the Frampton mosaics my attention had been drawn to Lefebvre's work on the production of space (1991). This encouraged me to think in terms of the ways in which interpretations of space might describe aspects of social relations. Lefebvre's emphasis on a "trialectics of spatiality" – in which distinctions can be drawn between perceived, conceived and lived space – suggested different ways of understanding the spatial configurations encountered within the Roman house (see also Soja 1996: 63–6). I was, therefore, inclined to find an interior design that might have "enriched the temporal dimension of space", generating something that might be described as "a theatrical space of hints and declarations" (Lefebvre 1991: 186–9; Perring 2002: 139).

In trying to relate the interior design to the ways in which the space might have been used, I have found it necessary to give most of my attention to the ideas that might have inspired the particular deployment of the images found at Frampton. This paper, therefore, is mostly concerned with the issue of 'conceived space' and the ideological intentions of those who designed the room in question. It is only peripherally concerned with the transformation which may be brought about through different uses and perceptions of space.

Decorative schemes found in the aristocratic houses of the ancient world were sometimes contrived to emphasise the spatial hierarchies involved in the 'ascent of privilege' described by Wallace-Hadrill (1994). This was an exaggerated feature of late antiquity, which witnessed an increasingly processional and revelatory approach to the design of both private and public architecture (Brown 1971).

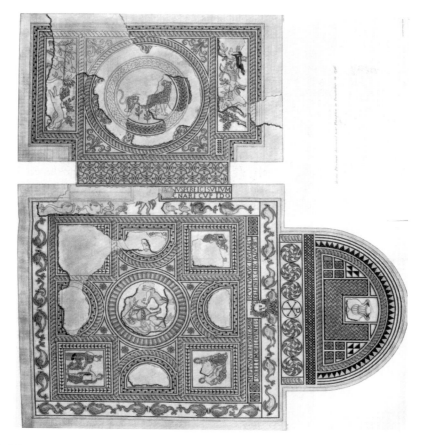

Figure 1. The mosaic pavements within the tri-partite room at Frampton, Dorset (from a coloured engraving by S. Lysons)

Such arguments can readily be applied to the evidence of Romano-British domestic architecture in general, and perhaps also to the building at Frampton in particular. The pavement at Frampon was set at one end of the building, and was reached along a portico-corridor decorated with geometric designs (for a more detailed discussion of the architecture of this building see Perring forthcoming). The Romano-British portico-corridor façade was likely to have operated in a similar fashion to the peristyle courtyard commonly found attached to the houses of Roman Italy and from which it was arguably derived (Perring 2002: 159). These colonnaded passages paid architectural homage to the stoa and gymnasia of the Hellenistic world, and established a suitable setting for the *ambulatio* or promenade with its attendant philosophical discourse (for a review of both the architectural evidence and written sources on the subject see Dickmann 1997: 123–5). The public architecture to which these domestic settings refer was also, at least in some instances, designed against the needs of civic ritual and religious procession (Bejor 1999). These architectural references to philosophical debate and religious procession need not have been very relevant by the time that the buildings at

Frampton were erected, when the portico façade was commonplace. But the very ubiquity of this feature attests to the importance of structured movement within the Roman houses of this period.

The arrangement of the mosaic images in the main room at Frampton suggests that this floor, like several others of the period, was designed to be seen from a series of different positions (Witts 2000). The room was divided into three separate areas, each with its own scheme of figurative mosaics. The spaces were separated one from the other by wide, almost certainly arched, openings where curtains may have hung. Motifs within the mosaics gave emphasis to the thresholds, defining the liminal nature of the boundaries found here but also providing conceptual links between the schemes deployed. The decoration of the different spaces marked out a dynamic pathway of images leading from the room's entrance to its innermost 'sanctum'. On one reading, therefore, these mosaics defined a processional and climactic use of the space: a closely argued three-part narrative, with a beginning, middle and an end.

The images chosen to mark the entrance to the room may have announced just such a narrative structure. The hunt scenes placed here marked the threshold and directed the visitor towards the more powerful images beyond. The hunt served as a metaphor for the quest for truth in late antique philosophy (e.g. Clement of Alexandria, *The Stromata* 1.2; Henig 1995: 155–6). In trying to account for the choices of images drawn upon in the decoration of the Frampton building this concept of a quest becomes an attractive one. The pavements contained frequent allegorical references to the mortality of the human soul, and the focal point of the entire decorative scheme appears to have contained a Christian message. A *chi-rho* monogram, a symbol of Christ occupied the chord of the apse. Although this motif might alternatively have been used here because of its association with post-Constantinian imperial power (as Henig 1995: 154–6), the other scenes and motifs found in this room suggest that the pavement was concerned with the salvation of the soul. In this context it is more likely that the *chi-rho* was used conventionally to represent the Christian saviour (as was also the case in the sister mosaic to Frampton at Hinton St Mary), rather than to describe temporal power. In either case most of the images in the room were orientated to be viewed from this cardinal point. This suggests that the images presented in this room could have been read in different ways from different perspectives. Visitors advancing into the room were given less information, and were in a position of comparative inferiority, to those already in occupancy of the room. The full range of information contained within the decorative scheme was not universally accessible. Knowledge, and by implication power, was structured hierarchically. The principal image that lay beyond this focal point, the conclusion of the narrative described in these mosaics, was the Bacchic chalice or *cantharus*. What could be more appropriate than a grail at the end of the quest!

Resisting the many tempting speculations that such an observation suggests, the main point to make here is that it is possible to consider the Frampton images within a narrative framework, albeit one in which the full clarity of the argument was reserved until the end of its reading. The antechamber, decorated with the hunt scenes, was introductory; the main body of text was found in the larger room beyond; whilst the smaller apse brought the scheme to some form of conclusion. Given the presence of the Christian symbol and the allegorical content of most of the other images found here it seems legitimate to see this narrative structure as leading towards some form of philosophical observation. This, then, was my working hypothesis in trying to describe and account for the art chosen to decorate the rooms at Frampton. It is, however, a much harder matter to tease out the detail of the arguments presented, and this must necessarily involve a considerable amount of conjecture.

The problem of the art of late antiquity is that it drew on an exceptionally rich iconographic vocabulary in making its 'hints and declarations' (Elsner 1998). The range of images deployed at Frampton – including representations of Bacchus, Bellerophon, Neptune and Cupid accompanied by a Latin epigram – place this pavement firmly within this classical tradition and show that the learning deployed here was of Graeco-Roman inspiration. This was a world where complex philosophies gave rise to intricate allegorical representations, drawing on a rich mythological and iconographic tradition. The allegorical interpretation of mythological texts was an important feature of the neo-Platonist thinking that dominated late antique philosophy and influenced the first Christian writers (Jonas 1958: 91). It can be argued that such ideas were inaccessible to an ill-informed rural Romano-British aristocracy that lived on the margins of the Roman world. For the purposes of this paper I take the contrary view, and assume that the proliferation of complex allegorical images found in late antique Romano-British art reflects on a mature intellectual engagement with the philosophical ideas that were then current. It was perhaps just such an intellectual environment that allowed Britain to subsequently produce Christian philosphers of the stature of Pelagius.

The eclectic nature of the images and the apparent lack of decorative coherence makes it possible to argue that the meanings of individual symbols and motifs at Frampton had somehow become subordinate, if not entirely lost, to their collective visual impact and a generalised message of erudite sophistication (Ling 1997). Alternatively, however, the complexity and sophistication of the iconographic vocabulary might reflect the arcane nature of the ideas expressed. The reading of images, the identification of the allusive arguments that give intellectual structure to the narratives that they present, relies on a range of shared understandings that are the product of both classical education and particular learning. This is not to deny the fact that different audiences would have engaged differently with the images and the ideas that they represented. It is unlikely that all visitors to the building at Frampton were intended to read and understand everything on display. In the ancient world, as in the modern, one of the purposes of a classical education was to elaborate a language of power that established rank and social boundaries. This language of learning formed cultural bonds that distinguished élite society from the lower orders, whilst defining gradations of taste and erudition within the elect. Our interest here is in the knowledge systems that operated amongst those competent to recognise and interpret the various layers of significance possessed by the images placed on the floors of this building. This, therefore, obliges us to turn to the religious and philosophical sources that might be referred to in pavements such as that at Frampton.

The mysterious object

There is not space here to do full justice to the pavements at Frampton. The building itself contained three main groups of rooms decorated with mosaics, each containing many individual images permitting a series of alternative interpretations.

Parallels can also be drawn with a wide range of other mosaic pavements, and with the iconographic choices found in other late antique art, especially the decorated silver found in the hoards of the period. Furthermore the interpretations of the evidence suggest several lines of inquiry into the nature of late Romano-British society. In particular it permits speculation on how the philosophical and theological arguments of the third and fourth centuries may have affected the social cohesion of Roman Britain and contributed to the changes evident in the power structures of the late fourth century. Some of these issues I have already touched on elsewhere, others I discuss in fuller detail in a forthcoming paper (Perring 2002; Perring forthcoming).

Here a more focussed and rather summary treatment must suffice. The object is not to prove my argument but to selectively explore some of its implications, in order to make some broader points about the nature of our use of ideas in forming archaeological interpretations.

One of the most particular characteristics of the Frampton pavement is its unusual combination of Christian and pagan elements. The floors here were from the same school as the better known mosaic at Hinton St Mary. In both cases there has been some speculation as to the possible significance of the syncretic approach to pagan myth and Christian symbol (Toynbee 1968; Huskinson 1974; Black 1986; Henig 1986 and Scott 2000).

The argument that I present elsewhere is that the images at Frampton were carefully contrived to present a series of allegorical statements about the nature and destiny of the mortal soul, set out in a dialectical fashion (Perring forthcoming). The emphasis placed on antithetical contrasts, from which synthesis could be achieved, hints at dualistic belief. The dualistic idea that the immortal soul was held captive in corrupt flesh was central to the Orphic followers of Bacchus. Some archaeological finds from Roman-Britain are unambiguously Orphic (Arthur 1977; Henig 1977), and the widespread popularity of Bacchus in the province is most readily understood in terms of the diffusion of Orphism. Orphic teachings and mysteries were in part developed from those Dionysius-Bacchus, and the beliefs that inspired them were both influenced by and influential on the neo-Platonic philosophy of late antiquity. Orphic ideas were in turn an important influence in the development of a dualistic tradition within the early Christian church (Legge 1964; Guthrie 1966: 253–5; Eisler 1925). In the course of the second and third centuries these dualistic Christians – better known as gnostics – were identified as heretic, and their belief systems both described and condemned in the anti-heretical writings of Irenaeus and Hypollitus, amongst others (Williams 1999; Rudolph 1983). Gnostics also believed that the spirit was imprisoned in hostile matter, and that salvation involved liberating the soul from its mortal chains. Salvation was the accomplishment of mystical knowledge gained through erudite study and the interpretation of signs and symbols (*gnosis*). Followers of the cult had to master secrets that revealed the soul's path through the spheres of human existence to immortal life (Jonas 1958: 45).

Several previous studies have identified gnostic and Orphic elements within Romano-British mosaics (Stupperich 1980: 300; Thomas 1981: 104–5; Walters 1982; Walters 1984), and although the evidence is open to question, the case for identifying gnostic influences at Frampton seems a strong one. It offers a credible context for the particular combination of images found here. Although the available sources suggest that these ideas were most widely diffused in the east and at their most vigorous in the second and third centuries AD, this reflects on the biases in the evidence. We know little of the spread of such ideas in the more remote western provinces since we lack sources. The fact that some of the firmest and most detailed denunciations of gnostic heresy were written by Irenaeus, as Bishop of Lyons, leaves little doubt, however, that these ideas reached the west. Their survival into the fourth and fifth centuries is documented in Egypt by both the recorded experiences of Epiphanius of Salamis and the extraordinary hoard of gnostic texts buried at Nag Hammadi. In the west we have episodes such as the suppression of the Priscillianist heresy in Spain to remind us that it was only in the course of the fourth century that orthodoxy was imposed on a plurality of Christian thinking. Although gnostic-style dualism returned to be an influence in medieval Europe, most famously amongst the Cathars, it is generally held that gnosticism in the west disappeared at the latest in the 6th century (Rudolph 1983: 367).

Regardless of the specific contributions made by Orphic, gnostic, Christian and neo-Platonic philosophies, my main purpose here is to suggest that the pavements were designed to present a dualistic proposition within a tri-partitite division of space: involving quest, mystery and revelation. In order to do so it is first necessary to very briefly describe the pavement itself. The three schemes of decoration can be separately described as follows.

Antechamber. The hunt scenes at the threshold flanked a central roundel containing the standing figure of the ecstatic god Bacchus. Bacchus was a twice-born god, whose return from death presented a symbol of immortality.

The main room. The central panel showed Bellerophon riding Pegasus and slaying the Chimaera. Four subsidiary panels in the corners depicted paired gods and mortals: including Adonis and Venus, and perhaps Attis and Sagaritis. An outer border of dolphins linked two panels of Latin text set alongside the figures of Cupid and Neptune. Cupid occupied the place between the antechamber and the main room, whilst Neptune was set facing towards the apse. The text describes the relationship between these elements, apparently celebrating Cupid's superiority. The dolphin was widely used in Bacchic and Orphic iconography, and later in Christian representations, to represent the human soul in search of escape from the mortality represented by the sea. Cupid too represents the divine spirit. Bellerophon is instead the mortal hero who challenges mortality and rides the divine Pegasus, offspring of ocean, but eventually fails to ascend heavenward. Similarly the stories of Adonis and Attis both refer to mortality and the relationship between human and divine. The most important contrast was that drawn between ethereal spirit (Pegasus-Cupid) and the chains of matter (represented in various references to Neptune and the oceans).

The apse. A cantharus or chalice occupied the main part of the apse, with a chi-rho set facing the mask of Neptune referred to above.

A clue to the reading of these images can be found in the contrasts drawn between elements that signify matter and mortality, and those of transcendent divine power. The space can be read as a dialectic argument (Figure 2), in which antithetical arguments were presented in a quest for a victory over death. The key feature is the *cantharus* that was found in the place of honour framed beneath the celestial apse in the innermost, third, space. This chalice could only be reached by passing through Christ, as represented by the chi-rho monogram. The *cantharus* was widely used as a symbol of the Orphic eucharist, the grail in which wine and water were mixed in a ritual practice inspired by the Graeco-Roman *symposium* (Slofstra 1995: 89). The very point of the later Christian eucharist was to bring about a miraculous transubstantiation through admixture. Participation in an early form of this sacrament may have been the main concern of the Frampton pavement, in which case the room was perhaps designed around the celebration of the gnostic eucharist.

Our best source on such practice is the *Gospel of Philip*, as found amongst the Nag Hammadi texts (NHC II, 3: 75, 15–24). This describes how the eucharistic chalice of water and wine contained the Holy Spirit, and that to drink it makes the perfect man. Although the eucharist may not have formed part of contemporary orthodox liturgical practice in the western church, it was already an important feature in Syrian church ceremony (Frend 1984–5: 149). Parallels can also be drawn between Syrian liturgical vessels and items found in late Romano-British hoards (de Bhaldraithe 1991; Perring forthcoming). The eucharist can be described as a

Antechamber

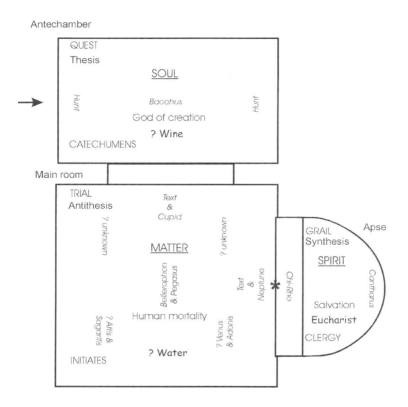

Figure 2. A summary of some of the themes and ideas that might be represented in the mosaic illustrated in figure 1.

mythic ritualization of the cycle of creation, death and resurrection, in which earthly substances were alchemically transmuted into divine (Jung 1979: 314).

If this room had been designed around eucharistic practice then, following the ritual practices that applied at the time, the antechamber would have served as a place for the catechumens in waiting, whilst the initiates participated in the ceremonies in the main room beyond. These ceremonies were in turn conducted by an elect clergy, stationed in the apse. The rituals assumed a hierarchy in which the bishops and clergy came first, ahead of the faithful (segregated according to their state of grace), and those uninitiated (Brown 1998: 40). This did not necessarily preclude alternative uses, and this room might have started life as a villa dining room where the patron also invited friends, clients and dependants to celebrate mass (Perring 2002: 169).

Several gnostic sects, in particular the Sethians, recognised three primal principles: those of human soul, earthly matter and divine spirit (Rudolph 1983: 90–2). Hippolytus describes how the soul, the human element of divine spirit, was believed to have been caught between darkness below, described as a formidable water, and light above (the contrast drawn between Cupid and

Neptune in the Frampton pavement may have made a similar point). This human spirit was a spark of divinity that had been caught and trapped in matter by the violence of wind on water (*Refutation of all Heresies* 5,14). The Orphics described this condition through reference to the fabrication of the human species from the ashy remnants of the Titans, destroyed by Jupiter, that had consumed Bacchus/Zagreus in his first emanation. In Valentinian cosmographies, humanity took its soul from the demiurge (the known god responsible for the creation of the world) and its flesh from matter. This awareness of the 'three-in-oneness' of existence inspired the use of antithetical contrasts as a means of achieving the ideal of synthesis.

The tripartite division of space at Frampton may therefore represent the division of existence into the three essential components referred to above. If this were the case the ante-chamber was not only the starting place in the quest for salvation, where catechumens waited on enlightenment, but was also the place of the soul. The soul here was ruled over by the demiurgic god of creation, personified as Bacchus. The first narrative declaration, therefore, was that of creation.

In this reading, the main room would therefore have been the place of matter, dedicated to the captive soul seeking blessed release (as represented by Bellerophon, the dolphins, Attis and Adonis). These captive souls were the initiates of the sect, aware of their unfortunate condition and awaiting revelation. The images in this area were the product of creation: man made mortal, destined to die but in search of divine release. The spark searching upwards. The texts in the border to the room were placed in prophylactic fashion, marking potent boundaries between the three conditions of existence represented by the three spaces.

The third and final chamber, the apse, was therefore reserved for the spirit. This was the place of the elect who through their knowledge (*gnosis*) of Christ and the celebration of his secret rites had achieved the necessary synthesis of sensual and material (the gnostic *pneumatic*). This spatial dialectic is that described in the ritual of the Eucharist, where wine and water became one. Indeed it is also possible to equate the outer room with wine (Bacchus), the main chamber with water (Neptune), and the apse with their mixing (the *cantharus*). In this reading the apse was the place where the main ritual uses of the room took place, the place where activities gave meaning to the architectural setting. There is an attractive coincidental symmetry to the way in which this third space can, with only gentle abuse of the ideas represented, be termed a 'thirdspace' of the imagined and enacted found in the social theories of Lefebvre (1991) and Soja (1996).

I suggest that the goal of the quest described on the floor at Frampton was symbolised by the eucharistic chalice, which here took on the attributes of a holy grail. Eternal life – the release of spirit – was the reward of this synthesis between soul and matter, divine and mortal, wine and water.

The grail

In this paper I have described two quests for enlightenment. The first quest I described was my own: my attempt to read the archaeological evidence represented by the pavements at Frampton. The second quest is the one that I attribute to the people who designed and studied these mosaics in the middle of the fourth century. These images were perhaps intended to describe a path to eternal life. The arguments drew on sophisticated cosmographies that were the result of centuries of philosophical study and reflection. It is important to remember that some of mythological scenes found at Frampton referred to legends that were already more than one thousand years old when the floors were designed. This ancient scholarship was the product of an interest in the past no less intense than that represented by the archaeological papers found in this volume, and a concern with theory that surely far exceeded our own. Theoretical Roman archaeology is no new thing.

Both of the quests described here can be presented within the context of a dialectical argument: involving quest, mystery and revelation. It should occasion no surprise that this Hegelian structure of thesis, antithesis and synthesis can be applied to both the present research and that represented in the design of the rooms at Frampton. Hegel's studies of the philosophy of religion, as described in his lectures of 1824, drew on the same neo-Platonist ideas that were subsumed within gnostic cosmographies (Hegel 1985). His description of the perfection of spirit, or 'geist', would have been readily understood by a gnostic audience, as would the emphasis he places on a 'triune' god. Hegel describes distinctions that can be drawn between matter, idea and spirit/god. Having tentatively established some points of contact between Hegelian and neo-Platonist philsosophy, it is a much easier matter to assert Hegel's influence on Marx, and in turn the Marxist character of Lefebvre's attempt to define a spatial trialectic.

In sum we can trace elements of a common intellectual approach in both the design of the Frampton pavements and in the interpretative agenda that I first brought to its study. Post-Enlightenment philosophy has, of course, taken us in very different directions in our quest for truth and understanding. But the fact of the quest itself is a shared one, and the language we use has common roots in the philosophy of late antiquity.

Department of Archaeology, University of York

Bibliography

Ancient sources

Clement of Alexandria, The Stromata: in *The Writings of Clement of Alexandria* (translated by W. Wilson 1867–9). Edinburgh: Ante-Nicene Christian Library.

Hippolytus (translated by F. Legge 1921) *Refutation of all Heresies*. London: Translations of Christian Literature, Series 1, Greek texts.

Nag Hammadi Codex (NHC) II, Gospel of Philip: in *The Nag Hammadi Library in English* (ed. J. M. Robinson 1977). San Francisco & Leiden: Harper & Rowe.

Modern sources

Arthur, P. 1977. Eggs and Pomegranates: an example of symbolism in Roman Britain. In J. Munby and M. Henig (eds) *Roman Life and Art in Britain*. Oxford: BAR British Series 41. 367–74.

Bejor, G. 1999. *Vie Colonnate. Paesaggi urbani del mondo antico*. Rome: Supplemento 22 alla Rivista di Archeologia, Bretschneider.

Black, E. W. 1986. Christian and Pagan hopes of Salvation in Romano-British mosaics. In M. Henig and A. King (eds) *Pagan Gods and Shrines of the Roman Empire*. Oxford: OUCA Monograph 8. 147–58.

Brown, P. 1971. *The World of late Antiquity*. London: Thames and Hudson.

Brown, P. 1998. *Late Antiquity*. Cambridge Mass: The Belknap Press of Harvard University Press.

de Bhaldraithe, E. 1991. Strainers and other instruments in early Church Ritual. In D. Watts *Christians and Pagans in Roman Britain*. London: Routledge. 231–3.

Dickmann, J-A. 1997. The Peristyle and the Transformation of Domestic Space in Hellenistic Pompeii. In R. Laurence and A. Wallace-Hadrill (eds.) *Domestic space in the Roman world: Pompeii and beyond*. Michigan: Journal of Roman Archaeology Supplementary Series 22. 121–136.

Eisler, R. 1925. *Orphische-dionysische Mysteriengedanken in der christlichen Antike.* Leipzig - Berlin: Olms.

Elsner, J. 1998. *Imperial Rome and Christian Triumph.* Oxford: Oxford University Press.

Frend, W. H. C. 1984–5. Syrian parallels to the Water Newton treasure? *Jahrbuch für Antike und Christentum,* 27–8: 146–50.

Guthrie, W. K. C. 1966. *Orpheus and Greek Religion: A study of the Orphic movement.* New York: Norton.

Hegel, G. W. F. H. 1985. *Lectures on the Philosophy of Religion: 3* (ed. P. C. Hodgson) Berkeley: University of California Press.

Henig, M. 1977. Roman Gemstones: figuretype and adaptation. In J. Munby and M. Henig (eds) *Roman Life and Art in Britain,* Oxford: BAR British Series 41. 341–6.

Henig, M. 1984. James Engleheart's drawing of a mosaic at Frampton, 1794. *Proceedings of the Dorset Natural History and Archaeological Society,* 106: 146.

Henig, M. 1986. 'Ita intellexit numine inductus tuo': some personal interpretations of deity in Roman religion. In M. Henig and A. King (eds.) *Pagan Gods and Shrines of the Roman Empire.* Oxford: OUCA Monograph 8. 159–70.

Henig, M. 1995. *The Art of Roman Britain.* London: Batsford.

Huskinson, J. 1974. Some Pagan mythological figures and their significance in early Christian art. *Papers of the British School at Rome,* 42: 68–97.

Jonas, H. 1958. *Gnostic religion.* Boston: Beacon.

Jung, C. G. 1979. Transformation symbolism in the Mass. In J. Campbell (ed.) *Eranos. Papers from the Eranos Yearbooks. 2: The Mysteries.* New York: Princeton University Press. 274–336

Lefebvre, H. 1991, *The Production of Space* (trans. D. Nicholson Smith). Oxford: Blackwell.

Legge, F. 1964. *Forerunners and rivals of Christianity.* New York: University Books.

Ling, R. 1997. Mosaics in Roman Britain: discoveries and research since 1945. *Britannia,* 28: 259–96.

Lysons, S. 1817. *Reliquiae Britannico-Romanae* iii. London.

Perring, D. 2002. *The Roman house in Britain.* London: Routledge.

Perring, D. forthcoming (2003). Gnosticism in fourth century Britain: the Frampton mosaics reconsidered. *Britannia,* 34.

Rudolph, K. 1983. *Gnosis: the nature and history of Gnosticism* (transl. R. Wilson), Edinburgh: T & T Clark.

Scott, S. 2000. *Art and Society in fourth-century Britain: villa mosaics in context,* Oxford: Oxford University School of Archaeology Monograph 53.

Slofstra, J. 1995. The villa in the Roman West: space decoration and ideology. In J. Metzler, M. Millett, N. Roymans and J. Slofstra (eds), *Integration in the Early Roman West.* Luxembourg: Dossier d'Archéologie du Musée National d'Histoire et d'Art 4. 77–90.

Soja E. W. 1996. *Thirdspace. Journeys to Los Angeles and other real-and-imagined places:* Oxford: Blackwell.

Stupperich, R. 1980. A reconsideration of some fourth-century British mosaics. *Britannia,* 11: 289–301.

Thomas, C. 1981. *Christianity in Roman Britain to AD 500.* London: Batsford.

Toynbee, J. M. C. 1968. Pagan motifs and practices in Christian art and ritual in Roman Britain. In M. W. Barley and R. P. C. Hanson (eds) *Christianity in Britain, 300–700.* Leicester: Leicester University Press. 177–92.

Wallace-Hadrill, A. 1994. *Houses and Society in Pompeii and Herculaneum.* Princeton: Princeton University Press.

Walters, B. 1982. Fourth-century 'Orphic' halls in Britain. *Mosaic* 7: 23–6.

Walters, B. 1984. The Orpheus mosaic in Littlecote Park England, *Mosaico Ravenna,* 433–42.

Williams, M. A. 1999. *Rethinking Gnosticism.* Princeton: Princeton University Press.

Witts, P. 2000. Mosaics and room function: the evidence from some fourth-century Romano-British villas. *Britannia,* 31: 291–324.

Becoming Consumers: looking beyond wealth as an explanation for villa variability

Chris Martins

Introduction

It is no longer unusual to find the word consumer in the title of papers on Roman Britain (e.g. Ferris 1995; Cooper 1996; Matthews 1997). The conduct known as conspicuous consumption (Veblen 1925) has become in recent years the dominant paradigm for explaining villa construction and aggrandizement. A consumer revolution is the context offered by Woolf (1998) for the widespread appropriation of Roman material culture to shape personal identities in Gaul. In a recent TRAC paper Fincham (2002: 34) argues that the concept of Romanization may essentially be understood as consumer behaviour.

This paper, drawn from continuing research, discusses evidence from seemingly high-status sites in the East of England using insights that arise from current consumer theory. The focus is on villa amenities or 'improvements' (wall plaster, mosaics, hypocausts, bath-houses etc.), asking in particular why the repertoire of such facilities varies so much in space and time. Whilst this approach might be labelled anachronistic and western-centric, it at least replaces a traditional economics-led understanding of the house-wealth relationship with those arguments drawn from anthropology, psychology and sociology that now inform consumption studies. These ideas are offered in order to open up the interpretation of villas to wider discussion. Because the paper is intended to cover much ground, shortcuts are being made. Consequently, methodological concerns arising from imprecise site definition, inexact chronology, incomplete excavation, inadequate reporting and inadvertent bias are acknowledged, but not examined (see Smith 1997: 9–12). The study concludes by asking whether the meaning of villas can be re-appraised in terms of personal and not just social identities.

Previous explanations for villa aggrandizement

Only recently has consumption behaviour been acknowledged as significant to villa development. This may reflect the negative overtones of the verb 'to consume' ('use up', 'waste', 'destroy' etc.), and a British disposition to disparage consumption in favour of production (Campbell 1994). Post-war archaeologists were possibly influenced by high-profile studies that denigrated society excesses (e.g. Galbraith 1962; Packard 1965; Nader 1973; Schumacher 1973). The enculturation model known as Romanization is commonly used to explain the villa ideal, with the owners typically perceived as civilised, mannered, gentlemanly or cultured (see Haverfield 1915: 37; Collingwood 1924: 64; Collingwood and Myres 1937: 210). It is an argument that endures (Ellis 2000: 191). For much of the last century there may have been unconscious identification with a British ruling class whose country house status was under threat from the *nouveaux riches* (Mordaunt Crook 1999; Strong 1996). The broad issue of affluence (or wealth, prosperity, ability to pay etc.) is raised (e.g. Richmond 1963: 110; Collingwood and Richmond 1969: 133, 146; Percival 1976: 95; Frere 1987: 298; de la

Bédoyère 1993: 80; Salway 1993: 411) and is used to explain different house standards (e.g. de la Bédoyère 1991: 121; Potter and Johns 1992: 88). This is underpinned by the reductionist neoclassical economic model of demand (see Himmelweit et al. 2001) which places emphasis simply on what things cost and the stereotypical person's rational concern to maximise utility (see critique of utility theory by Douglas and Isherwood 1979: 15–24). The approach is disparaged for its focus on functional use values, for assuming that needs are innate rather than socially constructed and because it ignores behavioural variables (see below). Villa amenities have also been seen as desirable comforts (e.g. Richmond 1969: 145; Branigan 1991: 96; Alcock 1996: 68) or even dinner party "conversation pieces" (Wacher 1978: 251).

Media references from the mid-1980s to conspicuous consumption (the 'Yuppies'; Donald Trump, etc.) provide a background to the popularity of the Veblen (1925) model as the orthodoxy for understanding villa construction and elaboration. This hypothesis is widely adopted to explain the strategies of the native elites to retain prestige and power after the Conquest through the adoption of Roman architecture, amenities and art, and later to demonstrate a social distance from an imitative class of newer villa owners (e.g. Millett 1990; Perring 2002). Elsewhere, the phrase is used specifically or euphemistically by Hingley (1989), Jones and Mattingly (1990), Millett (1992), de la Bédoyère (1993, 1999), Potter and Johns (1992), Dark and Dark (1997), Scott (1997, 2000), Smith (1997) and Ellis (2000). Characteristic language suggests that villas were "designed to impress" (Potter 1997: 32), "overawe visitors and social inferiors" (Millett 1995: 72), and to "keep up with, or surpass the Julii next door" (Wacher 2000: 51). However, some question whether wealth and prestige necessarily were displayed through the medium of villas (e.g. Reece 1988; Hingley 1989).

Challenging the conspicuous consumption model

Thorstein Veblen proposes that there is an instinctive competitive drive towards 'pecuniary emulation' (1925: chapter two). The accumulation of property becomes the "independent and definitive basis of esteem" (ibid. 29); the "possession of wealth confers honour" (ibid. 26); and those above seek to outspend those below, who are driven by envy. Criticised as bitterly prejudiced and merely satirical (Clarke 1986: 3), Veblen's focus on late nineteenth century America is regarded as too historically specific (Edgell 2001). His arguments are also labelled vague, untestable, uncertain about motives, unclear as to how the reaction of intended audiences of ostentatious display could be judged and improbable for making no allowance for the possible influence of other personal merits like intelligence or courage (Campbell 1995a). Highlighted by Mason (1981) are considerations of group psychology and structures of status and he distinguishes between conspicuous display which is "horizontally-directed" within a reference group and that (Veblenesque) consumption which is "vertically-directed" behaviour between such classes. Whilst personality is influenced by society, Mason (1981: 27) argues that it is possible for individual drives, needs and traits also to shape consumption decisions. Some might eschew self-esteem in favour of community-mindedness, opt for privacy not social aggrandizement, decide to reject wealth display or adopt imitative (i.e. within peer group) rather than emulative (i.e. between peer group) conduct.

Introducing consumer behaviour theory

In a way that is not fully explicit, archaeologists already use language and concepts derived from modern consumer behaviour theory to interpret villas. Recent references illustrate the risks involved in deploying an everyday consumerist vocabulary with apparently straightforward meanings.

Faulkner (2000: 132) describes late third century "sophisticates" expressing affluence, power and status through Roman-style architecture and art in line with the "prevailing fashion" and contributing to a "villa building craze" (ibid. 142). Decisions made by villa owners in respect of household decoration would be evaluated by members of their peer-group "at a local, provincial or empire-wide level" (Scott 2000: 169). Even geometric mosaics were evidence of "emulation amongst local elites" (ibid. 170). Ellis (2000: 9) acknowledges the likely effect of individual expression in house design and décor. He suggests that manifestations of wealth went beyond "conspicuous consumption" to the pursuit of influence (ibid. 182); but Roman amenities could be "simply attractive" and not acquired only as a device to secure political gain (ibid. 191). The period between the late second and early fourth centuries saw a "small and comparatively secure elite, competing with itself" (Perring 2002: 220). The fashion for *luxuria* "was driven by the need to search out new means of displaying status in order to retain a distinction between superior behaviour and the imitative aspirations of inferior classes" (ibid. 215). To Perring, villa architecture symbolised surplus, mastery and power (ibid. 43, 215).

Such arguments over-simplify the topic of consumption, the wider evolution of which is traced by Campbell (1991; 1995b), and for which overviews may be found in Bocock (1993), Corrigan (1997), Goodwin et al. (1997), Storey (1999) and Dant (1999). The potential for such theories to offer a challenging view of villa development will now be illustrated by presenting insights drawn mainly from a genre of consumer behaviour manuals, which combine academic insights with micro consumption studies.

The Romanists quoted above have not examined how or why the elites learned to consume. This behavioural change is understood today (Antonides and van Raaij 1998) as an outcome of new habit-structuring experiences, forms of classical conditioning and role modelling. Consumption is now seen (Solomon 2002) as contributing to personal concept and not just as a component of social identity. Through symbolic interactions with others in society, shared meanings arise which encourage people to consume in ways consistent with self concept, whether self-expressively (reflecting their unique individual qualities) or to symbolise their social relationships (Dittmar 1992: 89). But there can be 'actual', 'ideal', 'social', 'ideal social', 'expected' or indeed 'multiple' self-images (Schiffman and Kanuk 2000: 113, 118). A philosophical requirement is to distinguish human needs from wants (Sheth et al. 1999); the latter are influenced by wealth, reference groups and cultural context. Want-driven items deliver social and emotional benefits, are termed value-expressive and include status goals, pleasures and self-esteem. A question is how villas acquired their value-expressive (i.e. non-utilitarian) function reflecting the feelings, attitudes and aspirations of their owners? When discussing post-Conquest Britain it may be significant (especially because villas are so different from what came before) that consumption as self-definition can be particularly useful for those experiencing a new situation or role or who need symbolic possessions to round off their identity. This is known as symbolic self-completion theory (Solomon 2002: 136).

When explaining what motivates people to acquire, consumer behaviourists (e.g. Sheth et al. 1999) acknowledge the continuing universality and general validity of the model of human needs devised in the 1950s by psychologist Abraham Maslow, whilst allowing for variations in culture, individual and historical context. The five-stage hierarchy climbs from physiological and security concerns and the need for belongingness to the fourth level where esteem matters most and is sought through prestige, self-respect, status, and recognition. The highest level of need, for self-actualisation, acknowledges the importance of aesthetic and intellectual ideals. Among the consumption motives identified by psychoanalyst Ernest Dichter (Sheth et al. 1999: 350) are mastery over environment, status, individuality and social acceptance. The psychogenic needs recognised by psychologist Henry Murray (Sheth et al. 1999: 349) include dominance (to direct others) exhibition (to impress) and cognizance (to gain knowledge). People's values also shape their behavioural decisions and to be considered is whether a person is inner- or outer-directed, the former typically more independent, the latter more concerned with the social approval of others (ibid. 371). The relevance of personality traits to consumption is discussed below. Environment-Behaviour studies (Lang 2000: 86) take such human needs models into account when interpreting architectural function and Romanists may benefit from this more textured choice of motives to explain the housing spectrum than simply the discourse centred largely on power (e.g. Millett 1990; Perring 2002). Generally there is consistency (Solomon 2002) between things people own/desire and their personal values (self-image congruence theory: ibid. 137) and in these terms the repertoire of amenities introduced on villas may be understood as a 'consumption constellation' (ibid. 176). The symbolic meanings of the respective facilities relate to each other and display 'product complimentarity'. To be explained in villa studies therefore, are those cases where the anticipated groupings of amenities do not occur. The so-called 'halo effect' (Antonides and van Raaij 1998) is the perception that material wealth implies other positive characteristics for the person concerned, such as intelligence, power or success. Some aspects of consumption can be understood as hedonic (Sheth et al. 1999), providing sensory pleasures. These include bathing, sport, giving and receiving gifts or art appreciation. People also desire the experiences of novelty and variety, possibly at increasing levels, with this now recognised as a necessary inner drive to stimulate the central nervous system in the brain (Zaltmann and Wallendorf 1983).

Archaeologists can do more to deconstruct the idea of status. It can be classified as 'ascribed', if an outcome of birth; 'achieved', if earned; or 'desired', if an aspiration (Rice 1993: 261). Measuring this social standing can be complicated by the phenomenon of incomplete 'status crystallization' – inconsistent or unequal achievement of class criteria in any society (Solomon 2002: 396). Further complexities arise from generational change within a family, gender implications, the underlying subjectivity inherent in status positioning, the possible substitution of status symbols over time and knowing how intended audiences will react to them. If the consumer is already a member of the in-group whose approval is sought there is less dependence on stereotypical possessions to achieve this. Acquisitions that may be interpreted as publicly conspicuous – through their visibility in society, newness, luxury, or other status embellishing qualities – are the most likely to be influenced strongly by reference group comparison (Schiffman and Kanuk 2000). Weaknesses in the conspicuous consumption model as a guide to status have been discussed (above). There can be a life cycle for status symbols (Solomon 1999) with some obsolescent, others outmoded, some in passage, a few reviving and others avoided altogether or mocked through parody. Status is only one of eight types of value which consumers seek, alongside the experiences of efficiency, excellence, play, aesthetics, ethics, esteem and spirituality (Holbrook 1999). Social comparison theory may further inform archaeological interpretation by examining the relevance of particular reference groups to whom villa-owners may be responding. These are defined (Engel et al. 1995: 717) as primary (the family), comparative (neighbours), aspirational (those whose values there is a wish to emulate), as well as formal (an acknowledged network) and informal (friends). According to Wilkie (1994), the social power of the group over individual members of an elite can also be questioned, whether it derives from authority (recognised roles), knowledge (accepted expertise), identification (guided by others), pressure (actual or perceived coercion) or advantage (rewards for fitting in).

Ultimately people consume within a personal strategy of impression management (Leary 1996). Most aspects of behaviour (e.g. expressed attitudes, appearance, consumption) can be directed towards securing favourable inferences from others. This implies that the individual will live within a state of 'dramaturgical awareness' within a physical environment that contributes 'sets', 'props' and 'moods' to this process (Goffman 1959). Successful impression management strategies include the acquisition and manipulation of resources to create a sense of prestige and the use of appropriate symbols to display status (Tedeschi and Norman 1985: 307). Motives which encourage such self-presentation are perceived rewards like raised self-esteem, greater social influence, added power in relationships or enhanced social appeal. Self-presentation can also focus on the inner audience (Greenwald and Breckler 1985: 126), for self-enhancing purposes. People who are high 'self-monitors', paying special attention to the impressions they create, display the greatest self-awareness in public and are more susceptible to reference group pressures (Sabini 1995: 215). Mark Leary, a specialist in the study of self-presentation, believes impression management was as common in the ancient world as today (pers. comm.).

Consumption and the Roman villa

A suitably modernist introduction to this discussion will demonstrate how 'expensive' villas were. A subjective classification for such expenditure has been offered by Rivet (1969: 211) and more scientifically by Faulkner (2000: 71, 138) using the expertise of quantity surveyor Jack Newman. Faulkner-Newman accept the gross simplifications involved, among them chronological and stratigraphical uncertainties, variable building techniques and presumptions about 'costs'. Their estimates (a sample of 78 sites, at 1994 prices) suggest that villas 'cost' from under £100,000 to over £300,000, figures presented as 'construction unit values' to reflect the possibility that surplus labour was the likely resource (this could mean tenants but for a discussion of the presence of slaves on villas, see Samson 1999). Besides, the use of manpower is, itself, ostentatious consumption because workers had to be supplied, housed, fed, managed and instructed. Newman's method was to allocate a value to an average room, corridor, mosaic, hypocaust or bath-house, and compute the total 'expense' by each chronological phase. Utilising resources on this scale was arguably not needs-driven or logical-functionalist behaviour, but instead, discretionary, self-indulgent, irrational and psychologically motivated. But can this be demonstrated?

Case studies

Case-studies follow in which consumer theories help demonstrate how behaviour towards material culture in the Roman world may be better understood. These focus specifically on aspects of domestic architecture but similar approaches to personal possessions may be possible.

(a) Cinnabar and the 'snob' and 'Veblen' effects

In this example, the accepted correlation between interior decoration and status on villas is shown, using a consumption hypothesis, to afford scope for more detailed interpretation. Wall painting is acknowledged as a relatively costly but quite widespread expression of prestige in Britain (Davey and Ling 1982: 46). Although a typology recognises a panelling effect, architectural features or figurative work (Ling 1985) the interpretation of social motives is difficult, in contrast to Pompeii where more work has been possible (e.g. Wallace-Hadrill 1988, 1994, but see Tybout 2001). Because evidence is fragmentary, inferences about status typically are drawn from the size, shape and probable purpose of the room, the polychromy, intended symbolism, technical merit and the relative novelty or fashionability of the particular decoration.

The use of cinnabar (mercuric sulphide, the ancient *minium*) may cut across such considerations. Morgan (1992) highlights its scarcity value both in Britain and Italy. Mercury was mined only in southern Spain, refined in Rome and then imported to this country. Classical sources attest to the association between the pigment and personal standing; its special significance being attested by Vitruvius (*On Architecture* 7) and by the Elder Pliny (*Natural History,* 35) who identifies cinnabar as one of the brilliant colours (*floridi*) which the patron supplies at his own expense to the painter, as opposed to naturally occurring pigments. A price ceiling was set in Italy for cinnabar (Ling 1991: 209) and in Pompeii it is found only in the finest rooms in the most affluent homes (Ling and Ling 2000: 58) and in similarly prestigious settings in Rome (Rozenburg 1997). Morgan identified cinnabar in 27 out of 70 locations, among them Fishbourne Palace and half-a-dozen villas, most considered relatively luxurious (Bignor, Kingscote, Leicester (Norfolk Street), and Piddington). The use of cinnabar in Britain would be imbued with Imperial prestige, confirming an elite identification with the power and culture of Rome in much the same way that was the case with marble (Isserlin 1998). Special influence was perhaps required to obtain the material.

Consumer theory offers a more nuanced analysis. Cinnabar was coveted because it was expensive, though piecemeal finds make it impossible to know how much was used. Morgan shows that a square metre of fresco painting required 40g of the refined material, or eight sesterces at prices quoted by Pliny (33, 40). There were also the costs of procuring and importing cinnabar and the recommended protective waxing and oiling to stop it turning black. Two consumption motivations may be inferred (Leibenstein 1950), the so-called 'snob effect', a wish to be exclusive (demand would decline if others used the pigment) and the 'Veblen effect', where the requirement was that cinnabar was both costly, and its conspicuous price was also high. This is not just what others presume was paid, but what the property owner thinks that others imagine that it cost. A contrast may be drawn with Leibenstein's 'bandwagon effect' or acquisition merely to be fashionable, to belong, and which might characterise the widespread use of commonplace pigments.

A curiosity is the discovery of cinnabar in the small aisled villa of Empingham (Cooper 2000: 129). In a building without a mosaic perhaps its use was intended to impress influential people from nearby Great Casterton (Nick Cooper pers. comm.), but consumer theory suggests a more specific explanation. The newly rich, or those attempting to represent themselves as such (as opposed to families with long standing wealth), may consume in a conspicuous way out of 'status anxiety', to be seen to do the correct emblematic thing (Solomon 2002: 403). Such symbolic self-completion recognises flamboyant display as the means to acquire an identity in an unaccustomed role though the acquisition of the right symbols. The Empingham example challenges the presumption that only large villas represent wealth or prestige.

(b) House styles as a 'bridge' to a 'golden past'?

The idea that possessions can be an inventive medium for the creation of new symbolic meanings in society offers a theoretical approach to the explanation of anomalous building practices. Two housing forms in the East Midlands are exceptions to the generalisation that Iron Age timber round houses in civilian areas were succeeded by rectangular timber 'proto-villas' and in turn stone-built, increasingly 'developed' houses. The model is noted by Rivet (1964: 106–7) and in this study at Piddington (Friendship-Taylor 1997: 49).

   One is a tradition of stone-walled circular structures which emerged and continued notably in Northamptonshire, between the mid-second and fourth centuries AD (Keevill and Booth 1997). Various functional and social explanations are offered for the 'tenacious cultural trait' (ibid. 42) of round buildings. Most are accepted as having domestic uses and are often associated with high-status sites, though being less aggrandized (with exceptions) they are considered of relatively lower social importance than rectangular villas. The other example is the lasting preference in parts of Leicestershire and Lincolnshire for the rectangular aisled timber building. This style appeared as a partial successor to wooden round houses and by the late third and fourth centuries became a 'hybrid' household which featured 'Roman' improvements, whilst retaining indigenous practice in respect of the division of internal space (Taylor 2001).

   The consumer behaviour concept of 'displaced meaning' (McCracken 1990) offers an insight. His hypothesis, which can apply equally to nations, communities, cultures or individuals, is that a distance exists in life between experienced (unsatisfactory) reality and an imagined (desired) ideal. The discrepancy is resolved by 'meaning manipulation', the appropriation of possessions to serve as an illusory 'bridge' to a different place or time. This would be a golden age (a notion which McCracken shows was used in Ovid's *Metamorphoses*) that can be either long gone or to come. The object becomes a symbolic but solid access point to the displaced perfect ideal and a substitute in the mind for unattractive reality. Contemporary examples quoted by McCracken (ibid. 110–11) are the 'rose-covered cottage' in this country as redolent of someone's perfect future, and the 'log cabin' as being evocative in America of a virtuous past.

   Arguably, constructing round houses in stone enabled people to protect beliefs associated with a 'golden' (pre-Conquest) tradition, whilst for appearances they adopted a new building resource. Similarly, those opting for aisled buildings could retain their affection for a time-honoured construction in timber whilst adopting (outwardly) Roman embellishments and facades, for example at Denton (Smith 1964). Further support for this hypothesis may be evident at Winterton, where Stead (1976: 88) remarks on the 'curiously primitive' decision to use post-holes for the structural support of two aisled houses with the hitherto usual practice of using stone foundations 'deliberately discarded'. In these examples the housing form made palpable and also evoked an idealised synthesis of past experiences, continuing beliefs and projected hopes. There is a classical clue to the possibility that Roman society could be susceptible to such "rosy", self-justifying nostalgia. It arises from the attention drawn by late Republican historians seeking to eulogise the origins of Rome to the putative wooden hut of Romulus on the Palatine Hill (Wiseman 1994: 104). This reminds us that Romans were aware of, and manipulated, their pasts too. Perhaps the British examples drew upon a knowledge of this Roman context.

(c) Ancestral meanings and Roman villas

Material culture can convey status in ways which are not always overt, and the deterministic correlation between periods of economic prosperity and house aggrandizement noted by some Romanists (e.g. de la Bédoyère 1999) can be challenged. Many have not examined the implications of villa longevity and the possibility that, with the passage of time, buildings came to mean different things to later generations. Many villas evolved, albeit in phases, over a period of centuries, through a dozen generations. Often there was no apparent development for decades. A simple house-wealth interpretation (e.g. Faulkner 2000: 71) relates periods of such apparent stability to economic stagnation with bursts of upgrading viewed as resurgent conspicuous consumption.

To demonstrate how status symbolism need not necessarily reside in the obvious, McCracken (1990) cites the so-called patina system of consumption which operated in the medieval and Elizabethan periods. Class legitimacy was founded on what constituted an invisible code evoked by evidence of the wear and tear of possessions over time. Such indications of age communicated genuine prestige, old wealth and honour. The basis was a 'five generation rule' (ibid. 38), the period necessary to achieve authenticity through gentility. The 'cult of family status' (ibid. 137) linked lineage past, present and to come, and depended on patina to convey nobility. Although there are dangers in applying cross-cultural generalisations, it is possible that reverential emotions were attached to villas built generations earlier. One consequence may have been to imbue a particular family or kin-group with added social standing, another to equate prestige with the ancestry of the building and its originality, or lack of change. Equally, a particular wall decoration, mosaic, bath-suite or hypocaust might acquire iconic significance because it was old, serving as a direct connection with a founding generation. The importance attached to household ancestry (see Bodel 1997) is suggested by the villa mausoleum at Bancroft (Zeepvat 1994). The excavators were convinced that its location related to its connection with ancestors as the site had been continuously occupied from the late Bronze Age to the late Iron Age, after which it was used for a cremation cemetery until the mausoleum (considered a 'status symbol') was built (Bob Zeepvat pers. comm.). Furthermore, at Stanwick a hypocaust was constructed using re-cycled funerary sculpture conveying mythological scenes, and assuming the re-used stone was local this suggests there may have been monuments of greater prestige than the villa itself (Vicky Crosby pers. comm.). Such deliberate veneration of the past seems to have been the case at the House of the Menander in Pompeii (Roger Ling pers. comm.), where wall decorations date from the Second and Fourth Styles, a century apart. Also from Pompeii are examples of the patching of a revered mosaic, re-plastering which copied an earlier style, the re-cycling of pieces of esteemed decoration, and the revival of dated designs in unexpected settings (Ling 1993: 18).

These are situations where an awareness of consumer theory helps to avoid simple generalisations. A decision not to build/alter/decorate may itself be an issue of consumption and status.

(d) Consuming the view

Domestic architecture can be appreciated as offering scope for status display, but consumption decisions may embrace wider landscape values. Considerations which influenced villa location probably included proximity to or distance from other settlements, access to water including spring lines, topography and soil type, micro-climate, site ancestry and cosmological beliefs (Perring 2002). Additionally there may have been a desire for physical prominence, whether to view or be viewed, or both. The decision to appropriate the vantage point perhaps imbued such settings with added social significance by confirming the ability of owners to use wealth and influence to command attention and respect.

A possible further advantage is that it was well-attested behaviour in Roman Italy, and could remind observers of the proprietor's awareness of elite values close to Rome. Written sources highlight the importance attached to a panorama: see, for example, Pliny the Elder (*Natural History,* 4. 30); Cicero (*Ep.* 2. 3. 2. and 3. 1. 2); and Horace (*Ep.* 1. 16. 1), and whilst allowing for possible literary licence (Bergman 1995) also Pliny the Younger's description of the prospect from his Laurentine (*Ep.* 2. 17*)* and Tuscan *(Ep.* 5. 6) villas. Zanker (1998: 17) suggests that the new fashion for a villa lifestyle from the mid-second century B. C. embraced the view to identify with Hellenistic ideals of nature. Purcell (1987) understands this preoccupation with the view as an expression of dominance over nature, the owners' mastery of landscape, and control of resources.

It is difficult without literary evidence to confirm the importance of such psychological experiences of landscape in Britain. Certainly there were villas which, taking the opinion of excavators, were conspicuously sited with dominant views. Examples are Brantingham (Dent 1989); Dalton-on-Tees (Brown 1999); Scampton, near Lincoln (SMR records); Wharram Grange (Rahtz et al. 1986) and Mansfield Woodhouse (Rooke 1787). Equally, there were exceptions, for example Gargrave (Brian Hartley pers. comm.). Although further research is required because many factors are relevant, there are indications (subject to tree lines) that consumption directed towards a villa could be focused to extra effect if intended audiences could admire the setting from afar. Four possibilities arise, which could overlap. There is conspicuous siting to be visible generally, perhaps to dispersed non-elite homesteads. Second, an attractive location might be near a road, to win the approval of travellers, for example Brantingham (Dent 1989) overlooking the Brough to York road, or Drayton II, built in precise alignment with the Gartree Road (Cooper et al 1989). Similarly a riverside location might appeal, for example at Piercebridge (Harding 1984) or Stanton Low (Woodfield 1989). Another variant is to be within view of a nucleated settlement, for example the site of Greetwell near Lincoln (SMR records) or Norfolk Street villa near Leicester (Mellor 1981). There is also positioning to be noticed by villa owners of equal, higher or lower status. Nether Heyford (Stephen Young pers. comm.) could arguably be seen from three other villas (Nether Heyford II and Harpole I and II), the small town of Bannaventa and from Watling Street. Jeremy Taylor (pers. comm.) highlights a 'theatre of social display' featuring at least four intervisible villa sites overlooking a stretch of the middle Nene Valley near Irchester. The facades of the villas at Wollaston, Wollaston Quarry, Great Doddington and Earls Barton were structured so as to face each other, look down on two valley roads, and be viewed from below across a status-enhancing landscape of crops and vineyards.

(e) Consumer 'fashions' in wall decoration

Cultural meaning in the consumption and use of possessions is never fixed; a trajectory over time can be explored. Archaeologists often cite the modern construct of 'fashion' to describe/explain changes in style on Roman villas. Examples include references to changing colours of clothes (Liversidge 1973: 128); popular wall decorations (Alcock 1996: 70); the status bestowed through the adoption of Roman ways (Smith 1997: 279); conformity in villa typology (Wacher 2000: 51); and decisions to build in stone (Perring 2002: 37). Typically fashion is taken as a given cultural phenomenon rather than a complex expression of consumption.

Solomon (2002: 503) summarises the behavioural science perspectives involved. Fashion can be defined variously as a process affecting the social diffusion of cultural styles, as a shared code of symbolic meanings within society, or as a design currently in vogue. At one level it is an outcome of personal decisions- at the other, a reflection of societal values. Explanations for fashion change owe to individual psychology (e.g. drives to comply, be different, seek novelty), an economic rationale determined by availability and price (e.g. the Veblen, 'snob' and 'bandwagon' effects: above), or a sociological model influenced by the motive of social comparison (e.g. status symbols as the determinant of class). Stages within a fashion life cycle are broadly innovation – acceptance – obsolescence, but there can be short-term whims adopted by a few or long-lived trends taken up by many.

A study of clothes and jewellery in the ancient world (De Brohun 2001) concludes that society was distinctly fashion-conscious, with evidence of fads, rapid change and conscious innovation as well as notions of correct and 'power' dressing. As evidence, she quotes the criticisms of individuality in grooming by conformist moralists like Cicero and Seneca, the Elder Pliny reacting to crazes in perfumes, and Ovid describing rapidly changing hairstyles.

Whilst agendas for managing personal appearance in Rome and choosing wall plaster in Britain need have no meaningful relationship, there are cases where changes in interior decoration – which otherwise can survive for hundreds of years (Roger Ling pers. comm.) – need explaining. Overpainting is relatively easy, and typically a previous pattern is 'pecked' to ensure bonding. Davey and Ling (1982: 29) cite references to two such layers in Verulamium, three presumed within the second century in the Catterick *mansio*, four in a decade in the London *forum*, five during an 80-year period in the Lancaster fort bath-house, and six during the fourth century in the *praetorium* at Binchester fort. Villas illustrate a similar propensity for change. Examples are Castle Dykes (Lukis 1875) where three layers relate to a room within a bath-suite; Leicester (Norfolk Street) where plaster featuring two layers was found in the cellar (Mellor 1982); and also Harpham (Collier 1906), Redlands Farm (Edward Biddulph pers. comm.) and Winterton (Liversidge 1976). Possibly the fragmentary evidence of wall plaster might mislead: were these sections repairs?

Because evidence for such redecoration is relatively uncommon (although plaster remains are easily destroyed) it may be that of the three models for fashion change (above), those relating to wider economic and societal issues are least plausible. Instead, the decision may owe to individual values, alternative motives for which are identified below. A further explanation may be 'divestment ritual' (McCracken 1990: 87), action intended to obliterate associations with former householders. Earlier meaningful connections are expunged and re-constituted with new owners.

(f) Villa variability as consumer behaviour

Possessions are understood by consumer behaviourists as expressive of personality and as material symbols of personal identity. Only rarely is attention drawn in Roman housing studies to the possibility of decision-making at the level of the individual or a particular family (e.g. Wacher 2000: 51; Ellis 2000: 112) but this presumption is offered descriptively, not theoretically. Examples show it is not unusual to find apparent inconsistencies and idiosyncrasies in the consumption constellation displayed on villas, and consumer behaviour may offer an explanation. The simple villa at Carsington featured a central room, hypocaust, possible mosaic, probable bath-house and window glass, but no wall plaster (Ling and Courtney 1981: 73). At Winterton (Stead 1976: 86, 91), six cold baths were found, but not a heated one, and no rooms with mosaics had a hypocaust. Brixworth villa featured a bath house which was probably never utilised (Woods 1970: 4). Despite having hypocaust heating, wall plaster and an apsidal end, the main dining/reception room at Piercebridge villa featured only a flagstone, not mosaic, floor even though a contemporary bath suite had a mosaic (Harding 1984: 12). In contrast, at Dalton Parlours, the probable high status apsidal wing, featuring a Medusa mosaic and wall plaster, had no hypocaust (Wrathmell and Nicholson 1990 and Stuart Wrathmell (pers.comm.)). Easton Maudit villa (Charmian Woodfield pers. comm.) uniquely incorporated two round 'wings'. The exterior of Piddington villa was strikingly decorated (Bidwell 1996) and is not matched elsewhere in the Province. There were more hypocausts (at least six: Nick Cooper pers. comm.) during the life of the small aisled Drayton II villa than in an equivalent length of time at Fishbourne Palace, where there were just four (Black 1985: 77).

A problem, not helped by the vagaries of archaeological evidence, is to define the typical suite of villa 'improvements'. One approach has been made possible by using quantity surveyors' estimates (Newman, above) and is being pursued (Martins, in progress). It involves house-by-house, period-by-period comparison of the proportion of the overall 'construction value' of a property which can be accounted for by each amenity and by all such amenities. Since the underlying 'cost' presumptions will be the same for each building (in reality techniques may have altered over space and time), the varying percentages attributable to such 'embellishments' should provide a 'status-through-consumption' index for that villa, and for comparison with other villas. But this is still not an explanation for variation, and one premise, arising from consumer theory, is that the buildings were inevitably personalised. On what basis could such an argument be sustained? First, by acknowledging that the interlude for initial construction and/or subsequent improvements was a matter of months or a few years. Confirmation of short time-scales comes from Butser Farm and concerns the continuing re-creation of the Sparsholt villa (the late Peter Reynolds pers. comm.). Second, because there was such diversity, it may be presumed that, intentionally or unconsciously, a dialogue existed between the ideal of a particular villa type and that chosen by the owner. Third, there was the possible influence of Vitruvius (*On Architecture*, 6, preface), and perhaps other authorities. He advises "I cannot refrain from praising those owners of estates who, fortified by confidence in their own erudition, build for themselves … to spend their own capital to their own liking rather than to that of anyone else". Fourth, there are insights from environment-behaviour research. Lang (2000: 86) uses Maslow's human needs model (above) to theorize how personal motivations relate to buildings in a given social context. Architectural cues which match the level four needs of esteem and status include 'a sense of place', a 'sense of importance', 'recognition' and 'personalization' (ibid. 88). Finally, there are personality traits which may influence consumption (Schiffman and Kanuk 2000), including receptivity to innovation, responsiveness to social influence, degree of materialism and need for cognition. Others can be creativity, vanity, extroversion, hedonism or narcissism. Guided by impression management theory (above), predictive cues about personality can be observed from possessions and household settings (see Burroughs et al. 1991; Gosling and Jin Ko 2002). The 'house-as-a-symbol-of-the-self' thesis (Cooper 1974) draws on Jungian theories of symbolism and the collective unconscious to suggest that houses, externally and internally, reveal both the inner psyche and intended personal presentation. Environmental clues about intended identity must be recognised within society for the meanings to be accepted (Rapoport: 1982), and such individuality in expression was perhaps applauded in Roman Britain.

What follows is subjective, and owes to the suggestion (Gosling and Jin Ko 2002) that observer opinions of facilities can help interpret domestic environments. For villas such research might be based on annotated excavation plans, isometric modelling or a virtual reality programme and would seek insights into personal identity. Two cases illustrate the potential of the idea. The trait of voluntary simplicity may be apparent at Welton Wold villa overlooking the Humber, five km from Brough. This is conduct which eschews consumption values, preferring freedom from materialism (Kilbourne 1992) and has been noted in the ancient world (Belk et al. 1996). The five-room, late first to early fifth century stone-built house featured a central room and corridor but was never aggrandized; there was no evidence of tiles, mosaic, window glass or plaster, nor of wings, a hypocaust or bath-house (Mackey 1998 and pers. comm.). In contrast was the sophisticated nearby villa at Brantingham (Liversidge et al. 1973). Having made an early decision to adopt Roman-style architecture at Welton Wold was the decision taken that ostentation was thereafter unwanted behaviour? Winterton (six km from the Humber) presents the opposite case, suggesting the trait of materialism (Belk 1985). Highly materialistic consumers are particularly status-driven and concerned with social comparisons (Richins 1992). The massive wealth on display (Stead 1976 and specialist reports) from the late second to late fourth centuries included unusually early mosaics, later portrait and figurative pavements and wall plaster in a high proportion of rooms. It has been argued that materialism is a substitute for declining feelings of community (Antonides and van Raaij 1998: 533).

Concluding remarks

The case studies are not exhaustive, but illustrate the potential for using consumer theories to investigate villa evidence. I have attempted a deconstruction of traditional models for explaining architectural change. Arguably, archaeologists should use consumption terminology in more explicit and less simplistic ways. Assumptions that wealth always represents size and scale and that status symbols are necessarily ostentatious or unchanging can be challenged. Influential reference groups can be infinitely variable with a likely mix in Britain of domestic, local, regional, provincial and even inter-provincial audiences.

At another level, however, this study acknowledges the collaborative potential of relations between psychology and archaeology as a possible guide to past behaviour. A particular case is a new discourse focusing on the emergence of the individual (and individuality). This has been noted, for instance, in the wider use of toiletry objects in the first century AD (Hill 1997) and recognised in Roman Gaul in the creative responses to the options afforded by greater cultural choice (Woolf 1998: 12, 171; Woolf 2001). Similarly, it is implicit in this paper that there may be scope to examine the interface between the public image and the self-image of the elite.

Whereas it has been usual to discuss villas in terms of social identities, there may be scope to approach the concept of personal identities, too.

Traditionally the 'meaning' of villas has been sought in terms of an architectural or cultural typology, and more recently through an interpretation related to status and power. A further construal is possible: that manifestly overt consumption may signal a changing orientation of values within the individualism-collectivism construct of cultures (Wong 1997), with the new materialist tendency implying a preference for possessions over people (ibid. 202). Because of this, it may be speculated that villas provide a glimpse of the evolution of the independent self, unique and self-determining, and contrasting with the interdependent self in which identity is embedded within the social group (Dittmar 1992: 188). (This is a point worth making to social psychologists who do not acknowledge selfhood prior to the late medieval period – see Baumeister 1987).

If this can be argued it also extends Woolf's point (1998: 149) that rural settlement (including villas) is best viewed as a continuum of consumption, varying in scale and style. The opportunities to consume afforded by Roman governance might be seen less in terms of a cultural dialogue (i.e. 'Romanization') and more as a stimulus to psychological evolution. Villa variability may point to the process of consuming being used deliberately to fashion individual identity through possessions.

Department of Archaeology, University of Durham

Bibliography

Ancient Sources
Cicero (Translated by D.R. Shackleton Bailey 1979). *Cicero's letters to his friends.* London: Penguin Books.
Horace (Translated by Smith Palmer 1959). *The Satires and Epistles of Horace.* Chicago: University Press.
Pliny (Translated by H. Rackham 1961). *Natural History.* London: William Heinemann.
Pliny the Younger (Translated by B. Radice 1963). *Letters.* London: Penguin.
Vitruvius (Translated by F. Grainger 1962). *On Architecture.* London: William Heinemann.

Modern Sources
Alcock, J. 1996. Life in Roman Britain. *London: B.T. Batsford/English Heritage.*
Antonides, G. & Van Raaij, W. F. 1998. *Consumer behaviour. A European Perspective.* Chichester: John Wiley & Sons.
Baumeister, R.F. 1987. How the Self became a Problem: a psychological review of historical research. *Journal of Personality and Social Psychology,* 52.1: 163–176.
De la Bedoyere, G. 1991. *The Buildings of Roman Britain.* London: Batsford.
De la Bedoyere, G. 1993. *Roman villas and the countryside.* London: Batsford.
De la Bedoyere, G. 1999. *The Golden Age of Roman Britain.* Stroud: Tempus.
Belk, R.W. 1985. Materialism: trait aspects of living in the material world. In *Journal of Consumer Research* 12 (3): 265–280.
Belk, R. W., Dholakia, N. & Benkatesh, A. 1996. *Consumption and marketing. Macro dimensions.* Ohio: South West College Publications.
Bergmann, B. 1995. Visualising Pliny's villas. *Journal of Roman Archaeology* 8: 406–420.
Bidwell, P. T. 1996. The Exterior Decoration of Roman Buildings in Britain. In P. Johnson with I. Hayes eds. York: *Architecture in Roman Britain.* C.B.A. Research report 94. 19–32.

Black, E. 1985. Hypocaust heating in domestic rooms in Roman Britain. *Oxford Journal of Roman Archaeology, 4 (1): 77–92.*

Bocock, R. 1993. *Comsumption.* London/New York: Routledge.

Bodel, J. 1997. Monumental villas and Villa monuments. *Journal of Roman Archaeology, 10: 5–35.*

Branigan, K. 1991. Images–or mirrors– of Europe? An archaeological approach to the problem. In L. Alexander (ed.) *Images of Empire.* Journal for the study of the Old Testament supplementary series 122: 91–106.

Brown, J. 1999. Romano-British villa complex at Chapel House Farm, Dalton on Tees, North Yorkshire. Roman Antiquities Section. *Yorkshire Archaeological Society Bulletin, 16: 19–27.*

Burroughs, W. J., Drews, D. R. & Hallman W. K. 1991. Predicting personality from personal possessions: a self-presentational analysis. *Journal of Social Behaviour and Personality*, 65: 147–163.

Campbell, C. 1991. Consumption: the new wave of research in the humanities and social sciences. In F. W. Rudmin (ed.) *To Have Possessions: a handbook on ownership and property. Special Issue, Journal of Social Behaviour and Personality*, 6.6. 57–74.

Campbell, C. 1994. Consumer goods and the good of consuming. *Critical Review*, 8.4: 503–520.

Campbell, C. 1995a. Conspicuous Confusion? A critique of Veblen's theory of Conspicuous Consumption. *Sociological Theory*. 13.1: 37–47.

Campbell, C. 1995b. The Sociology of Consumption. In D. Miller (ed.) *Acknowledging Consumption.* London/New York: Routledge. 96–126.

Clarke, G. 1986. *Symbols of Excellence.* Cambridge University Press.

Collier, C. V. 1906. The Roman remains at Harpham. *Transactions of the East Riding Antiquarian Society, 13.2: 141–152.*

Collingwood, R.G. 1924. *Roman Britain.* London: Oxford University Press.

Collingwood, R. G. & Myres, J.N.L. 1937. *Roman Britain and the English Settlements.* Oxford: Clarendon Press.

Collingwood, R.G. & Richmond, I. A. 1969. *The Archaeology of Roman Britain.* London: Methuen & co.

Cooper, C. 1974. The House as symbol of the self. In J. Lang et al (eds.) *Designing for human behaviour.* Stroudsberg Pennsylvania: Dowden, Hutchinson & Ross. 130–146.

Cooper, N. J. 1996. Searching for the blank generation: consumer choice in Roman and post-Roman Britain. In J. Webster & N. Cooper (eds.) *Roman Imperialism: post-colonial perspectives.* Leicester School of Archaeological Studies. Leicester Monographs no. 3. 85–98.

Cooper, N. J. et al 1989. A report on the Geophysical survey and trial excavations at the site of the Roman villa near Drayton, Leicestershire 1988. *Transactions of the Leicestershire Archaeological and Historical Society, 63: 7–17.*

Corrigan, P. 1997. *The Sociology of Consumption.* London: SAGE publications.

Dant, T. 1999. *Material Culture in the Social World. Values, activites, lifestyles.* Buckingham: Open University Press.

Dark, K. & Dark, P. 1997. *The Landscape of Roman Britain.* Stroud: Sutton Publishing.

Davey, N. & Ling, R. 1982. *Wall Painting in Roman Britain.* London: Society for the Promotion of Roman Studies.

De Brouhn, J. B. 2001. Power dressing in Ancient Greece and Rome. *History Today*, 51.2: 18–25.

Dent, J. 1989. Settlements at North cave and Brantingham. In P. Halkon (ed.) *New light on the Parisi. Recent discoveries in Iron Age and Roman East Yorkshire.* East Riding Archaeological Society. 26–32.

Dittmar, H. 1992. *The Social Psychology of Material Possessions: to have is to be.* Hemel Hempstead: Harvester Wheatsheaf.

Douglas, M & Isherwood, B. 1979. *The World of Goods: towards an anthropology of consumption.* London: Allen Lane.

Edgell, S. R. 2001. *Veblen in Perspective. His Life and Thought.* London/New York: M.E. Sharpe.

Ellis, S. P. 2000. *Roman Housing.* London: Duckworth.

Engel, J.F. et al 1995. *Consumer Behaviour.* Fort Worth: Harcourt Brace Publishers.

Faulkner, N. 2000. *The Decline and Fall of Roman Britain.* Stroud: Tempus.

Ferris, I. 1995. Shopper's paradise: consumers in Roman Britain. In P. Rush (ed.) *Theoretical Roman Archaeology: Second Conference Proceedings.* Aldershot: Avebury. 132–140.

Fincham, G. 2002. Consumer Theory and Roman North Africa: a post-colonial approach to the ancient economy. In M. Carruthers et al (eds.) *TRAC 2001 Proceedings of the Eleventh Annual Theoretical Roman Archaeology Conference, Glasgow 2001.* Oxford: Oxbow books. 34–44.

Frere. S. 1987. *Britannia.* London/New York: Routledge/Kegan Paul.

Friendship-Taylor, R. 1997. Settlement and continuity? Two late Iron Age settlements and Roman sites in Northamptonshire. In R.M. and D.E. Friendship-Taylor (eds.) *From Round House to Villa.* The Upper Nene Archaeology Society. 47–51.

Galbraith, J. K. 1962. *The Affluent Society.* London: Penguin Books.

Goffman, E. 1959. *The Presentation of Self in Everyday Life.* Garden City, New York: Doubleday.

Goodwin, N.R., Ackerman, F. & Kiron, D. 1997. *The Consumer Society.* Washington D.C. : Island Press.

Gosling, S. D. & Jin Ko, D. 2002. A Room with a Cue: personality judgements based on offices and bedrooms. *Journal of Personality and Social Psychology,* 82: 379–398.

Greenwald, A. G. & Breckler, S. J. 1985. To whom is the Self presented? In B. R. Schenkler (ed.) *The Self and Social Life.* New York: McGraw-Hill.

Harding, D. W. 1984. *Holme House, Piercebridge: Excavations, 1969–70. A Summary Report.* University of Edinburgh Project paper no. 2.

Haverfield, F. 1915. *The Romanization of Roman Britain.* (3rd edition). Oxford: Oxford University Press.

Hill, J.D. 1997. 'The End of one kind of body and the beginning of another kind of body?' Toilet instruments and Romanization in southern England during the first century A.D. In Gwilt and C. Haselgrove (eds.) *Reconstructing Iron Age Societies.* Oxford: Oxbow.

Himmelweit, S. Simonetti, R. & Trigg, A. 2001. *Microeconomics.* London: Thomson Learning.

Hingley, R. 1989. *Rural settlement in Roman Britain.* London: Seaby.

Holbrook, M. B. 1999. Introduction to consumer value. In M.J. Holbrook (ed.) *Consumer Value. A framework for analysis and research.* London/New York: Routledge.

Isserlin, R. 1998. A spirit of improvement? Marble and the culture of Roman Britain. In R. Laurence and J. Berry (eds.) *Cultural Identity in the Roman Empire.* London/New York: Routledge.

Jones, B. & Mattingly, D. 1990. *An Atlas of Roman Britain.* Oxford: Blackwell.

Keevill ,G. D. & Booth, P. 1997. Settlement, sequence and structure: Romano-British stone built round houses at Redlands Farm, Stanwick (Northants) and Alchester (Oxon.). In R. M. and D. E. Friendship-Taylor (eds.) *From Round House to Villa.* The Upper Nene Archaelogical Society. 19–45.

Kilbourne, W. E. 1992. On the Role of Critical Theory in Moving Toward Voluntary Simplicity. In M. Richins & L. Rudmin (eds.) *Meaning, Measure and Morality of Imperialism.* Queen's University and the Association for Consumer Research. 161–163.

Lang, J. 2000. The 'New' Functionalism and Architectural Theory. In K.D. Moore (ed.) *Culture-meaning-architecture: critical reflections on the work of Amos Rapoport.* Aldershot: Ashgate Publishing . 77–102.

Leary, M. R. 1996. *Self-presentation.* Oxford: Westview Press.

Leibenstein, H. 1950. Bandwagon, Snob and Veblen effects in the theory of Consumer Demand. *Quarterly Journal of Economics,* 64: 183–207.

Ling, R. 1985. *Romano-British Wall Painting.* Aylesbury: Shire Publications.

Ling, R. 1991. *Roman Painting.* Cambridge: Cambridge University Press.

Ling, R. 1993. Keeping up with the Claudii. Painting and Roman Householders. *Apollo,* 138: 15–19.

Ling, R . & Ling. L. 2000. Wall and panel painting. In R. Ling (ed.) *Making Classical Art: process and practice.* Stroud: Tempus.

Ling, R. & Courtenay, T. 1981. Excavations at Carsington 1979–80. *Derbyshire Archaeological Journal,* 101: 58–87.

Liversidge, J., Smith, D.J. & Stead, I.M. 1973. Brantingham Roman Villa: discoveries in 1962. *Britannia,* 4: 84–106.

Liversidge, J. 1973. *Britain in the Roman Empire.* London : Sphere Books.

Liversidge, J. 1976. Winterton Wall-painting. In I.M. Stead (ed.) *Excavations at Winterton Roman Villa and other Roman sites in north Lincolnshire 1958–1967.* London: HMSO. 272–287.

Lukis, W.C. 1875. Castle-dykes. *The Archaeological Journal,* 32: 135–154.

Mackey, R. 1998. The Welton Villa– a view of social and economic change during the Roman period in East Yorkshire. In P.Halkon (ed.) *Further light on the Parisii: Recent research in Iron Age and Roman East Yorkshire.* East Riding Archaeological Society. 23–35.

Mason, R. 1981. *Conspicuous Consumption. A study of exceptional consumer behaviour.* Hampshire: Gower Press.

Matthews, K. J. 1997. Immaterial Culture: Invisible peasants and consumer sub-cultures in north-west Britannia. In K. Meadows et al (eds.) *TRAC 96. Proceedings of the Sixth Annual Theoretical Roman Archaeology Conference Sheffield 1996.* Oxford: Oxbow Books.

McCracken, G. 1990. *Culture and consumption: new approaches to the symbolic character of consumer goods and activities.* Bloomington & Indianapolis: Indiana University Press.

Mellor, J. 1981. Leicester. *Current Archaeology,* 8.10: 314–317.

Mellor, J. 1982. New discoveries from the Norfolk Street Villa, Leicester. In J. Liversidge (ed.) *Roman Provincial Wall-painting of the Western Empire.* BAR International Series 140. 127–40.

Millett, M. 1990. *The Romanization of Britain: an essay in archaeological interpretation.* Cambridge: Cambridge University Press.

Millett, M. 1992. Rural integration in the Roman West: an introductory essay. In M. Wood & F. Queiroga (eds.) *Current Research on the Romanization of the Western Provinces.* BAR International Series 5575. 1–4.

Millett, M. 1995. *Roman Britain.* London: Batsford/English Heritage.

Mordaunt Crook, J. 1999. *The Rise of the Nouveaux Riches.* London: John Murray.

Morgan, G. C. 1992. *Romano-British Mortars and Plasters.* Unpublished Ph.D. thesis at the University of Leicester.

Nader, R. 1973. *The Consumer and Corporate Accountability.* New York: Harcourt Brace Jovanovitch.

Packard, V. 1965. *The Status Seekers.* Harmondsworth: London: Penguin.

Percival, J. 1976. *The Roman Villa. An historical introduction.* London: Batsford.

Perring, D. 2002. *The Roman House in Britain.* London/New York: Routledge.

Potter, T. W. & Johns, C. 1992. *Roman Britain.* London: British Museum Press.

Potter, T. W. 1997 . *Roman Britain.* London: British Museum Press.

Purcell, N. 1987. Towns in Country and Country in Town. In E. MacDougall (ed.) *Ancient Roman Villa Gardens:* Washington D.C.: Dumbarton Oaks Trustees. 185–203.

Rahtz, P. Hayfield, C. & Bateman, C. 1986. *Two Roman Villas at Wharram le Street.* York University Archaeological Publications 2.

Rapoport, A. *The Meaning of the Built Environment.* London: Sage Publications.

Reece, R. 1988. *My Roman Britain.* Cirencester: Cotswold Studies.

Rice, C. 1993. *Consumer behaviour: behavioural aspects of marketing.* Oxford: Butterworth Heinemann.

Richins, M. 1992. A Psychographic approach to materialism. In M. Richins & L. Rudmins (eds.) *Meaning, Measure and Morality of materialism.* Queen's university and the Association of Consumer Research. 128–137.

Richmond, I. A. 1963. *Roman Britain.* Harmondsworth: Penguin Books.

Richmond, I. A. 1969. The Country Estates. In P. Salway (ed.) *Roman Archaeology and art, essays by Sir Ian Richmond.* London: Faber & Faber. 135–149.

Rivet, A. L. F. 1964. *Town and country in Roman Britain.* London: Hutchinson University Library.

Rivet, A. L. F. 1969. Social and economic aspects. In A. L. F. Rivet (ed.) *The Roman Villa in Britain.* London: Routledge & Kegan Paul.

Rooke, H. 1787. The Roman Villa at Mansfield Woodhouse. *Archaeologia,* 8: 363–376.

Rozenberg, S. 1997. Pigments and fresco fragments from Herod's Palace at Jericho. In Bearat et al (eds.) *Roman Wall Painting: materials, techniques, analysis and conservation. Proceedings of the International Workshop on Roman Wall Painting. Fribourg 1996.* 63–73.

Sabini, J. 1995. Social Psychology. New York: W.W. Norton.

Salway, P. 1993. *The Oxford Illustrated History of Roman Britain.* Oxford: Oxford University Press.

Samson, R. 1999. Slavish nonsense or the talking tool. In A. Leslie (ed.) *Theoretical Roman Archaeology and Architecture. The Third Conference Proceedings.* Glasgow: Cruithne Press. 122–140.

Schiffman, L. G. & Kanuk, L.L 2000. *Consumer Behaviour.* London: Prentice-Hall.

Schumacher, E. F. 1973. *Small is Beautiful. A study of economics as if people mattered.* London: Blond & Briggs.

Scott, S. 1997. The Power of Images in the late Roman House. In R. Laurence and A. Wallace-Hadrill (eds.) *Domestic Space in the Roman World: Pompeii and Beyond.* Journal of Roman Archaeology supplementary series no. 22. 53–67.

Sheth, J., Mittal, B., & Newman, B. I. 1999. *Customer behaviour. Consumer behaviour and beyond.* Fort Worth: Harcourt Brace College Publishers.

Smith, J. T. 1964. The Roman Villa at Denton. *Lincolnshire Architectural and Archaeological Society. Reports and papers.* 10.2: 75–104.

Smith, J. T. 1997. *Roman villas: a study in social structure.* London/New York: Routledge.

Solomon, M. R. 1999. The value of status and the status of value. In M.B. Holbrook (ed.) *Consumer Value. A framework for analysis and research.* London/New York: Routledge. 63–84.

Stead, I.M. 1976. *Excavations at Winterton Roman Villa and other Roman sites in North Lincolnshire.* London: HMSO.

Storey, J. 1999. *Cultural Consumption and Everyday Life.* London: Arnold.

Strong, R. 1996. *Country Life 1897–1997. The English Arcadia.* London: MacMillan.

Taylor, J. 2001. Rural Society in Roman Britain. In S. James & M. Millett (eds.) *Britons and Romans: advancing an archaeological agenda.* York: Council for British Archaeology Research Report 125: 46–59.

Tedeschi, J. T. & Norman, N. 1985. Social Power, Self-Presentation and the Self, In B. Schenkler (ed.) *The Self and Social life.* New York: McGraw Hill.

Tybout, R. 2001. Roman wall painting and social significance. *Journal of Roman Archaeology,* 14: 33–56.

Veblen, T. 1925. *The Theory of the Leisure class.* London: Allen & Unwin.

Wacher, J. 1978. *Roman Britain.* London: J.M Dent & sons.

Wacher, J. 2000. *A Portrait of Roman Britain.* London/New York: Routledge.

Wallace-Hadrill, A. 1988. The Social Structure of the Roman house. *Papers of the British School at Rome,* 56: 43–97.

Wallace-Hadrill, A. 1994. *Houses and society in Roman Pompeii and Herculaneum.* New Jersey: Princeton University Press.

Wilkie, W. L. 1994. *Consumer Behaviour.* New York: John Wiley & sons.

Wiseman, T. P. 1994. *Historiography and Imagination.* University of Exeter Press.

Wong, N.Y. C. 1997. Suppose you own the world and no one knows? Conspicuous Consumption, Materialism and Self. In M. Brucks & D. MacInnis (eds.) *Advances in Consumer Research.* Provo UT: Association for Consumer Research, 24: 197–203.

Woodfield, C. with Johnson, C. 1989. A Roman Site at Stanton Low on the Great Ouse, Buckinghamshire. *Archaeological Journal,* 146: 135–278.

Woods, P. J. 1970. Excavation at Brixworth, Northants. 1965–1970. vol. 1. The Romano-British Villa. *Northampton Museum & Art Gallery Journal,* 8.

Woolf, G. 1998. *Becoming Roman: the origins of provincial civilization in Gaul.* Cambridge: Cambridge University Press.

Woolf, G. 2001. The Roman cultural revolution in Gaul. In S. Keay & N. Terrenato (eds.) *Italy and the West. Comparative Issues in Romanization.* Oxford: Oxbow Books. 173–186.

Wrathmell, S. & Nicholson, A. 1990. *Dalton Parlours. Iron Age Settlement and Roman villa.* Yorkshire Archaeology 3: West Yorkshire Archaeology Service.

Zaltmann, G. & Wallendorf, M. 1983. *Consumer behaviour: basic findings and management implications.* New York: Wiley & sons.

Zanker, P. 1998. *Pompeii: public and private life.* Cambridge, Massachusets: Harvard University Press.

Zeepvat, R. J. 1994. *Bancroft. The Roman Villa.* Buckinghamshire Archaeological Society Monograph Series No.7.

Late Roman economic systems: their implication in the interpretation of social organisation.

Paul Johnson

Introduction

The aim of this paper is to discuss the ways in which we can use material evidence for the exchange of goods in order to investigate patterns of social organisation. In particular, it is the intent of this paper to explore the relationship between economic activity and social organisation in the Late Roman Empire. Much emphasis has been placed on the economic role of ceramic goods in the Late Roman Empire and work has been carried out which shows how changing social practices reflect changes in the way that goods are used and hence their appearance in the archaeological record. However, the focus on particular types of ceramic vessel excludes a wide range of goods which were in fact of a more fundamental importance in the everyday life of people in the Late Roman Empire. Previous studies have also failed to appreciate the way that less culturally specific goods can reflect patterns of social organisation through their spatial patterning. This paper will focus on the staple goods of grain and oil in order to suggest how the society of the Late Roman Empire may have functioned at its most basic level. Neither grain nor oil survive well in the archaeological record. As such, we must look to the containers and buildings in which they were stored to provide evidence for their presence.

This use of proxy indicators for the presence of these goods is not unproblematic, but it is practicable where a study of the goods themselves is not. We are fortunate in that it is possible to postulate the likely sites for the storage of grain in warehouse complexes such as those at Ostia and in Rome (Rickman 1971; Hermansen 1982). One can therefore assess the presence or at least the possibility of the presence of grain, if not the actual quantities which were stored. More detailed evidence can be accumulated through an examination of the movement of oil around the Mediterranean. This was transported both in large ceramic amphorae, which survive well in almost all conditions, and also by the later Roman Empire in oilskins, which unfortunately do not. The amphorae are unrivalled as a proxy indicator of the oil trade; one must however, be careful when dealing with the evidence from amphorae. Whilst some can be confidently identified with the transportation of oil due to the residues left on their inner surfaces, there is a noticeable 'grey area' where the contents are unknown. The recent developments in typological and fabric analyses also enable many of these amphorae to be accurately located to particular regions within a broad geographical context. In some cases it has even been possible to identify amphorae deriving from particular kiln sites (Peacock et al. 1990). Through a study of this evidence, one may garner a clearer understanding of economic and, by inference, social organisation in this period.

Background to the study of late Roman economic systems

This paper does not allow sufficient scope for a detailed and exhaustive discussion of all the previous studies of the Late Roman economy. However, it is extremely important to highlight some of the past approaches in order to contextualise the rationale behind the paper.

A particularly influential piece of scholarship in the field was Moses Finley's *The Ancient Economy* (1973); his ideas were to be fundamental in shaping many of the works which followed. Thought-provoking though this work is, Finley rarely considered the implications of economic behaviour for a society. He saw society and economy as linked, but deemed this to be a one-way relationship whereby social considerations defined economic practice. He was particularly concerned with the relationship between social hierarchies and economic activity. The main thrust of much of his argument concerned which 'professions' were deemed suitable by different strata of society, arguing that trade and agricultural production were exclusive pursuits undertaken by members of different classes. High status, concomitant with land ownership, is seen as the key to economic potential. Yet it is acknowledged that there are many professions open to the 'lower classes'. What Finley lacks is a real idea of how to work from the evidence of economic activity to a reconstruction of social practices.

The Marxist perspective of Rostovtzeff's *Social and Economic History of the Roman Empire* (1957) was highly influential in its time, suggesting that the Roman Empire had an economic base more complex than simple subsistence farming. Finley, however, believed a great deal of this to be rather vague and prone to unsupported generalisations (1973: 33). Studies of the economy and supply of bulk goods to Rome have, however, traditionally relied upon the historical sources for most of their evidence (Frank 1933–40; Sirks 1991; Tengström 1974; Whittaker 1983), partly because of a perceived lack of archaeological evidence and the lure of quantitative values for the scale of imports (Finley 1999: 25). Historians have also attempted to deduce population sizes for the city and the quantity of goods required to feed its population (e.g. Garnsey 1983; Hopkins 1980; Virlouvet 2000). This approach is severely limited due to inconsistencies in the sources and the modern readings of them.

Certainly by the 1980s Finley's work had begun to come under criticism and indeed led to revisions of the original work (Finley 1985; 1999). Following the second edition of *The Ancient Economy*, much discussion has taken place concerning the focus and relevance of Finley's work (Nippel 1991). More recent research has been published which confidently asserts that Roman Imperial expansion "should be linked to a major increase in commerce" (Patterson 1998: 150). Whilst this takes some account of the idea of the interrelation between changing social circumstances and economy the work is still based largely on ancient textual sources. The inescapable observation is that the majority of the work critical of Finley's conclusions was so dominated by the need to repudiate those very ideas that it inevitably did little to move beyond the basic concepts involved. The state of academic debate as outlined by Parkins (1998), has largely consisted of an argument over whether the ideas of Finley or Rostovtzeff are closer to the truth.

Recently attempts have been made (Mattingly & Salmon 2001) to move the debate about the ancient economy past the consideration of agricultural production to other economic practices occurring within or around towns. Unfortunately, as the authors admit, it does not address the question of the social implications of economic activity (Mattingly and Salmon 2001: 4). Whilst this represents a large step in the right direction by emphasising other forms of economic activity besides large scale trade in foodstuffs, it fails to take into consideration the most important aspect of any economic system: the people whom it serves. What is needed, and what this paper will attempt to do, is to contextualise the economy within its society and show how an understanding of one can shed light on the other.

The most recent and perhaps most effective attempt to move beyond the traditional models and paradigms associated with the study of the Roman Economy comes through a piece of work which is neither about Rome, nor specifically about the economy. Horden and Purcell's *The Corrupting Sea* (2001) places the emphasis back on the need for societies to use the resources available to them in order to make up shortfalls in agricultural production. That is not to argue for a kind of ecological determinism, as many of the goods exchanged were almost ubiquitous in their availability, but instead that all forms of economic activity are interlinked; one cannot separate producer from consumer and one cannot distinguish this from the wider social milieu. A mobility of goods is argued to have been accompanied by a similar mobility of the labour force, whether through itinerancy or through the forced movement ascribed to slavery. This begins to tie the social to the economic, since movements of people will, by definition, have an impact on society.

Much of the debate over the Roman economy has centred on the role of the state in the supply of the *Annona* and other goods to Rome. The argument has been dominated by the opposed views of Finley and Rostovtzeff regarding the complexity of the Roman economy and the extent of state involvement in the economic life of the Roman Empire. Much academic discourse has argued for extensive state involvement, especially where the supply of grain to Rome was involved (Casson 1980). Wickham's view whereby the late Roman trading system was dominated by, if not reliant upon, the demands of the state (1988: 193) may well be very close to the mark. More importantly, however, he makes explicit the connection between the economic activities of the state and those of the people living in the provinces (in this case Africa). Much of the work arguing for a centralised supply system has been primarily reliant on epigraphic evidence [e.g. Cébeillac-Gervasoni (1994) for the duties of the *Praefectus Annonae* (Casson 1980: 22–23)]. It has also been argued that as grain was so vital to the diet of the people of the ancient Mediterranean it engendered an unusual level of involvement from the state (Rickman 1980). The mechanisms for the collection of this grain are by admission not well known (Rickman 1980) and as such one must doubt the certainty of those whose arguments for high levels of state involvement are based on rather tenuous evidence. The creation of a *Procurator Portus Ostie(n)sis* under Claudius has been associated with the creation of the Claudian harbour at Portus (Houston 1980). This official has also been associated with the *Praefectus Annonae* and, as such, has been deemed to be responsible for the offloading and transhipment of the *Annona*. It would appear that in the later Empire, this official became the *Procurator Portus Utriusque* and was seen to be responsible for the *Annona* in the period after Septimius Severus (Houston 1980). That there was an official responsible for the Annona at Portus is unsurprising but the evidence fails to reveal much more about the way in which the Imperial government was involved in the supply of the Annona to the population of the city of Rome.

These studies and their biases have left a legacy of interpretation based on general models and ideal types, leaving us with a view of a late Roman economy which is restrictive and unduly dominated by the demands of the Annona supply to Rome. The *Annona* is undoubtedly an important part of the Late Roman economy, but its prevalence in both the literature and in the conception of the totality of Late Roman economics is misleading and problematic for anyone who wishes to form an understanding of the implications for the vast majority of Late Roman society. In order to fully exploit the potential of the evidence now available, it is essential to move beyond these paradigms and embrace a new approach which can shed light on the day to day economic interaction between the people of the Roman Empire.

New approaches to the problem

Whilst most recent studies of the Roman economy have failed to elucidate the social aspects of the economy altogether, those which have addressed this issue have not tested the ideas which they propose. What is needed, therefore, is a well grounded, theoretically informed archaeological investigation into the social implications of a given economic system. What we need to consider are the distributions of particular types of goods and the relative quantities in which they appear in a given context in order to understand patterns of distribution and consumption, and the social factors which may influence them. In order to accomplish this, we must more freely embrace theoretical viewpoints which enable us to move beyond an empirical assessment of the evidence and attempt to understand the social dimension of the archaeological record. This can be accomplished more fully where there is a large corpus of data, collected with these objectives in mind upon which to base an interpretation. However, in order to wholly appreciate what is needed, it is important to recognise both the potential and the shortcomings of the evidence now at our disposal.

Though the two are closely interrelated, society is not so much a facet of economic behaviour as economy is a result of social practices and demands. Economy could never function without society. All too often, economic studies have tended to ignore the human element; one must never forget that it is people who demanded these goods and thus caused them to be moved. Furthermore, it was people who actually transported them. Social practice is really the focus of all archaeological research. In this, Roman archaeology and the archaeology of late Antiquity should be seen as no different. The following section will demonstrate how this approach may be applied to the archaeological record.

Case study: Ostia

The Grandi *Horrea* are located by the ancient course of the Tiber just to the North of the *Decumanus Maximus* (Figure 1). They are easily the largest *horrea* yet discovered in Ostia and are important in understanding the processes behind the movement of goods into and through the town. Whilst we are somewhat hampered by the lack of detailed publication for the site, it has been proposed that they were still in use in the early fourth century (Calza 1953: 153) and there is much that can be said from a study of the standing remains and their relationship to their surroundings in the town. One can see that the *horrea* are oriented such that their only visible access fronts on to the riverside, an important functional aspect of a building dealing with riverine trade. However, when one also considers that there is no access into the building from any other direction, and that to the south the *horrea* are obscured by a series of small buildings fronting onto the street, this offers some important insight into the way that the building was used and how it related to the rest of the city.

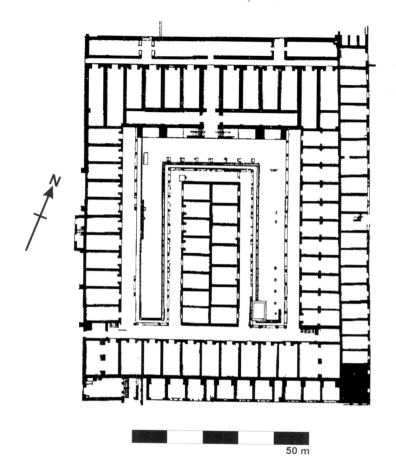

50 m

Figure 1. The Grandi Horrea (after Rickman 1971: 44)

The *Grandi Horrea* are particularly important as a type site for Ostian storehouses as they have been fully excavated and demonstrate the entirety of their plan. In particular, their standing remains demonstrate the presence of raised *suspensurae* flooring (Figure 2), as such these *horrea* must be treated as primarily being grain stores. As these have an entrance and frontage facing the river to the north one may expect them to have been situated in order to facilitate the movement of grain to and from the river. The overall pattern of *horrea* in Ostia (Figure 3) provides some interesting insights into the distribution of goods around the city. One can see that the larger *horrea* have all been identified as containing grain (Meiggs 1973). Although they have been seen as 'scattered' (Meiggs 1973: 282), the plan seems to suggest that they are actually concentrated toward the waterfront and in close proximity to the major public areas. This may indicate that there was a particular importance attached to grain. Or, alternatively and perhaps concomitantly, there was a much greater quantity of grain passing through the city and

Figure 2. Suspensurae flooring in the Grandi Horrea.

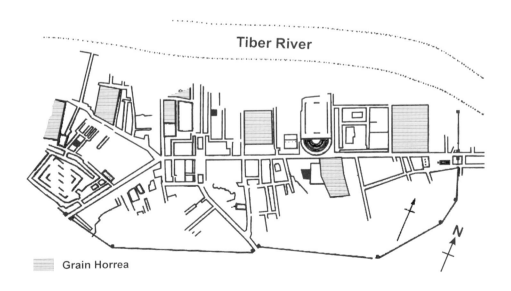

Figure 3. Distribution of known Horrea. (after Meiggs 1973: 284)

so it was considered expedient to place the storage facilities close to the water. The *horrea* identified with the storage of other commodities are almost without exception much smaller. Furthermore, they are all located further away from the river. It would not seem imprudent to suggest that this is indicative of a division between the goods intended for consumption and long-term storage in Ostia and those, such as grain, which formed part of the *Annona* and were destined for transport further up-river.

The economic implications of this are evident. The *Grandi Horrea* were a complex for the storage of grain, the most basic foodstuff in the ancient world, yet it was not constructed in such a way as to facilitate the supply of the population of Ostia. Furthermore, due to its relative size in comparison with other known *horrea* in Ostia, it must have accounted for a large part of the trade through the docks of the city. Its social implications, whilst less immediately apparent, are therefore significant. The proprietors of this complex must have been able to mobilise a large labour force in order to deal with the quantity of goods being stored in the *horrea*. This would have been at best a seasonal occupation due to the restricted sailing seasons in the ancient Mediterranean and implies that there was a large amount of labour available within the city on an ad-hoc basis.

The idea of short term or temporary labour has been postulated for the construction industry (De Laine 2000); why not for other purposes too? Indeed, De Laine suggests that unemployed labourers may have found work at the docks. This freedom for labourers to effectively hire themselves out wherever needed argues against ideas of tight control over or marked distinctions between various professions and might enable a wider re-assessment of the shipping mechanisms in place in the Late Empire.

It would be possible to see the existence of the various guilds as merely providing the organisation for the shipments, hiring free labour when needed for the physical task of actually moving these goods into and out of the warehouses. Without wider comparison, it is difficult to suggest any general patterns but this offers one possibility.

To illuminate further this point, it is necessary to draw on other material evidence. One of the very few well-published excavated sites at Ostia is the *Terme del Nuotatore* (Carandini & Panella 1973). The site lies to the south of the *Decumanus Maximus* (Figure 4) and is located away from the major thoroughfares of the city. The importance of this site is due not to its function as a bath house but rather to its mid-third century abandonment and use as a dump. Firstly, this in itself is suggestive of changing patterns within society which may have led to the disuse of a public bathing facility. This may be attributable to a general decline in the use of public bathing facilities or simply that the facilities formerly provided by the *Terme del Nuotatore* were now being provided elsewhere. Secondly, the nature of the deposits in the site would indicate that we cannot ascribe the disuse of the baths to a general abandonment or depopulation of the city. The presence of a large proportion of Tunisian oil amphorae datable to the fourth century (Keay 1984; 1998) would suggest a thriving import of commodities into the city, concomitant with the demands of a settled population.

Analyses carried out on the amphorae remains subsequent to excavation have revealed a startling increase in the proportion of African amphorae beginning in the late Severan period or by the late third century (Panella 1986: 65). By the fourth century the proportion of African amphorae had reached 45.1% of the total (Panella 1986: 66). Of these, amphorae which can be identified with the production and shipment of oil account for 53.1% of the total number of African amphorae. The area known as *ambiente XVI* disclosed amphorae remains in two discrete stratigraphic layers. The upper '*Strato I*' represents the post destruction layer of deposition following the mid third century abandonment of the site (Anselmino et al. 1977:

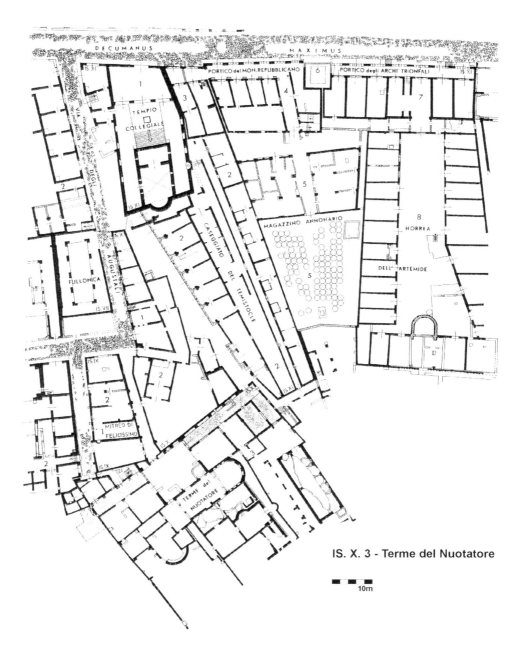

Figure 4. Location of the Terme del Nuotatore. (after Carandini 1973: Tav. I)

14). This layer contained a total of 1125 amphorae fragments (Anselmino et al. 1977: 244), a large proportion of which seem to have been African. This definition between two layers of deposition would seem indicative of an organised policy. If the deposits were ad-hoc it would be far more likely that there would be a single, undifferentiated stratigraphic layer covering the entire post-use period of the site. As it stands, there would seem to have been two discrete depositional episodes, each occurring over a short period of time with an interval between them. This is not a characteristic associated with a disorganised, continuously used dump. One can therefore postulate that the later deposition identified as *Strato I* is concomitant with increased imports of African goods following the redirection of the Egyptian grain fleet.

This sudden surge in the proportion of African amphorae can be confidently ascribed to the *Annona* shipments. However, these deposits also reveal details about the means by which these goods reached the populations of the cities to which they were transported. The location of these deposits, away from the major *horrea*, the main thoroughfares and piazzas echo the changes that can be seen in Rome in the same period. The lack of a replacement site for Monte Testaccio by the *horrea* of the Emporium suggests that this change in the pattern of amphora deposition is reflective of a changing pattern of distribution and consumption within Roman society. What is seen in the late third and early fourth centuries is a shift from the tightly controlled, centralised distributive network evidenced by the Dressel 20s that form Monte Testaccio (Remesal-Rodríguez 1998). It has been postulated that Monte Testaccio is composed of 1,334,000,000 kilograms of amphora sherds. This equates to roughly 53,359,800 whole amphorae which accumulated over a period of two centuries (Rodríguez-Almeida 1984; 1994).

The fourth century and the rise of the African oil amphorae see a more decentralised distributive network. This, in turn, is indicative of a relaxation of the state monopoly of imports and an increased reliance on quasi independent shippers to bring in the commodities required in the urban markets of Ostia and indeed, of Rome.

What is then seen from the admittedly limited evidence of these two sites is an often contradictory, yet undeniably illuminating, set of data. At the most basic level, the *Grandi Horrea* suggest that the economic focus of the city was outward looking, that its functional importance was the movement of goods up the Tiber towards Rome. From the restricted means of access to this building, we can further infer that there was a degree of separation between those goods destined for transhipment and those which would be distributed within the city. If we see the grain passing through the *Grandi Horrea* as being destined for Rome, the access into the building would suggest that goods destined for consumption in Ostia were stored and distributed from other locations.

This has resonance with the apparent division of oil between that destined for the *Annona* or the 'Rome levy' and that which was not; as recorded on the *Ilot De L'Amiraute* in Carthage (Peña 1998). The deposits at the *Terme del Nuotatore* would suggest that the city was still a centre of population in the Late Roman period but, as the bath house was abandoned there was some form of shift occurring in the social behaviour of elements of the population.

With such a limited data set one is only able to hypothesise about what this may mean. However, it can be suggested with a fair degree of certainty that the economic changes occurring in the fourth century were accompanied by significant alterations within the fabric of late Roman society. In Ostia we can see this as a shift in focus of activity and the structured re-use of an abandoned building as a dump for the refuse of the city. The quantity of material found in the *Terme del Nuotatore* alone is not sufficient to suggest a thriving population, but the structured manner in which the deposits were formed suggests that there was still control by some civic authority and as such is important in refuting ideas of a decline in either social organisation or the population of the city. It can be suggested that Ostia remained an important centre for the import and export of goods to and from Rome, hence important for the society of that city. Despite the construction of the harbours at Portus, the *Grandi Horrea* still fulfilled this function well into the late empire. If the grain stored there was not going to feed the population of Ostia, then it must have been some part of the wider trading networks which linked Rome to the Mediterranean as a whole.

Conclusion

This paper has presented a very brief overview of the complexities involved in the exploration of Late Roman society through the medium of economic evidence. The preceding discussion has been a conscious attempt to identify the questions which need to be answered in order to form a better understanding of this subject. Furthermore, it has begun to construct a framework upon which future thinking regarding the Late Roman economy can be based. Although there are problems with the current state of the evidence available for this type of study, this paper has espoused a different way of looking at these issues, and through attempting to apply this approach to the archaeological evidence we can see where its potential and its shortcomings lie. By looking at patterns of economic distribution, it is possible to infer patterns of social organisation as the various modes of distribution necessitated different social practices for their operation. In this case, one can suggest that these practices were linked to the provision of the *Annona* and therefore the governance of the Roman state. The scattered nature of deposits can be equated to a more dispersed pattern of distribution of goods prior to consumption and a decentralised yet organised system of disposal. This paper has also drawn attention to the problems inherent in making generalisations based on an understanding of one or two supposedly typical sites. The *Terme del Nuotatore* has itself often been used in this way, to provide a foundation for economic histories of the western Mediterranean. Yet it is still not fully understood in relation to other sites within the city of Ostia. The lack of systematic excavation has precluded a regional study within the city. However, this paper has demonstrated how one can approach the question of the way in which buildings like the *Grandi Horrea* may have been used.

This paper has been able to show that there is the potential to explore the evidence further and that there are still important questions to be asked of the data currently available for study. With the publication of more material from excavations at Ostia it should be possible to test further these ideas with respect to that particular city. However the real advances will come through relating this to the wider Mediterranean context. What is now required is a wider synthesis of the available data from sites around the Mediterranean, both published and unpublished, in order to explore what patterns may emerge from them.

The British School at Rome

Bibliography

Anselmino, L. A. Carandini and C. Panella. 1977. *Ostia IV. Le Terme del Nuotatore*. Studi Miscellanei 23.

Calza, G. 1953. *Scavi di Ostia. Volume I. Topografia Generale*. Roma: La Libreria dello Stato.

Carandini, A. and C. Panella. 1973. *Ostia III Prima Parte. Le Terme del Nutatore*. Studi Miscellanei 21.

Casson, L. 1980. The Role of the State in Rome's grain trade. In J. H D'Arms and E. C. Kopff, (eds.) *The Seaborne Commerce of Ancient Rome: Studies in archaeology and history*. Memoirs of the American Academy in Rome Vol. XXXVI. 21–34.

Cébeillac-Gervasoni, M. 1994. Ostie et le blé au IIe siècle ap. J.-C. In. *Le Ravitaillement en blé de Rome et des centres urbains des débuts de la République jusqu'au Haut Empire*. Actes du colloque international de Naples (1991). Naples-Rome: Ecole Française de Rome. 47–59.

De Laine, J. 2000. Building the Eternal City: the construction industry of Imperial Rome. In. Coulston, J. & Dodge, H. (eds.) *Ancient Rome: The archaeology of the Eternal City*. Oxford University School of Archaeology: Oxford. 119–141.

Finley, M. I. 1973. *The Ancient Economy*. London: Chatto & Windus.

Finley, M. I. 1985. *The Ancient Economy (2nd edn)*. London: Hogarth.

Finley, M. I. 1999. *The Ancient Economy*. Updated edition. Berkely, Los Angeles & London: University of California Press.

Frank, T. 1933–40. *An Economic Survey of Ancient Rome*, 6 vols. Baltimore: Johns Hopkins Press.

Garnsey, P. 1983. Grain for Rome. In P. Garnsey, K. Hopkins and C. R. Whittaker (eds.) *Trade in the Ancient Economy*. Berkeley & Los Angeles: University of California Press. 118–130.

Hermansen, G. 1982. *Ostia, Aspects of Roman City Life*. Edmonton: University of Alberta Press.

Hopkins, K. 1980. Taxes and Trade in the Roman Empire. *The Journal of Roman Studies*. Vol. 70. 101–125.

Horden, P. and Purcell, N. 2000. *The Corrupting Sea*. Oxford: Blackwell.

Houston, G. W. 1980. The Administration of Italian Seaports during the first three centuries of the Roman Empire. In J. H. D'Arms and E. C. Kopff, (eds) *The Seaborne Commerce of Ancient Rome: studies in archaeology and history*. Memoirs of the American Academy in Rome Vol. XXXVI. 157–172.

Keay, S. J. 1984. *Late Roman Amphorae in the Western Mediterranean*. British Archaeological Reports International Series 196.

Keay, S. J. 1998. African Amphorae. In. L. Saguí. *Ceramica in Italia: VI–VII secolo*. Firenze: Edizioni All'Insegna del Giglio. 141–155.

Meiggs, R. 1973. *Roman Ostia. 2nd edn*. Oxford: Clarendon Press.

Nippel, W. 1991. Finley and Weber. Some comments and theses. *Opus VI–VII*, 43–50.

Panella, C. 1986. Le Anfore. In A. Giardina, (ed.) *Le Merci gli Insediamenti*. Bari: Editori Laterza. 64–81.

Parkins, H. 1998. Time for change? Shaping the Future of the Ancient Economy. In H. Parkins, and C. Smith, *Trade, Traders and the Ancient City*. London and New York: Routledge. 1–15.

Patterson, J. 1998. Trade and Traders in the Ancient World: scale, structure and organisation. In H. Parkins, and C. Smith, *Trade, Traders and the Ancient City*. London and New York: Routledge. 149–167.

Peña, J. T. 1998. The Mobilization of State Olive Oil in Roman Africa: the evidence of late 4th-c. *ostraca* from Carthage. In J. T. Peña, *Carthage Papers: the early colony's economy, water supply and the mobilization of state olive oil*. Journal of Roman Archaeology Supplementary Series 28. 116–238.

Remesal-Rodríguez, J. 1998. Baetican Olive Oil and the Roman Economy. In S. J. Keay, (ed.) *The Archaeology of Early Roman Baetica*. Journal of Roman Archaeology supplementary Series 29. 183–199.

Rickman, G. 1971. *Roman Granaries and Store Buildings*. Cambridge: University Press.

Rickman, G. 1980. The Grain Trade under the Roman Empire. In J. H D'Arms and E. C. Kopff, (eds.) *The Seaborne Commerce of Ancient Rome: studies in archaeology and history.* Memoirs of the American Academy in Rome Vol. XXXVI. 261–276.

Rodríguez-Almeida, E. 1984. *Il Monte Testaccio.* Roma: Edizione Quasar.

Rodríguez-Almeida, E. 1994. *Excavaciones Arqueológicas en el Monte Testaccio (Roma).* Madrid: Institutio de Conservación y Restauración de Bienes Cultrales.

Rostovtzeff, M. 1957. *The Social and Economic history of the Roman Empire.* 2nd Edition. Oxford: Clarendon Press.

Sirks, B. 1991. *Food for Rome.* Amsterdam: Geiben.

Tengström, E. 1974. *Bread for the People.* Stockholm: Paul Åströms Förlag.

Virlouvet, C. 2000. L'approvigionamento di Roma imperiale. In E. Lo Cascio (ed.) *Roma Imperiale. Una metropoli antica.* Rome: Carocci. 103–135.

Wickham, C. 1988. Marx, Sherlock Holmes, and Late Roman Commerce. *The Journal of Roman Studies* Vol. 78. 183–193.

Whittaker, C. R. 1983. Late Roman Trade and Traders. In. P. Garnsey, K. Hopkins and C. R. Whittaker (eds.) *Trade in the Ancient Economy.* Berkeley & Los Angeles: University of California Press. 163–180.

Creolisation, pidginisation and the interpretation of unique artefacts in early Roman Britain

Gillian Carr

Introduction

Recent advances in understanding identity in Roman Britain have explored concepts of creolisation (e.g. Hawkes 1999; Webster 2001), which improve upon earlier models of Romanisation by allowing the non-élite native voice to be heard within the complex mix of hybrid Roman and non-Roman identities and counter-cultures which made up Roman Britain. Creole material culture is seen as an ambiguous mix of native and Roman cultures, and often reflects the political inequality seen in the colonial situation. Creolisation as model for interpretation "allows the subjected people the ability to accept or reject in part the package of Roman material culture which was available to them" (Hawkes 1999: 90). It can manifest itself as a Roman-style artefact or practice incorporated into an indigenous sphere of everyday life, and used as part of a social practice which differed to the way in which it might be used as part of the 'Roman'-style lifestyle (however it may have been defined).

How, then, are we to explain artefacts in Roman Britain which were entirely unique – items which do not appear to be hybrid mixes of either native or 'Roman'-style material culture? In this paper, I return to the field of linguistics to explore a concept related to creolisation and creole languages; I propose to investigate the concept of 'pidginisation', and 'pidgin' material culture, and whether this will allow us insight into the interpretation of unique artefacts. Such an investigation is presented as a possible methodology for dealing with new questions, and is very much work in progress. Later in the paper, I will illustrate my argument with a speculative reading of a single grave: that of the so-called 'Stanway doctor' from Colchester, the only known (or assumed) grave of a healer from either Roman or, indeed, Iron Age Britain.

Creolisation in theory

Creolisation theory has been put forward as a new model to replace 'Romanisation' as a way of understanding the processes at work in Roman Britain. As Webster (2001: 209) has argued, 'Romanisation' is a simplistic and outdated model which focuses on the capacity of individuals to find their own way of 'becoming Roman' (or not). It is presented as a civilising process, which was emulated at all levels of society. In her paper, Webster also explores other criticisms which have been levelled against 'Romanisation'. Importantly, she does not doubt that some élites came to identify themselves with the values of Roman civilisation; but asks with what success 'Romanisation' operated at lower social levels.

Because 'Romanisation' is 'simply another word for acculturation', Webster argues that it promotes a one-sided view of cultural change, which is not what the archaeological record of Roman Britain reflects. 'Romanisation' does not allow for a two-way exchange of ideas; does not address the cultural mixes that made up Roman Britain, nor the localised choices or developments of counter-cultures.

Webster proposed that we apply the linguistic term 'creolisation' as a substitute for 'Romanisation'. Linguistically, creolisation refers to two separate languages which are blended together to produce a third. It can also be used socially and culturally, often in a colonial context, to explain the adjustments which two societies make when they come together to form a third. As we shall see, creolisation has also been used in other fields of archaeology.

Several aspects of creolisation make it suitable as a replacement for 'Romanisation'. Creole dialects are rarely a neutral mix of the languages of which they are made; they often reflect the social relations of domination seen in the colonial context. There is always a dominant language, which contributes most of the vocabulary (the superstrate), and a minority language (the substrate). Similarly, in the colonial situation in Roman Britain, we see (the dominant) Roman material culture prevalent on most sites; however, we should not make the assumption that material culture, which to us looks 'Roman', was necessarily always perceived as 'Roman' or used according to 'Roman' cultural rules. This ambiguity is another important feature of creole material culture. Yet another important characteristic of creolisation is that, just as the blended dialect involves two languages (one dominant and the other not), any creole artefact is also a politically non-neutral blended mix that allows us to 'hear the native voice' in the way that discussions of 'Romanisation' rarely acknowledge.

To summarise, Webster (2001: 218) argues that ambiguity and hybridity are an important feature of creolised artefacts, and that creolisation emphasises the fundamental power inequalities between coloniser and colonised. Creolisation also gives us an insight into the 'negotiation of post-conquest identities' to help us better understand the variety of cultural mixes which would have existed after the Roman conquest. Moreover, creolisation leads us away from understanding Roman Britain in terms of a polarised world of Romans and Britons, and of 'either / or', with no grey areas in between; by understanding that Roman Britain comprised a complex mix of heterogeneous creolised identities and newly created cultural entities we can move away from such polarisation.

Creolisation as a concept: criticisms and justifications

Creolisation as a concept has different meanings in different contexts, including both the popular and the academic. The term 'creole' is used in Latin America and the Caribbean to refer to local born descendants of European families; in parts of the United States, the term refers to descendants of French families (Seymour-Smith 1986: 57). While it may be acknowledged that creolisation is often perceived to be associated with historically-specific processes in the Caribbean, creole languages are, in fact, found all over the world, from Haitian and Belizean creole to Swahili (possibly a creole made up of Bantu languages and Arabic). Pidgins, too, are geographically widespread, and found from Papua New Guinea (Tok Pisin) and Nigeria (Nigerian Pidgin) to China (China Coast pidgin). Creole languages are not *necessarily* (but often are) associated with the colonial context and slavery; in fact, it could be argued that English is (historically speaking) a creolised language itself. However, I would argue that the fact that creolisation is usually associated with the colonial context is part of its strength as a theory; it is a good tool with which to think and, with its associated concepts of ambiguity, political dominance and subjugation, it allows a more nuanced and informed study of the Roman period than the near-synonymous terms of 'hybridisation' or 'syncretism'.

Creolisation in practice

Webster (2001) was not the first person to discuss creolisation or creole artefacts. James Deetz's *In Small Things Forgotten* (1977) discussed the role of houses and artefacts used by early nineteenth century African Americans at the black settlement of Parting Ways, Plymouth. The houses at the settlement were not unlike the simple Anglo-American vernacular houses of the nineteenth century, but built according to the African American mind-set in terms of the use of space. Deetz also discussed the African American use of Anglo-American artefacts, especially ceramics, and how they were put to use in functional combinations (or broken and deposited) according to African American rules and ritual practices. For Deetz, creolisation was the "interaction between two or more cultures to produce an integrated mix which is different to its antecedents" (1996 [1977]: 213). Ferguson (1992) also discussed creolisation in relation to African American archaeology, examining the role, use and perception of African American culture on slave plantations and communities of the eighteenth and nineteenth centuries.

Elsewhere and more recently, the concept of creolisation has been applied to Roman Britain, and to food and religion in particular. Hawkes (1999) discussed the cultural meaning of the consumption and preparation of food. She asked whether food habits changed during the Roman period; whether different food was consumed; or whether dishes were merely prepared in a different way. She found that native practices continued and new ingredients were adopted, and that what was cooked and eaten was a creolised 'fusion', neither wholly Roman nor wholly native.

Building on earlier work (e.g. 1997a; 1997b), Webster (2001) discussed the creolisation of Romano-Celtic religion, using the example of Santeria, the creole religion of Cuba, which is a complex mix of American Indian survivals, Catholicism, and African influences. Santeria is an example of religious syncretism, and represents an adaptation (and not an adoption) of religious beliefs and practices, and is part of a process of intercultural negotiation. Webster asked whether similar processes were at work in the iconography of Romano-Celtic religion. Taking examples of a series of deities (which, although depicted anthropomorphically, were not Graeco-Roman gods), such as the horse goddess Epona and the horned god Cernunnos, Webster suggested that such deities were not depicted in human form before the conquest, but that, post-conquest, they were depicted as humans associated with animals or in a semi-zoomorphic form. Webster argued that pre-conquest zoomorphic deities were depicted in a human form for the first time after the conquest, but as inseparable from the animals with which they were associated. Such deities as Epona and Cernunnos cannot be regarded as "Celtic" or Roman, because they were the products of the post-Roman negotiation between Roman and indigenous beliefs and iconographic traditions. They were creole deities. There was a also a limit to their syncretism with Roman religion: both Epona and Cernunnos resisted being paired in a 'divine marriage' with Roman deities, and both rarely incorporated epigraphy.

Creolisation and Pidginisation

We have seen how the concept of creolisation has been successfully applied to material culture and, specifically, the material culture of Roman Britain. However, to return to linguistics, the traditional interpretation of a 'creole' is that it is used to refer to any language which was once a pidgin, and which subsequently has acquired native speakers and is capable of becoming the mother tongue of a speech community (Todd 1990 [1974]: 2), although this simplistic definition is slightly problematic because of the observed blurring between the two language categories (Jourdan 1991; Todd 1990 [1974]: 65). A creole can develop from a pidgin in two ways: it can develop in multilingual areas where an auxiliary language is necessary to communicate; or it can occur where people are deprived of the opportunity to use their mother tongue, as was the case in the Caribbean during the slave trade, where slaves from the same area were deliberately separated in order to prevent plotting; the only language available to them was thus any European language they had picked up. Their children consequently learnt this pidgin as a first language and as their mother tongue, which is when it became a creole (Todd 1990 [1974]: 3). A pidgin is thus a "marginal language, which arises to fulfil certain restricted communication needs among people who have no common language" (Todd 1990 [1974]: 1–2). It is a language which is native to neither speaker, and lacks a stable and regulated structure and grammar; when it becomes a creole, on the other hand, it acquires a stable and regularised grammar. Pidginisation is a linguistic process that occurs when people who do not speak the same language come into contact, and also involves the simplification of language. The meaning of verbal communication is often reinforced by intonation, gestures and mime (Todd 1980).

Creole languages are often languages with grammar created by children who are exposed to pidgin (which may have interesting implications for the archaeology of children, if the concept of pidgin material culture can be applied to this subject). Pidgin languages are not always (although can be) long lasting; in fact, many pidgins are what is known as 'contact vernaculars' and may exist for only one 'speech event' (known as a 'restricted' pidgin; 'extended' pidgins are used for longer). Pidginisation is a process which characterises casual, sporadic or random contacts (Todd 1980). Since some pidgins serve a single simplistic purpose, they often die out; however, if the pidgin is used long enough, with the next generation speaking it as their mother tongue, it becomes a creole language. Usually, the vocabulary of the pidgin (like the creole) is drawn from the language of the dominant group and, if the contact between the interacting groups remains superficial, the syntax is uncomplicated; such a marginal pidgin is usually limited in time and space. It disappears when the contact that gave rise to it is withdrawn (Todd, 1980: 19).

Can we apply such concepts to material culture, and talk of 'pidgin' artefacts? If so, how can we define and recognise them in the context of Roman Britain? I would suggest that two properties of pidgin material culture are that they would occur at the very beginning of Roman contact – at a time when any 'creolised' material culture was being used for the first time, i.e., by the first generation. Second, it may still be at a very experimental stage – not yet tied down by a stable and coherent 'grammar' or form, i.e., it may not always occur in the same contexts. It is, perhaps, during this stage when we may also see unique items of material culture – pidgins which last for 'one speech event' and then die out and are not used by the next generation; or rather, artefacts which are individual, single, creative responses to certain situations.

It is also useful to think of the 'life-cycle' of pidgins. Hall (1962) is generally credited with such a notion. As outlined above, pidgin languages usually come into existence for a specific reason and then quickly go out of use. By becoming the native language of a group of speakers, i.e., by becoming creolised, a pidgin acquires a longer lease of life, and thereby becomes a 'normal' language (Hall 1966: 126). Thus, by applying the concept of pidginisation to the archaeology of early Roman Britain, we are adding an awareness of the time depth and change in material culture experienced by the first generations who lived through the initial period of Roman contact.

Case study: The 'Stanway Doctor'

For the purposes of this paper, and of experimenting with and demonstrating the usefulness of the pidginisation metaphor to the archaeology of Roman Britain, I will explore the idea that the grave of the Stanway 'doctor' really was that of a healer, and that some of the other objects in the grave may have been related to healing. As part of this exploration, I will discuss some possible methods of medical procedure used by the healer. Although these obviously cannot be proved, I believe that such discussion and exploration is useful in the interpretation of the contents of the grave at Stanway. Although it must be strongly emphasised here that the assumed medical / healer status of the person buried at Stanway cannot be proved, there are certainly some intriguing and thought-provoking artefacts in the grave which are worthy of discussion. Just because the grave of the Stanway 'doctor' is unique, this does not mean that we should not try to interpret it; in fact, as I argue later in this paper, it is this very uniqueness that makes it suitable for interpretation using the pidginisation metaphor.

Finally, there are also problems with the use of the words 'doctor' and 'medicine' in understanding Roman Britain; as they are too 'presentist', the anthropological terms of 'healer' and 'healing' will be used instead, except, to avoid confusion, in relation to 'Roman medicine', for which a large literature exists.

Discovered in 1996 at Stanway, just outside Colchester, and dating to *c.* AD 50–60 (Crummy 1997a; 2002), the Stanway 'doctor' was among the dead at a funerary site of cremated high-status Britons who died in the later Iron Age and early Roman periods. The cremated bones were too fragmentary to determine the sex of the deceased (Crummy *pers. comm.*).

The burials at Stanway date from the late first century BC to *c.* AD 60 and overlapped the arrival of the Romans by a couple of decades (Crummy 1997b). They are part of a wider tradition of cremation in the south (e.g. the Westhampnett cemetery in West Sussex) and south-east (e.g. the cremations at King Harry Lane and Folly Lane in Verulamium) at this time. The richest high-status graves of this period, such as those at Welwyn Garden City and Lexden, clearly show evidence of 'Romanising' before the conquest.

The Stanway burials belonged to the period when the native stronghold of Camulodunum was at its most important. In all, there were five enclosures laid out in two rows at Stanway. The smallest (and earliest) seems to have been the nucleus of a small farmstead; the other four were funerary enclosures, and each contained funerary chambers. The burials within the chambers were high-status and are interpreted as having belonged to the 'ruling class'; a sign of their 'privilege' comes from the secondary burials inserted into the funerary enclosures (Crummy 1997b: 67).

The 'Stanway doctor' was one of at least seven of these secondary burials. Two of the other secondary burials also signified something about the identity of their occupants: one was buried with weapons and has been labelled a 'warrior', and the other was buried with an inkpot and is therefore presumed to have been literate. That the 'doctor' should be identified as such, and understood as a practitioner of 'Roman' medicine, does not appear to be in question. Creighton (2000, 188), for example, suggests that the 'doctor' was either a Briton who learned classical medicine in Italy or was a relative of Augustus' physician. Crummy (1997a; 2002) also identified the 'doctor' as such, because the tools with which he or she was buried look similar to, although are not exactly the same as, (again, supposedly) surgical instruments found in Bavaria (de Navarro 1955, Figure 2) and Hungary (Ebert and Südhoff 1913, cited in de Navarro 1955, Figure 3). One of the Stanway instruments is also Roman in style, and is thought to have been imported to Britain (Jackson 1997) – perhaps from Gaul. Although one can only speculate that these were definitely used as surgical instruments (and the physical association of the imported instrument with the others suggests this may be the case, although once again we cannot assume that 'Roman'-style instruments were used according to 'Roman' cultural rules), they may have had another function. It is also possible that these tools had not been the property of the deceased.

Besides the supposed 'medical' instruments or 'instruments of healing', a range of other objects were also found in the grave. While some of these are not unusual in rich cremation graves of the late first century BC / early first century AD, others are entirely unique, and we may only speculate about their function.

The range of objects includes a set of eight iron and copper-alloy rods (currently interpreted as cauteries or possibly for use in divination, Crummy 2002; c.f. Carr 2002), and a strainer bowl (interpreted as for use in making infusions for healing, Crummy 1997a: 7; 2002; c.f. Carr 2002). Other items in the grave, which have not been linked to healing (although this can be questioned), and which were all carefully and deliberately placed in position (as were the possible surgical instruments), included a gaming board with glass counters, an amphora, a samian bowl, a ceramic flagon, a copper-alloy pan, three brooches and various fragments of wood and textile. These will not be discussed further here, except to note that most of the 'surgical instruments' were carefully placed across the gaming board, perhaps thus indicating and implicating its use in healing rituals, *if* we are to assume that the instruments themselves definitely played a role in healing.

The thirteen 'surgical instruments' proved to be extremely interesting; not only are they the earliest identifiable selection of possible instruments of healing from Britain, but all but one of them (the import), have no parallel in the Roman world, differing subtly from Roman types (Jackson 1997). Jackson (ibid.) suggested that their 'idiosyncratic' appearance could be explained by the fact that they were made in Britain, probably at an early date, as it was only around the turn of the 1st century BC / AD that Roman instruments began to acquire their relatively standardised form. Baker (2001) has warned us that we cannot assume a standardisation of medical practice across the Roman Empire, because it consisted of many different societies, which would each have had their own ideas about healing. Thus, the use of medical tools may have been adopted in different places in accordance with local understandings of the body, illness causation and healing. The 'idiosyncratic' shape of the Stanway instruments may well not have been perceived as such by the Stanway 'doctor'. It is also interesting to note that all of the instruments were discovered intact except for a 'surgical saw', which had been broken into five pieces and the fragments placed in a tight group near the centre of the gaming board. Anthropological studies, such as that by Moore (1982a: 91–106; 1982b), have taught us that deposition is inextricably linked to cultural values; Baker (2001: 58) has noted this possibility for beliefs relating to the pollution of medical instruments, which might have been considered polluted if, for example, they had been used in an unsuccessful operation, and so would have to be deposited in such a way as to keep them from 'infecting' people or places. Although Baker did not consider the deposition of instruments within graves to fall into this category, such an interpretation might explain the condition of the surgical saw. It is possible that the Stanway 'healer' was not a healer at all, but a person who died after an unsuccessful healing ritual using the surgical instruments.

As mentioned earlier, a spouted strainer bowl was found in the grave, previously thought to have been used for straining alcohol such as ale, mead or some other native drink (Sealey 1999: 123–4). They are a later Iron Age / early Roman artefact, and their distribution shows that they were not Mediterranean types, but occur broadly in Britain, northern and central Europe (Sealey 1999: 122). A plug of organic material was found in the spout of the example from Stanway, which has now been revealed by pollen analysis to have consisted largely of the plant artemesia, although the species has not yet been determined (Crummy 2002).

Although artemesia can be used for non-medicinal treatments, such as for flavouring drinks, all forms also have perceived medicinal properties: *Artemesia abrotanum* or southernwood, aids menstrual flow; *Artemesia cina* or santonica gets rid of worms; *Artemesia vulgaris* or mugwort is a digestive stimulant; and *Artemesia absinthum* or wormwood is good for indigestion, worms and fever (Hoffmann 1996). It would seem, therefore, that, as one of its functions, it is not impossible that the strainer bowl could have been used for boiling, straining and pouring medicines of some sort, or was used for a concoction made by pouring boiling water on herbs (Sealey 1999, 123).

The eight metal rods were round in section. Four were of iron and four were of copper alloy. There were two small and two large of each, and they were found in association with eight copper-alloy rings. The two terminals of the rods were also different: one end flattens and splays out into a triangular shape, and the other end is knobbed. Their function is unknown, although, as mentioned above, speculation has provided two interpretations: that they were either cauteries or 'divination' rods. Howell (cited in Crummy 2002), however, notes that there are no known *similar* Roman examples of cauteries (cf. Jackson 1990: 20, Figure 7), and that the form of the rods resembles much later sixteenth century examples. Crummy suggests that, if they were divination rods, they may have been cast on the ground and the resultant configuration of all eight rods 'read' by someone who knew how. He also suggests that just a few of the rods could have been somehow 'selected', and the composition of the selection interpreted. As three of the eight rods had been extracted and carefully placed on the gaming board away from the others, this, once again, implicates the use of the gaming board in a ritual which may have been used in healing.

Healing practices in Roman Britain

Until recently, we have been content to assume that the native Britons would have seen the inherent 'superiority' of Roman medicine and, whenever they felt the need, would have visited the army doctor at the local fort (implied by Jackson 1988: 137), who practised a form of Roman medicine which was homogenous and standardised to that which was practised in Italy (implied by Davies 1970; Jackson 1988, 1990). Jackson (1988: 137) speculates, unsupported by archaeological evidence, that the work of military doctors would not have been restricted to soldiers alone and that, either on a formal or informal basis, people from the surrounding farms, villages and small towns may have visited the Roman forts for treatment. He also assumes that, in the long term, some of the military doctors would have become part of the local community themselves after retirement from the army, and continued to practise in a civilian setting. In this way, the army was supposed to have spread Roman medical knowledge and techniques, but also collected fresh information from locals. However, Jackson also mentions that few surgeries or consulting rooms have ever been positively identified, so these assumptions are not backed up by archaeological evidence.

Baker (2001) was the first to point out the possibility that Roman medicine was not a homogenous, standardised system (before this, the assumption was that medical care was standardised), and might not have been understood or practised in the same way throughout the empire. This is based, in part, on Baker's observation that there are variations in the use of Roman medical inscriptions and depositional practices of instruments among units who used such instruments, which may be linked to different cultural perceptions of the body and of healing in general (*ibid.*: 63). Although surgical instruments may look *similar* throughout the empire, Baker (*ibid.*: 56) again warns us that they may not have been used in a similar manner, may have been used in conjunction with other tools (with which they may have been deposited, but which the excavator may not have mentioned, not regarding them as 'medical'), may also have had several functions, or may have changed their meaning and function throughout their life-span. It would seem that we are on shaky ground to categorise the Stanway 'healer' as one who had learnt Roman medicine, simply on the basis of his or her instruments – or even to necessarily categorise him or her as a healer.

Given that Roman medicine was probably not, then, a homogenous practice, and given that Roman soldiers came from all over the Roman empire and beyond, Baker (2001) argues that it was likely that, as military doctors in the army were able to retain some form of their cultural identities in military matters (suggested by Saddington's assertion that different auxiliary units may have been allowed to continue fighting in their own manner (1997: 496)), then it is possible that they could have retained other aspects of their society, including their traditional healing practices. Thus, it is possible that Roman military medics practised a form of healing which was based on their own cultural understandings of illness causation, treatment and healing.

The creolisation of healing practices

How are we, then, to understand the Stanway healer? Why and how did he or she own such unique surgical instruments? While Jackson (1997: 1473) assumes that the healer had contact with Roman medical personnel and, 'presumably', an acquaintance with the precepts of classical medicine (even though the instruments are not the same as Roman types), we can question, at least, the latter assumption. If the instruments were made in Britain, we might presume that the 'doctor' might have *seen* Roman-style instruments before, or had at least heard a description of them, but only if we are to assume that he or she made them or had them made according to instructions as opposed to having acquired them in some other way, such as through trade. We should also bear in mind that the Stanway healer had other native tools, possibly for healing, including the strainer bowl, the rods, and possibly the gaming board. Why was there a mixture of native and 'Roman' styles?

Did the healer want to be able to cater to ordinary Britons and 'Romanised' élites / Romans alike? Was s/he trying to impress fellow natives with selected new techniques? Did the healer make them to resemble what s/he thought were the quintessence of Roman-style medicine, or were the instruments used in native rituals of healing in a way that 'made sense' to the healer, and not in the manner for which they were intended (or rather, for which a doctor in Rome might have used them)?

I would suggest another reason: the healer decided to make a deliberately ambiguous statement by using a cultural mix of both native and Roman-style (to the eyes of the healer, but perhaps not us) surgical instruments. Perhaps the aim was to allow the patient, spectators and, later, the mourners, to see what they wanted to see: Roman or native-style tools of healing. As we have seen, Webster (2001: 218) argues that ambiguity and hybridity are important features of creolised artefacts.

Webster argues that creole material culture can be drawn on to different degrees according to context – and can be imbued with different meanings in different contexts. I would suggest that this is precisely what we are seeing with the medical tools of the Stanway healer. S/he could have used the instruments in different ways in different contexts, sometimes emphasising the 'Roman'-style aspect of healing (whatever that may have been), and sometimes using the tools according to a set of values which were principally 'native' (however we may define this), depending on the identity or preferences of the patient. As Webster discusses, creolisation is frequently a process of *resistant* adaptation, as links with the past are often maintained in opposition to the dominant culture; but it can also serve to negotiate or adapt 'Roman' styles to serve indigenous ends. The Stanway medical tools, both those of native and (to the eyes of the healer) Roman-style, could have been used to treat everyone, although this does not mean that their use was politically neutral; they would have been used by the healer to make a statement about his or her identity, which could have varied, depending on context and patient.

Given that the indigenous Britons of the early post-Conquest period would have been unlikely to know anything about the theory or practice of Roman-style medicine, but may conceivably have seen Roman-style instruments, it would have been easy for the Stanway healer to combine the use of the tools with indigenous concepts of illness and healing, and to use them, as far as possible, in native healing ceremonies, imbuing them with a certain meaning – or, alternatively, s/he may have ignored them, emphasising the use of the indigenous tools instead.

Some indigenous élites, and certainly Roman soldiers, would have more experience of 'Roman'-style medicine (or at least, experience of medicine practised by a 'Roman' military medic from the local fort, which was not necessarily the same thing at all), through having visited doctors in the past or through having had the instruments used on their own bodies. When treating these kinds of people, the Stanway healer may have used the instruments in an entirely different way, perhaps playing down the use of the indigenous tools, such as the divination rods and, perhaps, the gaming board, and emphasising the use of the (to the eyes of the healer) 'Roman'-style instruments, perhaps using the strainer bowl to make infusions with imported rather than native herbs (although we do not know whether the artemesia was imported as we do not know its exact species), and utilising a different set of concepts of healing. This is not to imply that the healer had read the Hippocratic Corpus or had any training – s/he could have picked up different concepts of illness causation by talking to Romans, and perhaps 'bluffed' his or her way through a healing session, perhaps by letting the patient do most of the talking, and by picking up on certain expressions and concepts which could then be used on other occasions. As mentioned earlier, Baker (2001) suggests the possibility that even the medic in the Roman army may have practised a form of medicine that used many of their own traditional concepts (even when using 'Roman'-style medical instruments), depending on where they came from in the empire; thus, the use of familiar Roman-style instruments alone could well have been enough to convince the patient who had already had some exposure to this form of treatment.

Creolisation or pidginisation?

One of the group of artefacts within the grave of the Stanway healer is problematic, and it is difficult to see them in terms of creolisation because of their uniqueness. The 'divination rods', as I have mentioned, are not found anywhere else in Britain or the continent. Although it is possible that other examples may one day be found, how are we to understand such unique artefacts, other than as creative individual responses to unique situations? I would suggest that there is another way in which we can understand them; a way in which such creativity is taken into account: and that is by considering them as 'pidgin' artefacts.

Above, I suggested that pidgin material culture has three characteristics which might enable us to identify it. First, it would occur at the very beginning of Roman contact, at a time when any proto-'creolised' material culture was being used for the first time, i.e., by the first generation; second, that they would still be at a very experimental stage – not yet tied down by a stable and coherent 'grammar' or form, i.e., not always occurring in the same contexts. Third: it is, perhaps, during this stage when we may also see unique items of material culture – pidgins which last for 'one speech event' and then die out and are not used by the next generation; or rather, artefacts which are individual, single, creative responses to certain situations.

The concept of 'pidgin' artefacts helps us to understand the uniqueness of the Stanway healer. Although I would expect many 'pidgin' artefacts to date to the pre-conquest period, during the time of first Roman contact, I would not rule out the period of conquest or immediate post-conquest to be the date of others. Having been buried in AD 50–60, the Stanway healer is still young enough to be considered part of the first generation of Britons who lived through the conquest. Were the 'idiosyncratic' surgical instruments 'pidgins', which later went on to become the 'creoles' seen in other parts of the country, albeit rarely, and in a modified (or more Roman in style) form? Could the 'divination rods' be understood as 'pidgins'? They are certainly unique, and no version of them has been seen in any later period, although it is always possible that earlier or later versions were made of wood. Was the gaming board an example of a pidgin artefact which had yet to be grammatically 'tied down', regulated and made stable – which might be why this is the only example of one in a context possibly associated with healing (although we cannot know for sure whether it was used as part of the healing ritual); other examples all appear in rich graves which (we assume) were not associated with healers or healing equipment, which may be their 'grammatically stable' context.

Linguistically, the boundary between pidgins and creoles is now understood to be blurred (Jourdan 1991), so that some pidgins and creoles may exist simultaneously in the same socio-linguistic niche, thus reflecting the fluid nature of individual and collective praxis and agency (*ibid.*: 189); thus, we should not be surprised to see pidgin and creole material culture in the same context for the same reasons.

Creolisation, identities and alternative readings

Creolisation involves, by its nature, a discussion of hybrid identities. In order to discuss those identities we need to label them, which inevitably leads to descriptions of 'Romans' and 'natives'. These categories are, however, problematic, as discussed elsewhere (e.g. Cooper 1996; Barrett 1997; Freeman 1993; Hill 2001; Hingley 1997). Roman Britain comprised a mixture of hybrid (or might we label them 'creolised'?) identities, cultures and counter-cultures. The terms 'native' and 'Roman' imply two opposing homogeneous, static and monolithic groups with an internally homogeneous material culture; the archaeological record shows that this was obviously not the case. Additionally, as Hill (2001: 12) reminds us, identity is not fixed at birth – it can and does change.

Any 'Roman' material culture imported to Britain was itself probably not 'purely Italian', but rather a hybrid mix. Indeed, when discussing the 'Roman' identity of Britain, Reece states that it "became more Gaulish, more Rhinelandish, more Spanish, a little more Italian, a very little more African, and a little more Danubian" (Reece 1988: 11). Thus, when we discuss the surgical instruments of the Stanway healer, we should not necessarily see them as 'Roman' or 'Roman-inspired'. They may have been traded from Gaul (or elsewhere in the empire), perhaps also inspired from others which may have once been inspired by a 'Roman' source. In fact, rather than imagining that the Stanway healer (or other Britons) saw the group of artefacts in the grave as a combination of 'native' and 'Roman' tools, it is entirely possible that, to them, these objects reflected a network of cultural interactions. As James (1999: 92) argues, the British élite were part of a wider political and cultural European circle of peers, with whom they allied, intermarried and shared an ideology and lifestyle. To follow this argument, rather than seeing the instruments as something 'Roman', 'foreign' and 'them-not-us' – something that the healer had to use or not use, depending on context and customer, it is possible that all of the artefacts in the grave represented part of this network of interactions and trading of which the healer (assuming his or her status was that of an élite, judging from the apparent wealth of the grave) was a part. However, this combination of origins for the contents of the Stanway healer's grave can also be seen as a creolised mix. For the purposes of this paper, I have preferred to focus on the interpretation of the contents of the grave in terms of 'creole' and 'pidgin' material culture simply as a way of exploring the way we understand unusual and unique material culture.

Conclusion

In death, the Stanway healer was buried with at least some of his or her tools of healing. Different mourners may have recognised different goods in the grave as tools of the trade, depending on their own identity. The flexibility or ambiguity of the grave goods would have allowed the spectator to see what it was appropriate for them to see, the Roman-style or indigenous tools of healing. The grave itself was a mixed context in that we, as archaeologists, are not seeing the instruments as they were used in daily practice, although their positioning in the grave can suggest certain associations and meanings. We do not know when or for what the tools were used, or with what words and gestures they were accompanied. We do not know if we have recognised the full range of artefacts connected with healing within the grave, or whether the healer possessed other instruments, which were not consigned to the grave; it is certainly possible that organic objects in the grave have perished. We do not even know the process(es) of selection of grave goods. What we can suggest, however, is that the healer chose to maintain indigenous practices whilst simultaneously adopting aspects of the dominant material culture as a way of negotiating and making a statement about his or her identity in the early post-conquest period; something that patients were perhaps also doing by choosing the Stanway healer to be their medical practitioner.

Department of Archaeology, University of Cambridge

Acknowledgements

Many thanks are owed to Philip Crummy and Paul Sealey for advice on, and discussion of, the Stanway 'doctor'; to Patty Baker, for commenting on this paper and curbing the excesses of my imagination and over-enthusiasm; to Ralph Jackson, for liberal use of his yellow highlighter pen; to Jane Webster, for her positive feedback; and to Simon James, for suggesting alternative interpretations and for his support of the idea of 'pidginisation'. However, any errors in the opinions and theories expressed remain my own.

Bibliography

Baker, P. 2001. Medicine, culture and military identity. In G. Davies, A. Gardner and K. Lockyear (eds.) *TRAC 2000: Proceedings of the Tenth Annual Theoretical Roman Archaeology Conference, London 2000*. Oxford: Oxbow Books. 48–68.

Barrett, J. 1997. Romanization: a critical comment. In D. J. Mattingley (ed.) *Dialogues in Roman Imperialism*. Journal of Roman Archaeology Supplement 23. Portsmouth: Journal of Roman Archaeology. 51–64.

Carr, G. 2002. A time to live, a time to heal and a time to die: healing and divination in Later Iron Age and early Roman Britain. In P. Baker and G. Carr (eds.) *Practices, practitioners and patients: New approaches to medical archaeology and anthropology*. Oxford: Oxbow Books.

Cooper, N. 1996. Searching for the blank generation: consumer choice in Roman and post-Roman Britain. In J. Webster and N. Cooper (eds.) *Roman Imperialism and Post-Colonial Perspectives. Proceedings of a symposium held at Leicester University in November 1994*. Leicester: Leicester Archaeology Monographs No. 3. 85–98.

Creighton, J. 2000. *Coins and Power in Late Iron Age Britain*. Cambridge: Cambridge University Press.

Crummy, P. 1997a. Britain's earliest doctor? *Rescue News*, 73: 7.

Crummy, P. 1997b. *City of Victory: the story of Colchester – Britain's first Roman town*. Colchester: Colchester Archaeological Trust.

Crummy, P. 2002. A preliminary account of the doctor's grave at Stanway, Colchester, England. In P. Baker and G. Carr (eds.) *Practices, practitioners and patients: New approaches to medical archaeology and anthropology*. Oxford: Oxbow Books. 47–57.

Davies, R. 1970. The Roman military medical service. *Saalburg Jahrbuch*, 27: 84–1–4.

Deetz, J. 1977 [1996]. *In Small Things Forgotten: an archaeology of early American life*. New York: Anchor Books.

Ferguson, L. 1992. *Uncommon Ground*. Washington and London: Smithsonian Institution press.

Freeman, P. W. M. 1993. 'Romanization' and Roman material culture. Review of M. Millet's *The Romanization of Roman Britain: an essay in archaeological interpretation*. Cambridge 1990. *Journal of Roman Archaeology*, 6:438–445.

Hall, R. A. 1962. The life cycle of pidgin languages. *Festschrift De Groot (Lingua 11)*: 151–156.

Hall, R. A. 1966. *Pidgin and Creole Languages.* Ithaca: Cornell University Press.

Hill, J.D. 2001. Romanization, gender and class: recent approaches to identity in Britain and their possible consequences. In S. James & M. Millett (eds.) *Britons and Romans: advancing an archaeological agenda.* York: Council for British Archaeology Research Report 25.

Hawkes, G. 1999. Beyond Romanization: the creolisation of food. *Papers from the Institute of Archaeology,* 10:89–95.

Hingley, R. 1997. Resistance and domination: social change in Roman Britain. In D. Mattingly (ed.) *Dialogues in Roman Imperialism.* Journal of Roman Archaeology supplement 23. Portsmouth: Journal of Roman Archaoelogy. 81–100.

Hoffman, D. 1996. *Complete Herbal: a safe and practical guide to making and using herbal remedies.* Shaftesbury: Element Books.

Jackson, R. 1988. *Doctors and Diseases in the Roman Empire.* London: British Museum Press.

Jackson, R. 1997. An ancient British medical kit from Stanway, Essex. *Lancet,* 350:1471–1473.

James, S. 1999. *The Atlantic Celts: ancient people or modern invention?* London: British Museum Press.

Jourdan, C. 1991. Pidgins and Creoles: the blurring of categories. *Annual Review of Anthropology,* 20:187–209.

Moore, H. 1982a. *Space,Text and Gender: an anthropological study of the Marakwet of Kenya.* Cambridge: Cambridge University Press.

de Navarro, J. M. 1955. A doctor's grave of the Middle La Tène period from Bavaria. *Proceedings of the Prehistoric Society,* 21:231–247.

Reece, R. 1988. *My Roman Britain.* Cirencester: Cotswold Studies 3.

Saddington, D.B. 1997. The 'politics' of the auxilia and the forging of auxiliary regimental identity. In W. Groenman van Waateringe, B. L. Van Beek, W. J. H. Willems and S. L. Wynia (eds.) *Roman Frontier Studies 1995.* Oxford: Oxbow Monograph 91. 493–6.

Sealey, P. R. 1999. Finds from the cauldron pit. In N. R. Brown (ed.) *The Archaeology of Ardleigh, Essex.* Chelmsford: Heritage Conservation, Essex County Council in conjunction with Scole Archaeological Committee 1999, East Anglian Archaeology Report No. 90. 117–24.

Seymour-Smith, C. 1986. *Macmillan Dictionary of Anthropology.* London: The Macmillan Press Ltd.

Todd, L. 1980. Pidginization and Creolisation. *Annual Review of Applied Linguistics,* 1: 19–24.

Todd, L. 1990 [1974]. *Pidgins and Creoles.* London and New York: Routledge.

Webster, J. 1997a. A negotiated syncretism: readings on the development of Romano-Celtic religion. In D.J.Mattingly (ed.) *Dialogues in Roman Imperialism.* Journal of Roman Archaeology, 165–84.

Webster, J. 1997b. Necessary comparisons: a post-colonial approach to religious syncretism in the Roman provinces. *World Archaeology,* 28.3:324–38.

Webster, J. 2001. Creolizing the Roman Provinces. *American Journal of Archaeology,* 105: 209–225.

Breaking Ground or Treading Water? Roman Archaeology and Constructive Implications of the Critique of Meta-narratives

Stephanie Koerner

Introduction

It is difficult to overstate the importance of the Roman Empire, both as a source and as a paradigmatic example, in the long-term history of western social theory and philosophy. In antiquity, Roman political philosophers developed sophisticated theories about human origins and knowledge, and what these implied for evaluating contemporary pedagogical and political ideals (e.g. Cicero [106–43 BC] 1942). A number of the most significant changes in the history of western intellectual culture have turned on reinterpretations of categories and narratives rooted in two ancient ideal types: Plato'[s philosopher-king and Cicero's poet-orator (Mooney 1979).

In late antiquity, contrasting theories about the Roman Empire were used to formulate what became the foundational paradigms for western culture in general (Collingwood [1949] 1956). For example, Eusebius of Caesaria's [ca. AD 260–339] *Historia ecclesiastica* (1952) and Augustine of Hippo's [ca. AD 354–430] *De civitate Dei* (1963) center on theories about the emergence and expansion of the Roman Empire. The two bishops' perspectives differ in a number of respects, relating to opposing positions on relationships between Church and Empire. In Eusebius' *Historia ecclesiastica*, the entire history of the world (sacred *and* profane) is conceived as an evolutionary process guided by Divine Providence. In this view, humanity is to be restored to its original 'royal nature' through the evolution, expansion, and transformation of the Roman Empire to Christianity. Objecting to the radical implications of such a view, Augustine (1963) emphasizes a fundamental division between the origins and evolutionary trajectories of *the city of God 'wandering on the earth' (the Church)* and *the profane worldly city of man (Rome)*. But their works share several features, which may signal the earliest horizon of what late twentieth century scholars refer to with the term, 'western meta-narratives'. Both Eusebius and Augustine combine principles drawn from Graeco-Roman philosophy and Judeo-Christian apocalyptic teleology (Funkenstein 1986). Both envisage the Roman Empire as *the* paradigmatic example for understanding fundamental truths about human nature, knowledge, and relations between sacred and profane world history. Eusebius envisages the Empire as the means whereby sacred ideals and human realities will be joined in a unified order, while, for Augustine, the Empire reveals the reasons why humans *fail* to realize such an order.

Throughout the Middle Ages and Renaissance, images of the emergence, expansion, and decline of the Roman Empire figured centrally in debates over political authority, religious institutions, social boundaries, and the scope of human knowledge (for instance, Valla [1407–1457] 1962; Machiavelli [1469–1527] 1965). In early modern times, these images were opened to new interpretations relating to the contrasting orientations of the Enlightenment and Romantic movements (e.g., Momigliano 1966; Schnapp 1996). During the nineteenth and early twentieth centuries these images were further embellished, in relation to large scale archaeological projects commissioned by national institutions, contemporary national, imperial and colonial ideologies (e.g., Trigger 1984, 1995; Webster and Cooper eds. 1996; Atkinson, Banks, and O'Sullivan eds. 1997; Hingley 2000), and meta-narratives concerning the Birth of Modernity and the Scientific Revolution (Toulmin 1990; Dupré 1993).

The second half of the twentieth century saw remarkable change take place throughout the human sciences and philosophy relating to what some scholars call the 'critique of meta-narratives' (Adorno 1974; Foucault 1980; Lyotard 1984; Bourdieu 1990). Many debates turn on categories that have been taken for granted for over two centuries (Toulmin 1990; Koerner and Gassón 2001). Until around the 1960s, such dichotomies as those of subject-object, mind-body, nature-culture, individual-society, evolution-history, science-values, epistemology-ontology, and western-non-western, formed a common basis for defining disciplinary boundaries, classifying subjects of study, and debating predominant paradigms for research. The last decades have seen precisely these categories come under convergent (if not identical) forms of scrutiny in fields as diverse in subject matter as the philosophy of science, social anthropology and Roman archaeology (e.g., Biagioli ed. 1999; Descola and Pálssen eds. 1996; Hingley 2000). Little by little researchers have become concerned with the extent to which categories, which went hitherto unremarked, hinge upon problematical narratives concerning human nature, knowledge and the diversity of cultures of different times and places.

The late twentieth century critique of meta-narratives is, of course, neither the first nor perhaps even the most influential. The history of western culture has not been a continuous trajectory, but marked by heterogeneous points of view, critiques of contemporary claims about universal truths and social realities (Rorty 1989; Hale 1993), and attempts to go beyond the shared presuppositions that underwrite apparently antithetical absolutist and relativist positions (Grassi 1989; Toulmin 1990). Interestingly, the Roman Empire has played important roles in such situations as well (Mooney 1979; Dupré 1993). Augustine's *De civitate Dei* (1963) centered on discrepancies between claims that the Roman Empire could realise the purposes of the city of God and what he identified as the factors most responsible for the development of the Roman Empire, namely: greed and desire of power. For another example, the critique of medieval generalizations about the Roman Empire played essential roles in Renaissance humanists' campaign against Scholastic paradigms for intellectual culture and political authority (Berlin 1976; Grassi 1980; Funkestein 1986).

For the Theoretical Roman Archaeology Conference (henceforth TRAC) held in Canterbury, England, March 5–6, 2002, Andrew Gardner and I organized a session entitled, 'Breaking Ground or Treading Water. Theoretical Agendas for the 21st Century'. One of our aims was to explore the bearing that recent developments in the field may have upon cross-disciplinary concerns to go beyond traditional meta-narratives concerning human nature, history and knowledge. Instead of limiting the session to considerations of what 'X' social theory can do for Roman archaeology, we sought to create a context for exploring Roman archaeology's relevance to these concerns. Thus the papers included in the session offered various perspectives on key issues posed by the meta-narratives critique, including:

(a) The need for alternatives to paradigms for the human sciences and philosophy, which render invisible the diversity of human experience and ways of life.
(b) The challenges facing attempts to go beyond the opposition of science and values, which underwrites both objectivist and relativist points of view.
(c) The need for multi-disciplinary contextual alternatives to approaches derived from universalising unity and disunity models of science.
(d) The challenges facing attempts to carry forward interesting constructive directions suggested by the critique of meta-narratives.

This paper has two objectives. The first is to present something of the historical and philosophical background of the concerns that motivated the session. To this aim, I will attempt to outline the main foci of the critique of meta-narrative. The paper's second objective builds upon two responses in Roman archaeology to this critiques, namely: (a) the growing interest in arguments against the notion that the human self is prior to its embodied and material preconditions (e.g., Foucault 1980; Bourdieu 1990) and (b) the concern to focus attention on the discrepant experiences of human agents (e.g. Said 1993). I will highlight some of the issues that these responses pose, and consider Roman archaeology's relevance to several promising constructive implications of the meta-narratives critique. Emphasis falls on what the issues at stake suggest concerning the usefulness of an approach to the historicity of agency, in which ethics plays a key role. Such an approach may have advantages for going beyond problematical meta-narratives, including those concerning the homogeneity of the Roman Empire, which continue to have an impact on perceptions of the modern world. It may also be relevant to the question of whether the discrepant experiences that human beings have of their life-worlds can make a difference not just in particular *events*, but in *conjunctures* that reconfigure the *longue durée* (cf. Husserl [1936] 1970; Braudel [1949] 1966).

Dualist paradigms for human nature and knowledge

Despite the diversity of the works of the major contributors to the critique of meta-narratives, it is possible to identify several common foci. One is the critique (or deconstruction) of the epistemic bases of dualist paradigms for *human nature* and *knowledge*. At issue is the series of essentialist categories that underwrites the notion of a transcendental, timeless, and placeless human agent, which has functioned for over two centuries as the supposedly universally valid foundation for understanding all human thought and behaviour. This critique has powerful implications. It reveals the interdependence of a wide range of dualist categories, including those of subject-object, mind-body, nature-culture, science-values, western - non-western, as well as Roman - non-Roman). It challenges claims about the existence of an a-historical standpoint from which one can make judgements about reason, knowledge, appropriate action, and what is definitive of being human.

Historical meta-narratives

Secondly there is the critique of the narratives (the plots of predominant philosophies of *history*) on which the aforementioned paradigms for *human nature* and *knowledge* hinge. Concerns with the consequences of these meta-narratives are reflected in the critical literatures on nineteenth and early twentieth century theories about the supposed importance to all of humanity's history of the Scientific Revolution, Birth of Modernity, and modern Western culture's triumph over nature. This critique has important methodological, theoretical, socio-political and ethical implications too. It challenges the ways in which these narratives standardise the criteria whereby cultures (and human experience, in general) can be said to vary (e.g., Friedman 1992; Miller ed. 1995; Wilk 1995; Koerner 2001). It calls into question the ways in which the above mentioned dichotomies have been used not only to obscure discrepant experiences, but to render some human beings 'invisible' to the *ethical* faculties of their fellows (e.g., Gaitta 2000; Geertz 2000).

Essentialist ontologies and the consequences of dualist theories of the conditions of historical (and archaeological) knowledge

The meta-narratives at issue today vary in a number of respects. The most significant differences relate to contrasts between the philosophies of history of the major contributors to the Enlightenment and Romantic movements. Contrasting interpretations of the Roman Empire figured importantly in these philosophies, as well as in contemporary national, colonial, and imperial ideologies. The challenges facing attempts to go beyond these apparently antithetical philosophies are difficult to overstate. The latter continue, for instance, to underwrite apparently unresolvable debates over 'processualist' and 'post-processualist' paradigms for archaeological research. Bruce Trigger's observations touch upon this matter:

> European thought has been dominated for over 200 years by a pervasive dichotomy between rationalism, universalism and positivism on the one hand and romanticism, particularism (or 'alterity'), and idealism on the other. The first of the philosophical packages was initially associated with French liberalism, the second with German reaction [Dumont 1991]. Both ethnic nationalism and post-modernism (which is the essence of post-processualism) are products of the romantic side of the polarity (Trigger 1995: 263).

The polemical nature of such meta-narrative follows from the points on which they agree. Several examples of shared features can be mentioned:

(a) A dependence on teleological plots, which envisage modern western culture as a standard for classifying and explaining the diversity of cultures of all times and places.
(b) Explanations that centre on such dichotomies as nature-culture, subject-object, individual-society, western-non-western.
(c) A shared notion of a timeless placeless 'individual', which is treated as a node through which social systems or cultural histories operate.
(d) A dependence on theories about the conditions of historical (or archaeological) knowledge, which are underwritten by essentialist ontologies, i.e., theories about what *is* (being) and what kinds of things there *are* in the world.

The structural dimensions of modern meta-narratives are of considerable antiquity, dating at least back to the works of Eusebius and Augustine mentioned above. According to Collingwood ([1949] 1956: 49), any narrative with structures rooted in such ancient frameworks and underwritten by essentialist ontologies, will necessarily be *universal, providential, apocalyptic*, and *periodised*. The implications of essentialism for the persistence of problematical generalisations about human history have been another focus of critiques of meta-narratives. The problem has been touched upon by a number of papers presented in recent TRAC conferences, including several papers presented in the TRAC 2002 session 'Breaking Ground or Treading Water' and the session, entitled, 'Meaningful Objects', organized by Hella Eckhardt.
    Since earliest Greek and Roman antiquity, all essentialising ontologies have been structured around two opposing poles. On one side is the notion of an absolute unity and permanence of all things. On the other is the notion of absolute dis-unity, or pure flux (Mcguire and Tushanska 2001). Questions about change (in particular, historical change) are rendered problematical by this supposed opposition. The most influential way to represent this situation was put forward by Aristotle [384–322 BC] in the *Metaphysics* ([1908] 1960). Aristotle's approach centered on the question: If something can be said to be subject to change, what is the essence of that something?

He offered three possible answers: (1) the unchanging aspect, (2) the changing aspect, and (3) both, that is, the interaction of changing and unchanging aspects. In the views that underwrite the ancient and modern meta-narratives, which we are considering, the important answer is (1), and the others have to be reducible to it.

The consequences of this emphasis on the supposed *unchanging* essence of things include the disregard of questions about how things come into being, and reduction of ontology's task to classification. Thus, ontology is supposed to address questions like: What (underlying substances) makes particular items what they are? What distinguishes them from one another? What timeless substances distinguish different categories of entities? Appropriate responses to these questions are supposed to add up to universally valid generalizations about the range of categories in terms of which all things existing at all times can be classified (McGuire and Tushanska 2001: 45–47).

The roles that essentialism plays in perpetuating problematical historical generalizations are considerable. Essentialism permits only a-historical theories about the conditions of historical knowledge (such as those structured around a subject-object dichotomy), and historical descriptions and explanations based on terms that conform to these theories (such as those forming the dichotomies, nature-culture, individual-society, western - non-western, Roman - non-Roman). In both cases, essentialism permits only terms that are deemed suitable for talking about what things are at all times.

All this relates to the problem that essentialism restricts us to only two options when it comes to historical description and interpretation. Modern versions of these options are structured around variations on the Cartesian opposition of two essentially different types of things: *perceiving things* (including the 'minds' of people and, until quite recently, God) and *extended things* (all the rest, like the physical world and society). One option is to treat history as a perceptual experience, which occurs in the minds of individual subjects. Thus, history is to be treated as an aspect of the 'representational content' of the 'mental states' of individuals. The other option is to treat history as an 'extended thing' that can occur in a number of states or forms, such as the social types: band, tribe, chiefdom and state, or the 'collective representations' associated with these types.

These options have been instrumental in creating and perpetuating very problematical perspectives on human beings and history. In order to satisfy their requirements, we must ignore all qualities, which are deemed unnecessary from an essentialist point of view. There are many famous examples of this situation. One, which had profound impacts on the works of Hegel ([1831] 1975), Marx and Engels ([1846] 1975), Morgan ([1877] 1963) Durkheim ([1914] 1960) and Weber ([1904] 1958), as well as various nineteenth and twentieth century political ideologies, is Immanuel Kant's account of the relationship between the histories of nature and culture. The most famous version is presented in what Kant entitled, an 'Idea of a Universal History from a Cosmopolitan Point of View' ([1784] 1963). Prior to Kant, the relationship between these histories (and between human beings' natural and cultural aspects) was seen as a problem, which complicated the scientific (epistemic) status of the human sciences and historiography (Cassirer 1960). Kant's ([1784] 1963) solution centred on treating (a) culture as a necessary outcome of the history of nature (indeed the means whereby 'nature's hidden plane' was to be realized), and (b) an antithesis of nature and culture as explanatory of the course humanity's history had taken (Collingwood [1949] 1956). In this view, the histories of nature and culture form a unilinear series of stages in the evolution of human capacities for 'reason' and 'moral freedom'. Kant's series starts with a hypothetical time when nature consisted only of particles and Newtonian principles of Matter and Motion (cf. Kant [1755] 1963); leads to the emergence of 'primitive' forms of human consciousness and social life; and eventuates in the 'Copernican Revolution', rational modes of consciousness, and the unification of social ideals and realities in the modern state (Kant [1784]

1963). Essential to this philosophy of history and knowledge, is a new conception of human nature. The later centres on a new image of the 'individual' human subject: simultaneously the source of all meaning and value, and reduced to a node through which relationships between human consciousness (subjectivity) and the (object) world evolve.

Comparisons can be drawn between such modern 'invisible hand' explanations and premodern notions of 'Divine providence'. But absent from the latter are the notions that motivate the former concerning the absolute autonomy of human history, and the mind of the individual human subject as the source of all meaning and value. We will return to this theme shortly.

Researchers have responded in various ways to critiques of essentialist modes of reasoning. One of the constructive responses has been the growth of interest in dynamic relational alternatives. Several papers presented in the 'Breaking Ground or Treading Water' and other TRAC 2002 sessions reflected this interest. A critical requirement of a satisfactory alternative is that we no longer treat the question of what things are in an essentialist way: as a static sum of supposedly self-evident properties and parts. In a relational alternative, 'to be' does not mean being belonging to a particular pre-existing type or category. Instead, as McGuire and Tuchanka (2001: 96) explain, it means "to act upon and to be acted upon, or to constitute oneself/itself and to be constituted... Any entity is constituted by its ways of being, and the latter are established in the course of its ongoing activity." Such an ontology can be expected to have an impact on the ways in which we conceptualise the conditions of archaeological knowledge, and may be carrying forward some of the most constructive implications of the meta-narratives critique in Roman archaeology.

The transformation of the concept of the subject, and the privatization of ethics

It is important for considerations of similarities between ancient and modern meta-narratives not to overshadow contrasts. Many features shared by the latter lack pre-modern precedents (cf. Koyré 1968). Here is space only to focus on two features. One is the role modern meta-narratives give to the dichotomies: nature-culture, subject-object, and individual-society. The other is a radically transformed notion of a 'subject', one which has given rise to what Hannah Arendt ([1961] 1977: 147) refers to as the 'privatisation of freedom' (and its corollary, the *privatisation of ethics*). These features underwrite the a-historical notion of a human 'self' (subject), which has become a focus of critical attention in the recent archaeological literature on agency (e.g., Dobres and Robb 2000), as well as the critical literatures of the human sciences and philosophy, in general (e.g., Barnes 2000; Geertz 2000).

These features of modern meta-narratives did not develop in a vacuum (Toulmin 1990). They are rooted in the responses to the need for new social structures and modes of solidarity, which emerged in the wake of the Thirty Years War (1618–1648). Social changes had counterparts in intellectual culture. A notable example of the latter was the notion that it might be possible to develop new *social* ideals and institutions on the basis of principles, which the emerging physical sciences were using to investigate (and manipulate) *nature*. The question posed was that of whether one could model both universally valid explanations of regularities in nature and new modes of social organization on mathematics and logic (e.g., Hobbes [1651] 1962; see, for example, Shapin and Schaffer 1985).

In the views of a number of Enlightenment scholars, Descartes' [1596–1650] epistemology and Newton's [1642–1727] mathematical laws of Matter and Motion suggested that the answer to this question could be yes (Descartes 1984–91; Newton [1687] 1934). Descartes' (1984–1991) epistemology hinged on an ontological distinction between the *rational freedom of moral intellectual decision in the human world*, and the *causal necessity of mechanical processes in the natural world of physical processes*. This radically transformed traditional notions of the 'subject', with profound implications for the status of ethics in modern epistemology. Louis Dupré (1993: 112–114) explains that, throughout most of the history of western intellectual culture, the subject was an ontological principle, which referred to the underlying essence of things (and the ontic foundation of all things was God or an ideal Nature). In Cartesian epistemology, the individual human subject was forced to function as the primary source of all meaning and value (Blumenberg 1983).

The emergence of debates over the extent to which this situation was a *cause* for *uncertainty* took place in the midst of serious social, theological, and epistemic crises (Toulmin 1990: 45–88; Dupre 1993: 113–115; Funkenstein 1996: 290–327). During the sixteenth century, writers such as Disiderus Erasmus, Francois Rabelais, William Shakespeare, Michel de Montaigne and Francis Bacon suggested that the self (human agent) was the *source* of all uncertainty (Toulmin 1990: 19–20, 57–56). The solution that Descartes proposed established the foundations of the status of ethics in modern epistemology. It turned issues of moral (as well as social and ontological) uncertainty into an epistemological problem. Specifically, Descartes translated these issues into philosophical *'doubt'*, and made doubt the basis of a method for attaining epistemological certainty (Toulmin 1990: 45–89; Dupré 1993: 114–116).

But it was not until Kant's times that modern moral philosophy separated this supposed inner realm of 'mental substance' from the causal network of the social and physical universe. Kant articulated this separation in the approach to relationships between human nature, history and knowledge, which was outlined above. This approach hinges upon:

(a) A conception of human nature and knowledge that restricts discussion of ethics to individual intentions generated by the mind's (or consciousness') capacities for 'reason' and 'moral freedom' (Kant [1790] 1955).

(b) A meta-narrative concerning relationships between the histories of nature and culture (or in Kant's terms, 'transcendental metaphysics') in which the individual subject functions as the node through which the 'final cause' of human beings' capacities for 'moral freedom' is realised, namely: the 'perfect civic constitution' (Kant [1784] 1963).

Arendt ([1961] 1977: 147) notes that the withdrawal of moral freedom (the capacity of human beings to act otherwise) from the material physical and social order ('out there') to the inward domain of individual mental states may have realised an objective, which modern thought had pursued from the onset, namely: 'the privatisation of freedom'. Once meaning and value could be seen as the product of a supposedly disembodied individual mind, it could be conceptualised as independent of its historically contingent social and ethical implications. In this connection, moral privatisation (the privatisation of freedom and ethics) removed ethics from its traditional status *at the centre of epistemology and ontology*, and reduced social life to inter-individual systems of contractual structures. Here, we may glimpse the foundations of the a-historical conceptions of the individual (self), which critics of meta-narratives have called into question, and which is receiving much attention in the recent archaeological literature on agency (e.g., Dobres and Robb 2000). We may also be able to gain an appreciation of the complexity of the problems that some new lines of research in Roman archaeology, which touch upon the historicity of agency, are attempting to address.

Ethics and a satisfactory ontology of agency

Researchers have responded in a variety of ways to the issues posed by the dimensions of the critique of meta-narratives, which are outlined in this paper. My aim in this final section takes its departure from two recent developments in Roman archaeology, which may relate to cross-disciplinary considerations of the constructive implications of this critique. One is the growing interest in arguments against the notion of a human self that is prior to its embodied and material preconditions (e.g., Foucault 1980; Bourdieu 1990). The other is the concern to focus attention on the discrepant experiences of human agents (e.g., Said 1993).

The former raises issue with approaches to the intentionality of human behaviour, which have been structured around a supposed gap between the 'mental states' of individual subjects and an object world 'out there'. An interest in a alternative approaches is reflected in a number of new lines of research in philosophy and the human sciences, and several papers on 'material culture' and 'social identity' presented at TRAC 2002. The later concern is represented in the literatures in critical theory, post-colonial studies, publications on domination and resistance in the Roman world (e.g. Webster and Cooper 1996; Mattingly ed. 1997; Hingley 2000), and several papers presented at TRAC 2002 that focused on the heterogeneity of the Roman Empire. This concern implies a complex range of issues, including: How might we best reconceptualise intentionality, and human capacities to act voluntarily (or to 'behave otherwise')? What makes it possible for human agents to act against existing socio-historical constraints, and to transform the circumstances from which these arise? Can human experiences of discrepancies between how things *are* and how things *ought to be* make a difference not just to particular *events*, but in *conjunctures* that reconfigure the *longue durée*?

I admire much of the recent epistemological work motivated by concerns to go beyond traditional notions of a timeless, placeless disembodied agent. These notions hinge on a dichotomy between how concrete embodied human beings *are* and how rational 'mental states' *ought to be*. They figure essentially as treatments of human beings as interchangeable atomistic nodes through which (the invisible hand' of) social systems and cultural histories operate (Koerner and Gassón 2001). But I am worried that if we come too close to reducing agency to its material and embodied preconditions, we may not be able to address the key issues posed by studies seeking to focus on discrepant experiences.

It might be useful to broach this matter from the perspectives offered by new frameworks for going beyond dualist paradigms for the conditions of archaeological knowledge, and philosophical insights relating to the historicity of human agency. Two notable examples of the former are those advanced by John Barrett (2000) and Christopher Gosden (1994). Barrett's contribution to the TRAC 2002 session took its starting point from the framework he has proposed for going beyond essentialist notions of an archaeological 'record', and a-historical conceptions of human agency (cf. Patrik 1985; Barrett 1988, 1994, 2000). The framework centers on a distinction between 'structuring conditions' and 'structuring principles' (Barrett 2000). The former are defined as the historically contingent embodied and materialised conditions of possibility for human agency. The latter are defined as the means whereby human beings inhabit structural conditions: "they are expressed in the agents' abilities to work on those conditions in the reproduction and transformation of their own identities and conditions of existence" (Barrett 2000: 65). The relationship between the two is not reducible to a dichotomy between mental states locked into the minds of individual subjects *versus* a world of objects (including society) somehow 'out there'. It implies processes of perception and modes of objectification, which occur in a wide range of historically contingent implicit and explicit modes (cf., Miller 1987; Bourdieu 1990; Brandom 1994). In such a view, there is no such thing as a 'self' that is prior to its embodied and material preconditions. Yet such a view does not require that we risk reducing thought to practice (cf. Foucault 1980) or abandon notions of human selves and intentionality altogether.

Robert Brandom's work, *Making it Explicit. Reasoning, Representing and Discursive Commitment* (1994), indicates why this is the case. Brandom shows how we can replace traditional dualist notions of *representation* by the open-ended concept, *expression*. The latter enables us to replace the traditional opposition between (a) *internal* and *external* representations with (b) a range of *implicit* and *explicit* socially situated processes of objectification that carry the materiality and mutuality of human relationships forward over time. Brandom also explains why the latter approach is important for pursuing some of the most promising implications of notions of 'social agency' *without abandoning the importance of intentionality for understanding processes of individuation*. If we ignore these processes, we cannot account for how humans can interact (Arendt [1958] 1989). Brandom explains that:

> Only a creature who can make beliefs explicit – in the sense of claiming and keeping discursive score on claims – can adopt the simple intentional stance and treat another as having beliefs implicit in its intelligent behavior. Just so, only a creature who can make attitudes towards the beliefs of others explicit – in the sense of being able to ascribe scorekeeping attributions – can adopt the explicitly discursive stance and treat others as making their beliefs explicit, and so as having intentionality (Brandom 1994:639).

The importance of these observations extends well beyond the point that processes of individuation make possible the interaction of human beings. Our treatment of our fellow humans as possessing intentionality is essential to the constitution of ourselves. *We not only make our shared epistemic and ontological commitments (our collectivity) explicit, we make ourselves explicit as social agents making that collective explicit.*

Notably, these observations do not hinge upon an essentialist ontology of a timeless, placeless individual. They also have very direct bearing upon Barrett's (2000) distinction between 'structuring conditions' and 'structuring principles', and issues posed by Gosden's (1994) emphasis on the 'materiality' and 'mutuality' of human ways of life. In *Social Being and Time* (1994), Gosden writes that:

> ...the term 'materiality' refers to human relations with the world, 'mutuality' looks at human-interrelationships. Materiality and mutuality are linked here for the simple reason that they are inseparable. Full social relations can only be set up though making and using things; full relations with the world only come about through people working together (Gosden 1994: 82).

Brandom's arguments relate to questions about how 'structuring principles' articulate with 'structuring conditions' (Barrett 2000) and how 'materiality and mutuality' (Gosden 1994) are linked. They point towards the importance of ethics for a satisfactory ontology of such linkages, and indicate why we do not need to resort to 'invisible hand' meta-narratives in order to account for these linkages. Indeed, we may be able to abandon the dichotomy between how concrete embodied human beings *are* and how rational 'mental states' *ought to be* on which such meta-narratives hinge.

Your and my experience informs us that human beings are mutually accountable and mutually susceptible social creatures. Furthermore, as Barry Barnes (2000) points out, our interaction is informed by our experience that human beings are creatures that act voluntarily. Focusing on ethics enables us to understand the ways in which human beings freely chose and freely act as mutually accountable and mutually susceptible creatures, and that they do so while affecting and being affected by each other as creatures of this kind. Our interaction as human agents is always situated in contingent ethical relationships (commitments), which make self-understanding possible. Our relationships to the world (ontological, epistemological, social, material, historical commitments) emerge out of our ethical relationships to one another as mutually susceptible, mutually accountable, (intentional) beings (Brandom 1994; Barnes 2000; McGuire and Tuchanska 2001). Such a view takes us beyond a-historical dichotomies of *agency* and *structure*, and enables us to develop alternatives to notions of agents, which reduce human beings to "timeless, featureless, interchangeable and atomistic individuals, untethered to time or space" (Gero 2000: 38). It rejects the very dichotomy of *being* and *acting* of the *self* in the world and the acting for *others* in history on which metaphysics traditionally hinges.

Furthermore, focusing on the importance of ethics for a satisfactory ontology of agency makes it clear that societies are not just sums of atomic individuals. Norbert Elias (1991: 12, 17–19) and others have noted that societies are very particular sorts of 'wholes'. It has been misleading to represent human communities as harmonious unities without "contradictions, tensions, or explosions," or a "formation with clear contours" (Elias (1991: 12). Openness, changeability and potential for internal tensions may characterise the histories of all communities. One of the implications of our considerations is that the 'wholeness' of communities is not a function of interacting atomic entities, consisting of natural and cultural parts, as Hobbes ([1651] 1962), Kant ([1784] 1963), and others suggest. Rather, whatever we are treating as the 'wholeness' of communities may consist of the implicit and explicit fields of thought and practice, which constitute the life-worlds of mutually susceptible and mutually accountable ethical agents, who have differing experiences of the world as such beings.

These comments may relate to some of the concerns motivating recent research on discrepant experiences, and questions of whether experiences of discrepancies between how things *are* and how things *ought to be* can make a difference not just in the outcomes of particular events, but in conjunctures that reconfigure patterns in the longue durée. These are the kinds of issues that motivated Edmund Husserl's ([1936] 1970) conception of the significance of ethics for understanding the life-worlds of human beings. In *The Crisis of European Science and Transcendental Phenomenology* ([1936] 1970) Husserl challenged the long tradition of philosophies of history structured around such dichotomies as those of subject-object, mind-body, and is-ought. For Husserl, human beings are not atomistic, interchangeable nodes through which social systems or cultural histories operate. A human life-world can be envisaged as a prism of diverse fields of experience, including the inanimate world given in sensation, the vital world that is given to us as embodied living beings, and an ethical dimension in which other human beings are apprehended as centres of meaning and value. These fields are interrelated, and our discussion above of the mutual susceptibility and accountability of human beings may illuminate something of the nature of their interconnections. For Husserl, the ethical field cannot emerge without the others. However, in the experiences of human beings, the ethical field is prior to the others since it is constitutive of them.

These considerations may be useful for avoiding risks associated with some recent proposals of alternatives to views of the human self as prior to its embodied and material preconditions. The present paper focuses on the problems some proposals pose for addressing questions of how discrepant experiences are possible, and whether such experiences can have an impact on long-term historical processes. Notably, following Husserl, single discrepant experiences and single ethical acts 'irradiate' the other fields of human experience because they can take on a paradigmatic quality. Expressed in the terms which are employed in this paper, these acts can render explicit experiences of discrepancies between how things are and ought to be *on the very scales on which human meanings and values are generated.* Thus, insofar as they attest (make explicit) the existence of an ethical field, single ethical acts can transform life-worlds. In this view, it may be the structure of human experiences of meanings, values and practice (or what Barrett 2000 calls 'structuring principles') that lead to conjunctures in the *longue durée*, and the emergence of new cultural forms or 'structuring conditions'.

Some suggestions for future considerations

In this paper, I have attempted to present something of the historical and philosophical background of the concerns that motivated the 2002 TRAC session, 'Breaking Ground or Treading Water. Theoretical Agendas for the 21st Century'. One of the aims of the session's participants was to explore Roman archaeology's relevance to issues posed by the cross-disciplinary critique of meta-narratives. Much of the beginning of this paper has been devoted to highlighting the importance of the roles played by the Roman Empire (both as a source and as a paradigmatic example) in the history of these meta-narratives, and of social theory and philosophy in general. I have also tried to provide a general picture of the main foci of the meta-narratives critique. In so doing, my aim has been to illustrate something of the kinds of concerns that motivated the papers presented in the session, and why specialists in Roman archaeology are likely to be able to make particularly useful contributions to this critique.

The second aim of this paper concerns the challenges facing attempts to carry forward the constructive implications of the meta-narratives critique. My approach took its departure from two interesting responses in Roman archaeology to this critique, and a tension between them, which complicates their strengths. I attempted to show how we can go beyond the problem by combining new frameworks for the conditions of archaeological knowledge (e.g., Gosden 1994, Barrett 2000) with philosophical insights bearing upon an ontology of the historicity of agency, which gives ethics a key role (e.g., Husserl [1936] 1970; Arendt [1958] 1989, 1961; Miller 1987; Brandom 1994, Barnes 2000). The proposed approach may be useful to research on the heterogeneity of the Roman Empire, as well as broader questions of whether discrepant experiences of how things *are* and *ought to be* can make a fundamental difference not just in particular *events*, but in *conjunctures* that reconfigure the *longue durée*. In view of (a) the roles that problematical pictures of the Roman Empire have played in the history of western social theory and philosophy, and (b) the wealth of evidence which is available to Roman archaeology concerning major conjunctures in historical processes, studies of these conjunctures may be highly relevant to cross-disciplinary debates over how to carry forward the constructive implications of the meta-narratives critique.

University of Manchester

Acknowledgements

Warm thanks to my friend and session co-organizer, Andrew Gardner, the participants in the session, and the editors of the TRAC 2002 proceedings volume.

Bibliography

Ancient sources

Aristotle [1908] *Metaphysics*, translated by W. D. Ross. In W. Ross (ed.) *The Works of Aristotle*. Oxford: Clarendon Press. Vol. 8.

Augustine of Hippo 1963. *The City of God* [*De civitate Dei*]. London: Oxford University Press.

Cicero, M. T. 1942. *De Oratore*, Books I and II, translated by E. W. Sutton, Book III, translated by H. Rackham. London: Loeb Classical Library.

Eusebius of Caesarea 1973. *The Ecclesiastical History of Eusebius Pamphilus*, translated by L. Kirsopp. Cambridge: Cambridge University Press.

Modern sources

Adorno, T. 1974. *Minima Moraia: Reflections from a Damaged Life*, translated by E. F. N. Jephcott. London: Verso.

Arendt, H. [1958] 1989. *The Human Condition*. Chicago: University of Chicago Press.

Arendt, H. [1961] 1977. *Between Past and Present. Eight Exercises in Political Thought* New York: Penguin Books.

Atkinson, J. A., Banks, I. and O'Sullivan, J. (eds.) 1997. *Nationalism and Archaeology*. Glasgow: Cruithne Press.

Barnes, B. 2000. *Understanding Agency: Social Theory and Responsible Action*. London: SAGE Publications.

Barrett, J. 1988. Fields of Discourse. Reconstituting a Social Archaeology. *Critique of Anthropology*, 7(3). 5–16.

Barrett, J. 1994. *Fragments from Antiquity: an archaeology of social life*. Oxford: Basil Blackwell.

Barrett, J. 2000. A Thesis on Agency. In M. A. Dobres and J. Robb (eds.) *Agency in Archaeology*. London: Routledge. 61–68.

Berlin, I. 1976. *Vico and Herder. Two Studies in the History of Ideas*. New York: Viking Press.

Biagioli, M. (ed) 1999. *The Science Studies Reader*. London: Routledge.

Blumenberg, H. 1983. *The Legitimation of the Modern Age*, translated by R. M. Wallace. Cambridge, MA.: MIT Press.

Bourdieu, P. 1990. *The Logic of Practice*, translated by R. Nice. London: Polity Press.

Brandom, R. 1994. *Making it Explicit. Reasoning, Representing and Discursive Commitment*. Cambridge, MA: Harvard University Press.

Braudel, F. [1949] 1966. *The Mediterannean and the Mediterannean World in the Age of Philip II*, 2 vols, translated by S. Reynolds. New York: Harper and Rowe.

Cassirer, E. 1960. *The Logic of the Humanities*, translated C. Smith Howe. London: Yale University Press.

Collingwood, R. G. [1949] 1956 *The Idea of History*. N.Y.: Oxford University Press.

Descartes, R. 1984–91. *The Philosophical Writings of Descartes* translated by J. Cottingham, R. Stoothoff and D. Murdoch. Cambridge: Cambridge University Press.

Descola, P. and Pálssen, G. (eds.) 1996. *Nature and Society. Anthropological Perspectives*. London: Routledge.

Dobres, M. A. and Robb, J. (eds.) 2000. *Agency in Archaeology*. London: Routledge.

Dupré, L. 1993. *The Passage to Modernity. An Essay in the Hermeneutics of Nature and Culture*. New Haven: Yale University Press.

Durkheim, E. [1914] 1960. The Dualism of Human Nature and its Social Conditions. In K. H. Wolff (ed.) *Essays on Sociology and Philosophy*. New York: Harper. 325–340.

Elias, N. 1991. *The Society of Individuals*, translated by E. Jephcott, M. Schröter (ed.) Oxford: Basel Blackwell.

Foucault, M. 1980. *Power/Knowledge: Selected Interviews and Other Writings 1972–1977*, translated by L. Marshall, J. Mepham, and K. Soper, C. Gordon (ed.) New York: Pantheon Books.

Friedman, J. 1992. The Past in the Future: History and the Politics of Identity. *American Anthropologist*, 94(4): 837–859.

Funkenstein, A. 1986. *Theology and the Scientific Imagination. From the Middle Ages to the Seventeenth Century*. Princeton: Princeton University Press.

Gaitta, R. 2000. *A Common Humanity. Thinking about Love and Truth and Justice*. London: Routledge.

Geertz, C. 2000. *Available Light. Anthropological Reflections on Philosophical Topics*. Princeton: Princeton University Press.

Gero, J. 2000. Troubled Travels in Agency and Feminism. In M. A. Dobres and J. Robb (eds.), *Agency in Archaeology*. London: Routledge. 34–39.

Gosden, C. 1994. *Social Being and Time*. Oxford: Basil Blackwell.

Grassi, E. 1980. *Rhetoric as Philosophy. The Humanist Tradition*. University Park: The Pennsylvania State University Press.

Hale, J. R. 1993. *The Civilization of Europe in the Renaissance*. London: Simon and Schuster.

Hegel, G. W. F. [1831] 1975. *Lectures on the Philosophy of History*, translated by H. B. Nisbet. Cambridge: Cambridge University Press.

Hingley, R. 2000. *Roman Officers and English Gentlemen. The Imperial Origins of Roman Archaeology*. London: Routledge.

Hobbes, T. [1651] 1962. *Leviathan*. New York: Collier Books. Shapin.

Husserl, E. [1936] 1970. *The Crisis of European Science and Transcendent Phenomenology*, translated by D. Carr. Evanston, Illinois: Northwestern University Press.

Kant, I. [1755] 1969. *Universal Natural History and Theory of the Heavens*, translated by W. Hastie. Ann Arbor: University of Michigan Press.

Kant, I. [1784] 1963. Idea of a Universal History from a Cosmopolitan Point of View. In *On History*, translated by L. White Beck.Indianapolis: Bobbs–Merrill.

Kant, I. [1790] 1955. *Critique of the Faculty of Judgement*, translated by J. H. Bernard. New York; London: Henry G. Bohn.

Koerner, S. 2001. Archaeology, Nationalism, and Problems Posed by Science/Values, Epistemology/ Ontology Dichotomies. *World Archaeology Bulletin*, 14: 57–96.

Koerner, S. and Gassón, R. 2001. Historical Archaeology and New Directions in Environmental Archaeology: Examples from Neolithic Scandinavia and Venezuela (400–1400 AD). In U. Albarella (ed.) *Environmental Archaeology: Meaning and Purpose*. Dordrecht: Kluwer Academic Publishers. 177–210.

Koyré, A. 1968. *From the Closed World to the Infinite Universe*. Baltimore: The John Hopkins University Press.

Lyotard, J.F. 1984. *The Postmodern Condition: A Report on Knowledge*, translated by G. Bennington and B. Massumai. Manchester: Manchester University Press.

Machiavelli, N. 1965. *Machiavelli. The Chief Works*, translated by A. Gilbert. Durham, NC.: Duke University Press.

Marx, K. and Engels, F. [1846] 1975. *The German Ideology: Collected Works*, 5 vols. New York: International Publishers.

Mattingly, D. J. (ed) 1997. *Dialogues in Roman Imperialism. Power, Discourse, and Discrepant Experiences*. Oxford: Oxbow Books.

McGuire, J. E. and Tuchanska, B. 2001. *Science Unfettered. A Philosophical Study in Sociohistorical Ontology*. Athens: Ohio University Press.

Miller, D. 1987. *Material Culture and Mass Consumption*. Oxford: Basil Blackwell.

Miller, D. (ed) 1995. *Worlds Apart: Modernity through the Prism of the Local*. London: Routledge.

Momigliano, A. 1966 *Studies in Historiography. Collected Essays by Arnold Momigliano*. London: Weidenfield and Nicolson.

Mooney, M. (ed.) 1979. *Renaissance Thought and its Sources*. New York: Columbia University Press.

Morgan, L. H. [1877] 1963. *Ancient Society*, L. White (ed.) Cambridge, MA.: The Belnap Press of Harvard University.

Newton, I. [1687] 1934. *Mathematical Principles of Natural Philosophy*, translated by A. Motte and F. Cajori. Berkeley: University of California Press.

Patrik, L. E. 1985. Is There an Archaeological Record? *Advances in Archaeological Methods and Theory*, 8: 27–62.

Rorty, R. 1989. *Contingency, Irony, and Solidarity*. Cambridge: Cambridge University Press.

Said, E. 1993. *Culture and Imperialism*. London: Chatto and Wardus.

Schnapp, A. 1996. *The Discovery of the Past: The Origins of Archaeology*. London: British Museum Press.

Shapin, S. and Schaffer, S. 1985. *Leviathan and the Vacuum Pump. Hobbes, Boyle and the Experimental Life*, including a translation of Thomas Hobbes's *Dialogue Physicus de Natura Aeris* by S. Shaffer. Princeton: Princeton University Press.

Toulmin, S. 1990. *Cosmopolis: The Hidden Agenda of Modernity*. Chicago: University of Chicago Press.

Trigger, B. 1984. Alternative Archaeologies. Nationalism, Colonialist, Imperialist. *Man*(NS), 19: 355–370.

Trigger, B. 1995. Romanticism, Nationalism, and Archaeology. In P. L. Kohl and C. Fawcett (eds.), *Nationalism, Politics and the Practice of Archaeology*. Cambridge: Cambridge University Press.

Valla, L. [1540] 1962. *Opere*, 2 vols. Turin: Bottega d'Erasmo.

Weber, M. [1904] 1958. *The Protestant Ethic and the Spirit of Capitalism*. New York: Scribner's Press.

Webster, J. and Cooper, N. J. (eds.) 1996. *Roman Imperialism. Post-Colonial Perspectives*. Leicester: Leicester University Press.

Wilk, R. 1995. Learning to be Local in Belize: Global Systems of Common Difference. In D. Miller (ed.), *Worlds Apart. Modernity through the Prism of the Local*. London: Routledge. 110–133.

A brief comment on the TRAC session dedicated to the interdisciplinary approaches to the study of Roman women

Patricia A. Baker

Introduction: why study Roman women?

This paper is intended only to be a comment on the session 'Interdisciplinary approaches to Roman Women' held at TRAC in 2002. The session, unfortunately, did not attract many speakers (only two, originally three). When I noticed the lack of interest I originally intended to cancel the session, but with further consideration I felt this would not be fair to the two participants. I also thought that rather than be defeated by the lack of interest the seminar should be held as an opportunity to open up discussion about why women in the Roman world are not being paid much attention in modern scholarship, and question why a session inviting scholars specialising in Roman woman from other disciplines did not elicit greater participation from those scholars. The original intent of the session was to bring together scholars who study Roman women from archaeological as well as non-archaeological approaches, such as philology, art history, philosophy and history for example. As someone with a specialism in the archaeology of ancient medicine, I must interact with scholars on an interdisciplinary level, and it has been noticed that there is often an air of indifference, and in some cases even hostility, both from and towards scholars with a different expertise. The same is noticeable with the study of Roman women: examinations made in the fields of philology and ancient history relating to women are rarely referred to by archaeologists, and, on the other hand, archaeological material is rarely mentioned by non-archaeologists. The indifference generally seems to be caused by a lack of understanding of how separate disciplines are studied and approached. Although TRAC is an archaeological conference, it is one that provides an arena in which theoretical interpretation can be openly discussed, and by allowing for interaction between other areas of study that operate in theoretically interpretative and informed manners, scholarship on Roman women can only be made richer, more informed and interesting. Thus, a session based on interdisciplinarity would have been a means to initiate such discussion.

Another intention for the session was to invite conversation between scholars who specialise in studies of Roman communities in the Mediterranean with those who examine the Roman provinces. Generally TRAC papers tend to focus upon provincial Roman archaeology; nonetheless it is the Theoretical Roman, rather than Theoretical provincial Roman, archaeology conference. In relation to this particular topic scholarship has been done on women for both regions, but again conversation between the two does not seem to have been forthcoming – a geographical divide still exists. It was hoped to bridge this gap, too, since it cannot be expected that Roman women lived and acted in a vacuum either as a single entity encompassing the entire Roman world, or as uniform sets of women living in separate provinces without contact or any influence from Rome or other provinces, cities or groups of people. It therefore made sense that specialists should be in contact with one another rather than remain separated. In spite of the intentions to broaden the discussion on Roman women and make archaeological evidence open for discussion by non-archaeologists, the interest has not been forthcoming, and questions must be addressed as to why this is the case.

There are possibly three general reasons for the lack of participation. The first may have been because the Classical Association conference (CA) was being held at the same time. It is possible that some speakers at the CA might have volunteered papers for TRAC if the timing of the two did not conflict. Yet this is not necessarily the main reason. Somewhat exceptionally, I am someone who fairly regularly attends both conferences and at each there are always different groups of participants; rarely does one see someone who would normally attend TRAC at the CA, and vice versa. This second reason is possibly indicative of the geographical division already mentioned, in that there is a definite divide between those who are Classicists studying the Mediterranean and those who study the Roman provinces. The third contributing factor for the lack of interest, and for the session as a whole, is more likely due to the paucity of people studying Roman women. Few scholars seem to focus their work on women, and as someone with a strong interest in the subject (Baker 1999), it is apparent that there is not much published material to draw upon, and what there is mainly comes from the study of women in ancient Greece rather than Rome. This problem of limited attention has been noted in a recent paper by Hill (2001) on identity in Roman Britain, where it is pointed out that women are rarely mentioned or considered as important elements in the province and they generally tend to be overlooked. This holds true not only for the study of women in the Roman provinces, but for the entire Roman empire. It is this third aspect that requires further consideration. Why, after three decades of gender and feminist archaeological and anthropological criticism on the subject of women in general, are Roman women not being studied?

A brief review of the study of Roman women

There are relatively few works on Roman women, and from a specific archaeological perspective there are even fewer studies to be found. The general concentration of works on the subject of Roman women tend to be on Roman laws and politics (e.g. Gardner 1985, 1986; Savunen 1995), the Roman family (e.g. Corbier 1991; Dixon 1992) and investigations on the depiction of Roman women in art (e.g. Kampen 1991; Mikocki 1990, 1995). Overall these studies generally tend to focus upon women of the upper classes and those who held imperial status. There seems to be a lack of concern for the common woman, possibly because there is more obvious evidence available for the empresses and the upper class women. Yet, there are a number of means by which one can attempt to learn about the 'average' woman, rather than simply concentrate on imperial females. Although in-depth philological studies can inform us on Roman women, archaeological evidence can be used to learn much about the mundane aspects of daily life and attitudes towards females that might not have been recorded in the written record. One of the few attempts to initiate a study of women in Roman archaeology was begun by Allason-Jones (1989), who looked specifically at women in Roman Britain. Although the study was innovative for the field of Romano-British studies, consideration was not given to scholarly work that had been undertaken on gender and women in both anthropology and prehistoric archaeology (e.g. Ardener 1975; Ehrenberg 1989; Ortner and Whitehead 1981; Rosaldo and Lamphere 1974; Sørensen 1988). By the time Allason-Jones' book was written there was a vast amount of literature in the theoretical areas of feminist and gender studies, which pointed out that simply 'adding' women to studies was not a strategy for understanding them in their cultural context. Unfortunately, this is ultimately what Allason-

Jones' book has done, in spite of all the conscientious intentions to break away from the traditionally male-based study of the Roman world. Rather than seeing the book as a starting point for studying Roman women from an archaeological perspective and moving on to critically question the Roman, or more specifically, provincial cultural understanding of women in the Roman period, Allason-Jones' study seems to be taken by some scholars as being the ultimate and final statement on the subject. As mentioned, simply discussing women was something critiqued by feminist anthropologists in the 1970s and early 1980s (e.g. Strathern 1981) when it was argued that women had to not only be mentioned, but also considered in their cultural context, asking what it meant to be female in a particular culture. Allason-Jones book does not attempt to answer this in much depth, and it is this point that needs to be addressed in future studies on women. There have been attempts to examine women more critically in Roman Britain as mentioned in Hill (2001: 15–16), with works by Hingley (1990), Scott (1995) and van Driel-Murray (1995), and there is also the unpublished PhD thesis by Rodgers (1998) on women and art in Roman Britain, for example. These are exceptional, however, and in general little has been done from an archaeological point of view. To look at the subject more critically, there is a need to further discussions of Roman women using a far more interdisciplinary approach, as this will open discussion amongst a wider community of scholars.

The problem is compounded by the fact that the study of Roman women is continuously discussed separately in conference sessions dedicated solely to women, rather than being incorporated into mainstream sessions at conferences. This reflects the situation at the TAG (Theoretical Archaeology Group) conferences up until the early 1990s, where sessions on gender and feminism were not only separated from mainstream sessions, but in some instances men were excluded from participation and attending. This only served to make feminist and gender studies the exclusive domain of female scholars. Traditionally the study of women (and children, although the topic is not considered in this paper, but it suffers from similar problems [e.g. Moore and Scott 1997]) has been separated from the rest of scholarship because it was the only means by which to develop the subject. Quite early on this separation was deemed to be problematic by anthropologists; in the 1970s it was pointed out that women are an integral element to society so should not be discussed in isolation (Rosaldo and Lamphere 1974). Questions were later raised about why the study of women was being sidelined and not included within the main conference sessions that ultimately involved (implicitly or explicitly) the study of men. According to Strathern (1981: 683), men are considered by western scholars to be the mainstream component in a society, therefore, what they did in the past has always been considered a societal norm, and thus, until recently, little thought had been given to separating studies of masculine roles in books or conferences (e.g. Foxhall and Salmon 1998). The reason postulated by Strathern is because men are perceived as having a particular place in history and are therefore studied in the forefront, rather than having to be discussed in a separate subculture or even ghettoised, as are women. This says more about modern viewpoints of women, and how it is projected onto understandings of women in the past. There is often the assumption that if there is little obvious or apparent evidence in the historical (here meaning all evidence of the past) record then there is little use in studying something, because it is considered that it was not important in the past. It demonstrates a modern preconception about certain sections in societies, reflected back onto past societies; that is that women are seen as second class citizens and not deserving of much attention. They are frequently portrayed as being tied to the household without much say in their society – entirely lacking in effective agency. Unfortunately, Allason-Jones book and recent paper reinforces this (e.g. 1989; 2000).

There is a view that female power/agency operated at a mundane level, that of the domestic sphere, but it did not extend beyond this level. This image of Roman women has been carried through scholarship without much attention as to how it was created, or without questions being raised as to whether the common understanding of Roman women related to how they were understood by their societies.

Although women in the Classical world are less visible than men, this could be an issue of representation created by scholars, who are generally men and who do not find it necessary to locate the female. Perhaps scholars should be looking for the possibility of less visible women and the habituated or intrinsic power they might have held. Anthropological studies have shown that often minority groups in societies have frequently demonstrated an invisible power (e.g. Friedl 1986; Ilcan 1996). At the moment it cannot be said with certainty that all women in the Classical world were seen as minority groups, given the scholarship and assumptions made about them. Such agency is not so immediately apparent, but upon closer examination significant and meaningful power relationships can become visible, and the invisible minority will often control the more visible in certain aspects of their lives, demonstrating that they are not fully subordinate. One example of this comes from an anthropological study made by Friedl on the position and power of women in the village society of Vasilika, Greece between the 1960s and 1980s (Friedl 1986). The main thesis of her work points to the structural opposition, or polarisation in a Greek village society where men are seen as being dominant and women subordinate. She challenges the outward appearance of the society and looks closely at the roles women play in this particular village. In general the women of Vasilika are associated with the private (the household), whilst men are linked to the public sphere in places such as the *kaffenion* (coffee shop) and therefore are more obvious in the public domain. Since men are visible to the outside observer and women are not, it is the male authority that is apparent; yet, upon close inspection, Freidl noted that the outward appearance of life in the village was producing the wrong impression, because she learned that the women in the village held power because they control the household, and ultimately the household controls the public sphere. Thus, Friedl's work teaches us not to focus all attention on what seems immediately apparent, because the invisible may be equally important, if not more so; this might hold true for women in the Roman world.

Friedl's work along with many other studies, although influential on our understandings of women, have not achieved an amalgamation of scholarship on males and females, that is true gender studies. There is still a separation between gender and feminist studies and what is seen as mainstream scholarship. This was commented on in 1996 by del Valle in her introduction to *Gendered Anthropology* where it was noted that it is not only studies on women that are relegated to subdivisions, but studies of genders (13–16). Gender studies, although questioning gender identity rather than simply female identity, are somehow associated with scholarship on women. Male anthropologists, according to del Valle (1996: 13), claim they cannot study gender because they will not understand women, but even when they study men rarely are issues raised about the cultural construction of masculinity (for an exception see Foxhall and Salmon 1998). Strathern, as quoted in del Valle (1996: 14), argues that it is not simply that women are excluded from studies by men, but that gender studies do not apply to the paradigm of modern thinking because we are dealing with a male world and a male way of thinking. Without a complete change in academic thinking, will gender studies always be relegated to the sidelines of academic importance?

Suggestions to improve studies of Roman women

Much has been made about gender being a performance, this is to say that gender is created through human behaviour and action. It is not completely biological, but rather it is something that is learned and acted out in accordance to the rules of a society (Butler 1993 and for a further discussion of this see Busby 2000). To understand the ways in which people conceive gender and the ways in which practices and dispositions are engendered, one must try to gain access to how different societies play out their engendered roles. For example food production is often associated with female activity. The questions must be asked how is the task engendered, how is food made available and who makes it and why? From an archaeological perspective, much could be made of clothing and the ways in which outward styling contributed to the construction of gender. One could examine where certain items might have been worn, which could also be useful in the context of burials. Moreover, space and temporality must be addressed, for, as mentioned earlier, the Roman empire was not a single entity, but one of vast cultural variation and temporal periods. We must not expect that women in Britain were the same as those in Italia, Hispania or Germania. Even within the provinces themselves, variation was to be expected, and one cannot expect that the roles of women would have remained static through time. New interactions would have been made between different groups and changes within a society would have occurred. A complex hybrid of situations created through a colonial experience would most likely have occurred. We who study women in the Roman empire are lucky in that we have a potentially vast amount of information available to us to make the most of our understandings, and archaeologically we have a rich field. There are for example, a number of relief sculptures that depict women doing jobs in markets, and girls playing games that provide us with another view into the Roman world, a view that does not seem to be taken advantage of in many studies. We also have to look far more closely at our material remains to see if they can be defined in terms of gender, or at least gender association. Moreover, consideration must be given to the cultural diversity in the Roman empire, which could imply that there might have been many different gender relationships in operation. Even if women were tied solely to household activities this actually makes them very visible in the archaeological record in relation to productive activities. Thus, one could build upon the work of Allison (1997) and look to production activities, deposition, use of pottery and other 'household' items. Furthermore, the archaeology can be enhanced by other fields of study: epigraphic remains that mention women, historical sources and even poetry and plays can all provide more of an insight into the Roman world. All of these sources should be incorporated to study women from all perspectives in the Roman world. We should not divide archaeology, history and philology, each should be considered to have an equal degree of validity and inclusion. Moreover, self-critical theoretically aware arguments with the inclusion of critiques on feminist and gender studies must be incorporated into our research. To deny them will not advance the study of Roman women. Finally, I would suggest that scholars specialising in Roman women and/or gender should consider presenting papers in mainstream sessions at conferences (and not just TRAC), as a means of demonstrating the importance of considering women in scholarly studies. This would make studies of women more accessible, and known to scholars with other specialisms, which may be a means to open up this field of research.

Although the aims of the session were not met, it did lead to an interesting discussion on how to carry the field further, but with the small attendance only those few who are aware of these issues were able to comment; thus it seemed necessary to point this problem out in writing. It must be made clear that there is still much work to be done on integrating the study of Roman women into the broader realm of classics, and this can only be done through interdisciplinary discussion.

School of European Culture and Languages,
University of Kent at Canterbury

Acknowledgements

I would like to thank the two speakers, Angela Morelli and Rebecca Redfern for participating in the session and for presenting very interesting papers. I would also like to thank all who took part in the discussion at the end of the session for suggesting ways to take the study further. Finally I would like to thank Joshua Pollard and Adrian Chadwick for reading and making comments on the draft of this paper. Needless to say all comments are the author's own.

Bibliography

Allason-Jones, L. 1989. *Women in Roman Britain.* London: British Museum Press.

Allason-Jones, L. 2000. Women and the Roman Army in Britain. In A. Goldsworthy and I. Haynes (eds.) *The Roman Army as a Community.* Portsmouth, Rhode Island: Journal of Roman Archaeology Supplement 34. 41–51.

Allison, P. 1997. Why do excavation reports have finds catalogues? In C.G. Cumberpatch and P. W. Blinkhorn (eds.) *Not so much a Pot, More a Way of Life.* Oxford: Oxbow Monograph 83. 77–84.

Ardener, S. (ed.). 1975. *Perceiving Women.* London: Malaby Press.

Baker, P. 1999. Soranus and the Pompeii Speculum: the sociology of Roman gynaecology and Roman perceptions of the female body. In P. Baker, C. Forcey, S. Jundi and R. Witcher (eds.) *TRAC 98: Proceedings of the Eighth Annual Theoretical Roman Archaeology Conference, Leicester 1998.* Oxford: Oxbow Books. 141–150.

Busby, C. 2000. *The Performance of Gender: an anthropology of everyday life in a south Indian fishing village.* London and New Brunswick, New Jersey: Athlone Press.

Butler, J. 1993. *Bodies that matter: on the discursive limits of 'Sex'.* London and New York: Routledge.

Corbier, M. 1991. Family behaviour of the Roman aristocracy, Second century BC to Third century AD. In S. Pomeroy (ed.) *Women's History and Ancient History.* Chapel Hill: University of North Carolina Press. 173–196.

Del Valle, T. 1996. Introduction. In T. del Valle (ed.) *Gendered Anthropology,* London and New York: Routledge.

Dixon, S. 1992. *The Roman Family.* Baltimore and London: John Hopkins University Press.

Ehrenberg, M. 1989. *Women in Prehistory.* London: British Museum Press.

Foxhall, L. and J. Salmon (eds.) 1998. *Thinking Men: masculinity and its self-representation in the Classical Tradition.* London and New York: Routledge.

Friedl, E. 1986. The position of women: appearance and reality. In J. Dubisch (ed.) *Gender and Power in Rural Greece.* Princeton: Princeton University Press. 42–52.

Gardner, J. 1985. The recovery of dowry in Roman law. *Classical Quarterly,* 35: 449–453.

Gardner, J. 1986. *Women in Roman Law and Society.* London: Croom Helm.

Hill, J.D. 2001. Romanization, gender and class: recent approaches to identity in Britain and their possible consequences. In S. James & M. Millett (eds.) *Britons and Romans: advancing an archaeological agenda.* York: Council for British Archaeology Research Report 25.

Hingley, R. 1990. Public and private space: domestic organisation and gender relations among Iron Age and Romano-British households. In Samson (ed.) *The Social Archaeology of Houses.* Edinburgh: Edinburgh University Press. 125–149.

Ilcan, S. 1996. Fragmentary encounters in a moral world: household power relations and gender politics. *Ethnology,* 35(1): 33–49.

Kampen, N. B. 1991. Between public and private: women as historical subjects in Roman Art. In S. Pomeroy (ed.) *Women's History and Ancient History.* Chapel Hill: University of North Carolina Press.

Mikocki, T. 1990. Les Impératrices et les princesses en déesses dans l'art Romain. *Eos,* 78:209–218.

Mikocki, T. 1995. *Sub Specie Deae les Impératrices et Princesses Romaines Assimilées à des Déesses.* Rome: Giorgio Bretschneider Editore.

Moore, J. and E. Scott (eds.) 1997. *Invisible People and Processes: writing gender and childhood into European Archaeology.* London: Leiciester University Press.

Ortner, S. B. and H. Whitehead (eds.) 1981. *The Cultural Construction of Gender and Sexuality.* Cambridge: Cambridge University Press.

Rodgers, R. 1998. *Imagery and Ideology: aspects of female representation in Roman Art, with special reference to Britain and Gaul.* Unpublished Ph.D. thesis, Durham University.

Rosaldo, M. Z. and L. Lamphere (eds.) 1974. *Women, culture and society.* Stanford: Stanford University Press.

Savunen, L. 1995. Women and elections in Pompeii. In R. Hawley and B. Levick (eds.) *Women in Antiquity.* London and New York: Routledge. 194–206.

Scott, E. 1995. Women and gender relations in the Roman Empire. In P. Rush (ed.) *Theoretical Roman Archaeology: Second Conference Proceedings.* Aldershot: Avebury.174–189.

Sørensen, M. L. S. 1988. Is there a feminist contribution to archaeology? *Archaeological Review from Cambridge,* 7(1):31–50.

Strathern, M. 1981. Culture in a netbag: the manufacture of a subdiscipline in anthropology. *Man,* 16(4): 665–668.

Van Driel Murray, C. 1995. Gender in Question. In P.Rush (ed.) *Theoretical Roman Archaeology: Second Conference Proceedings.* Aldershot: Avebury. 3–21.

Sex and the City: A biocultural investigation into female health in Roman Britain

Rebecca Redfern

Introduction

The examination of the effects of urbanism on the health of archaeological populations has not been exhausted within Britain, with little integrated work attempted on Romano-British populations (for example, London). Therefore, this study aimed to investigate whether the Romano-British urban environment and culture can be reflected in the remains of individuals buried in urban cemeteries dating from the second to fourth centuries AD. However, due to time restraints, the paucity of readily available rural data, and the limited excavations surrounding rural cemeteries, it must be considered that the osseous changes seen in the cemetery populations discussed in this paper may not have been specifically caused by urban environments.

The study of this period is important because not only is there is a wide variety of source material, but also because it was during the Roman period that urbanism developed for the first time in Britain. This introduced the native population to a new set of pathogens, diet, medical care, hygiene, sanitation, and living conditions. It was also undertaken in order to improve the understanding of Romano-British health, which for too long has rested upon the Poundbury Camp (Dorset) and Cirencester (Gloucestershire) data sets. Understanding past communities cannot be achieved without considering their health statuses. This can be achieved through palaeopathological analysis, which permits a direct, unequivocal understanding and analysis of the well being of our ancestors. Recently there have been calls to fully integrate palaeopathological evidence, especially by Esmonde Cleary, who has emphasised this need within his frequent papers on cemeteries. In his words, "palaeopathology has yet to be deployed to full effect in the study of Romano-British material" (1992: 29).

The study within this paper combines palaeopathological data with a gendered reading of the archaeological evidence, and also considers bioarchaeological evidence of the living environment to investigate the health statuses of urban dwellers. This information is set in a biocultural framework which is defined as "[one which assesses] the biological condition of human populations ... its consequences for the biological and cultural reproduction of the society ... to consider the selective effects of culture on the population under study and its survival" (Bush and Zvelebil 1991: 5). As interpretations of health are given within a cultural context, this provides some control over which interpretations are valid (Ortner 1992: 8; Wood et al. 1992: 358), as does the integration of bioarchaeological data (Bush 1991: 6).

This investigation has several interpretational problems. First, the cemeteries were used for long periods of time and, therefore, the information regarding health from these samples represents the whole of the Roman occupation. Second, who was living in towns and from where did they come? Unfortunately, this will not and cannot be answered unless ancient deoxyribonucleic acid (aDNA) and isotopic analyses are undertaken on all skeletal material from this period. We must, therefore, consider that some individuals buried in the urban cemeteries lived a rural way of life.

Methods

Archaeological Context

Table 1: Total number of individuals used in study.

Cemetery	Male	Probable Male	Female	Probable Female	Total
Colchester	171	6	129	17	323
Chichester	19	9	12	2	42
Ilchester	–	28	13	2	43
York	311	21	42	17	391
Poundbury Camp	251	–	226	1	478
Cirencester	220	9	78	15	322
London	96	17	36	12	161
Total	1068	90	536	66	

Table 2: Examples of rural palaeopathology from Dorset (unsexed and unsexable adult data excluded)

Cemetery	Periosteal Reaction	Tuberculosis	Fractures	Cribra orbitalia	Lack of osseous change	Total
Tolpuddle Ballm (McKinley 1999)	3 females, 2 males	1 male	1 female, 2 males	2 males and 1 female	13 individuals	16 females 10 males
Southern By-Pass (Rogers 1997)	1 male		3 females 1 males		6 females and 2 males	9 females 6 males
Western Link (Jenkins 1997)					1 females and 2 males	3 females 5 males

In the preliminary research for this analysis, it was hoped that changes through time could be identified by examining each century individually in order to emphasise the urban development and fluctuating numbers of urban dwellers. However, due to the difficulties of dating some inhumations and the problems of splitting material temporally, this was not possible. It was also initially proposed to compare urban and rural cemeteries, but there was a lack of available excavation reports of sufficient detail, and the time constraints governing research did not permit the collation of rural cemetery data from archives. Despite this, data from just three rural cemeteries in Dorset was collected as a sample study. Table 2 shows the incidence of disease in these cemeteries. Current research by the author will also investigate health changes in Dorset from the Iron Age to the post-Roman period to address rural / urban health differences in the Romano-British period (see Redfern 2002). It should also be mentioned here that cremated and disarticulated material were excluded from analyses in this paper due to disparities of publication, analysis and identification of pathology (McKinley

2000: 413), unclear contexts, and because the total numbers of individuals from sites were frequently not calculated using this data.

Data Collection

The data was collected from information published in the microfiches of site and specialist reports (where available). The London data set was sourced directly from the Museum of London Archaeology Service Archive. These sites were chosen because they were fully published (or available), and they are acknowledged as being 'urban' centres within Roman Britain.

As different authors published the data, the disparities between each report were evident. This was especially noticeable in the level of detail in the descriptions and in the inclusion or omission of necessary data, particularly for dental disease. Therefore, in order to use the data, the information was separated using the age categories described by Scheuer and Black (2000: 469), where 'infants' are those under three years old; 'children' are three to seven years old; 'juveniles' are those of eight to ten years old; 'adolescents' are ten to twenty-two years old; and 'adults' are those over twenty-two years old. All information regarding osteological change was categorised according to Aufderheide and Rodríquez-Martin (1998). This was done in order to demonstrate the range of changes as well as the palaeopathology found during this period. In order to analyse more closely the relationship between periostitis (inflammation of the upper surface of the bone (periosteum) which leads to the laying down of new bone), enamel hypoplasia (a defect of the tooth enamel) and cribra orbitalia (pin-prick sized holes in the roof of the eye orbit, which group together and may increase in size, caused by iron deficiency and / or a parasitic infection) in the different age and sex categories, periostitis was further subdivided from infectious disease as it can also be caused by trauma (Roberts and Manchester 1999: 130). In some cases individuals were described with osteological changes that are no longer regarded as reliable within palaeopathology, and these were either re-assigned or ignored. The results of the research generated by the analysis of specialist reports are restricted for the most part by inter-observer error, as well as by constraints of publication, which limit photographs and the length of reports. The frequent lack of accurate descriptions and total number of elements have often resulted in many diagnoses being rejected because of a lack of certainty, for example, whether female vertebral body collapse was due to underlying osteoporosis or trauma (see Resnick and Niwayama 1988: 1813–1821).

Dental disease, which is recognised as an important insight into past health statuses (Freeth 2000) was excluded from this analysis due to the lack of data within reports regarding the total number of teeth, and the totals of left and right dentition. Consequently, it was not deemed useful to include it in this particular study; however, dental data will be included in a future study by the author examining rural and urban health.

As the research presented here seeks to find correlations between the environmental evidence for the living environment and the palaeopathology of the cemetery samples, the discussion will concentrate upon evidence for infectious and metabolic diseases, stress indicators, trauma, surgery and fractures.

Palaeopathological approaches

Palaeopathology, as defined by Lovell, "aims to reconstruct the history and geography of diseases, to illuminate the interaction between disease and cultural processes, to document the evolution of diseases over time, and to understand the effect of disease processes on bone growth and development" (2000: 217). For this to be achieved, studies rely upon a wide research base, including medical anthropology, social anthropological research in traditional societies, clinical data, and inclusive studies of past populations (see McElroy and Townsend 1996; Sargent and Johnson 1996; Merbs 1983). This is also the essence of a biocultural approach as "it is only at the interface of archaeology and cultural and physical anthropology, within the framework of the biocultural approach, that the study of health in past societies can be fully developed" (Bush 1991: 7–8). For instance, an analysis of the implications of dietary stress relies upon data for both the environment and possible cultural stressors produced by the social environment (Bush 1991: 6); this data will thus be generated by anthropological and archaeological data (see Eisenberg 1991).

Roberts remarks that the interpretation of palaeopathological data cannot be undertaken unless clinical texts and data from anthropology are used (1991: 225). This approach has been proven by Jurmain's work on osteoarthritis (1999: xii); Jurmain states that the analysis of human remains must incorporate clinical and anthropological data in order for reliable interpretations to be achieved. Studies of enamel hypoplastic defects have also shown that analysis of modern clinical and anthropological data can be used to understand past prevalences (see Lukacs et al. 2001; Goodman et al. 1987) and to explain trends within prehistoric populations (Goodman and Song 1999; Goodman and Rose 1991). The use of clinical data is also central to the analysis of ancient trauma, as Walker (1997: 160) has shown that clinical literature contains valuable comparative data and models, which can be used to determine patterns of palaeo-trauma. Consequently, in this research, these sources of evidence have been used in order to attempt an inclusive understanding of the health affects of Romano-British urban environments.

As with any discipline, there are limitations to the analysis of past health. Ortner (1992: 8) has summarised that which we cannot always excavate, interpret or understand, but which are crucial in understanding health in the past:

1) The age at which the individual contracts the disease;
2) The individual's nutritional status;
3) The immune response of the person;
4) The biology of infectious agents;
5) The disease's portal of entry;
6) The effectiveness of any method of treatment;
7) Social conditions that can affect the transmission of disease.

These factors are further hindered by the fact that archaeological human remains reflect the osteological changes which were present / active at the time of death (Goodman 1993: 281–2). What must also be remembered is that the osseous lesions on the skeletal remains of past populations represent a small percentage of the total disease load in a population (Wood et al. 1992: 634; Waldron 1994: 36–41; Ortner et al. 1992: 337).

Palaeopathology must be used in combination with bioarchaeological evidence in order to understand the transmission of diseases, especially in urban environments; as McGrath (1992: 14) notes, human behaviour is instrumental in influencing disease transmission, and is often crucial in determining the success of vector transference.

Past concepts of health

Concepts of disease and illness are socio-culturally dependant; diagnoses of disease are reliant upon what the observer believes to be significant, as well as their ideas of health and disease (see Baker and Carr 2002); for instance Hippocratic doctrines on disease transmission compared to modern understanding of microbe transmission (Armelagos et al. 1977: 72). The symptoms taken into account may be very different to our own concepts of disease causation, and what constitutes a symptom; for instance, some morbid characteristics of sickness may sometimes form part of an aesthetic ideal and are therefore ignored (Polunin 1977: 85– 88) e.g. the romanticisation of tuberculosis (Roberts 2000: 52). The opinions used in diagnosing a disease may actually reflect socio-political factors affecting the social unit (Armelagos et al. 1977: 82). These concepts also impact upon the treatment and care given to individuals (Hughes 1977: 156–7; Ackerknecht 1977), especially those who may have been disabled (c.f. Roberts 2000).

Investigations of health and treatment in the Roman period have shown that there were differences in treatment and use of medical equipment depending on the part of the Empire in which you lived, where you came from, and where your doctor trained, as well as the influence of social and economic statuses of both the patient and the doctor (Fleming 2000; Jackson 2000; Baker 2001). Therefore, the care and treatment received in Roman Britain may have been very varied, reflecting individual views of health and sickness.

Urbanism

Urbanism is a key area of research within Roman archaeology and palaeopathology because it is such a unique un-natural environment. Urbanism is and was created by people and subsequently influences the health of those who live in an urban environment. The effect of the urban environment on health is of great importance in understanding Romano-British urban living. Such a study has not previously been investigated following the biocultural approach presented here. Storey's examination of pre-industrial urban health highlighted many relevant points: food would have been sourced from the surrounding areas and therefore any fluctuations in quantities would have also affected urban dwellers. Many infectious diseases are transferred more easily in denser communities, and closely packed housing can lead to contamination of water supplies; furthermore, migrants into the area can act as agents of disease (Storey 1992: 33). All of these points need to be borne in mind when considering Romano-British urbanism in regard to palaeopathology.

Several works on British urbanism have been undertaken, for example Brothwell (1994: 129–136), Waldron (1989: 55–73), and Manchester (1992: 8–14). However, none has specifically focused upon the Romano-British period. The main differences between rural and urban areas are through the modes of transmission and frequencies of disease only, not the diseases themselves (Manchester 1992: 9). Consequently, many changes seen in individuals may reflect diseases that were transmitted in rural areas and were not specifically caused by urbanism.

When investigating urbanism in past populations, data concerning migrants in developing countries can be used to understand the affects of urbanism, as exemplified in Allason-Jones' work 'Urban angst in Roman Britain' (2001 unpublished). As stated previously, the use of anthropological research is key to understanding past health statuses.

Romano-British urban areas

The setting of towns has been reviewed by Salway, who notes that health was also considered during the planning phases. He cites Vitruvius's 'scientific' explanation that "if the town is on a coast and faces south or west, it will be unhealthy, because the southern sky in summer heats up as soon as the sun appears" (*De Architectura* i.4.1–6). However, as Salway admits, at the time of the Claudian invasion of Britain, Vitruvius's advice, written in the reign of Augustus, may have seemed out of date (1985: 67).

Throughout time, towns have been places of public buildings and services. Present in British towns were basilicas, theatres, shops, temples, fora and baths (de la Bèdoyére 1992: 23–6), all important vectors and manipulators of disease (McGrath 1992: 16). However, this does not necessarily mean that they were *more* unhealthy than rural areas, or more likely to cause certain diseases (c.f Manchester 1992).

James's recent work which attempted to distinguish between civilian and military areas in Roman Britain has highlighted several key points which are of relevance to this research, especially concerning whether the environmental evidence from military contexts can be used to infer living conditions elsewhere in the urban areas. There is no evidence to suggest that civilians were banned from entering and living in or near fortresses. He suggests that we "must recognise that we are always dealing with a 'soldier-civilian' mix" (2001: 83–4). Therefore, we must assume that women as camp followers and 'wives' of the soldiers were exposed to the same living environment as the men, and had similar or the same access to medical treatment as men.

Bioarchaeological evidence for the living environment

Environmental evidence is our major access point in re-creating a sense of the Roman urban environment, especially as we lack the written sources, available for Rome, which might have described British urban living (see Scobie 1986). Dobney et al.'s review of the environmental evidence from Britain demonstrates that insufficient contexts have been excavated (1999: 18–20) and, as most of the evidence has been retrieved from London and York, we are reliant upon these datasets to understand Romano-British urban environments. Therefore, it is acknowledged in this paper that this provides a biased view of the urban environment. However, unless future research and analysis is undertaken and published, this will not change.

The environmental evidence discussed in this paper uses faunal material, macro and microscopic flora remains, and entomological evidence. These are often used in collaboration with each other, following Kenward and Hall's indicator groups which are defined as "a collection of recordable data of any kind which, when occurring together, can be accepted as evidence of some past state of activity" (1997: 665).

Local environment

The local environment is an important agent in determining the health of any individual. Therefore, unless this is understood, the interpretation of the palaeopathology is limited. In this study, the definition of the local environment follows Evans and O'Connor (1999: 62 & 64). Integrated bioarchaeological data from urban areas has been characterised by an indicator group which has been interpreted to represent areas of rotting organic material composed of domestic refuse, including food remains, faecal material, fleas, lice and woodworm, with the flora indicating disturbed ground (Hall and Kenward 1995: 393).

Figure 1. Reconstruction of Roman urban living.

The data from 1 Poultry in London is particularly important to this study because timber buildings and plots were preserved. This dataset provides one of the most detailed available; however, as London was the capital, the results may be atypical. Data from other areas such as Dorchester or Carlisle provide a wider view and are reviewed by Dobney *et al.* (1999). Environmental samples from 1 Poultry have indicated that the homes had dumps of household rubbish in their yards in which were also kept pigs and chickens. The houses provided shelter for the black rat, which is another vector of disease. Wells were dug into the house yards to provide water for the inhabitants (Rowsome 2000: 30 & 34–5; Jackson 2000: 46); if the rubbish was able to contaminate these sources, the wells would become excellent habitats for fatal diseases such as cholera and dysentery (Roberts and Manchester 1999: 12). The effluent from animals would make the water dangerous, as coliform bacteria may develop which, if ingested can cause gastrointestinal infections (http://www.vh.org/ Patients/ IHB/Peds/ Safety/

DrinkingWater/DrinkingWater.html).   In other examples of living areas, such as Pompeii, latrines were often situated in kitchens (Jackson 2000: 53). This may also have been the case in Britain.

Excavations and finds from both 1 Poultry and Walbrook indicate that industry was not separated from domestic contexts, as people lived close to forges and tanneries, and the run-off from these industries entered the local water supply (Perring and Brigham 2000: 412–4; Jones 1980: 2; Rowsome 2000: 34). This would have exposed people to air pollutants, rotting animal carcasses and poisons.

Internal parasites

The health of the urban communities is also reflected by parasite evidence (see Figure 2); at Poundbury Camp head lice and internal parasites were preserved in the plaster packing; at Carlisle a crab louse was recovered from organic layers; and, at York, deposits contained faecal material infested with whipworm and roundworm (Hall and Kenward 1995: 386; Kenward 1999). The parasites can be used to reflect urban living, where people may be living in a more faecally polluted environment compared to rural areas (Knight 1982: 91)

The preservation of head lice – still attached to hair shafts at Poundbury Camp, can be used to infer that people were also probably suffering from internal parasites, that they had poor personal hygiene, and that some may have been living in cramped conditions which were suitable for the spread of infectious diseases (Rheinhard 1992: 238).

Many individuals from Poundbury Camp with whip- and roundworms recovered from their pelvic regions (Jones 1993: 197–8) also had osseous responses associated iron deficiency (Roberts and Manchester 1999: 165–170). Stuart-Macadam's analysis of iron deficiency at the site suggests

Figure 2. Hair louse preserved on hair shaft from Poundbury Camp

that these anaemic responses may have been caused by the parasite infestations (1991: 103 & 105). However, the creation of an anaemic response can also be produced in order to inhibit the effects of the infestation (Ryan 1997: 51; Weinberg 1992: 135–6; Stuart-Macadam 1991: 105).

Dietary evidence

Diet is crucial in understanding the health of Romano-British urban dwellers, because it played a part in their susceptibility to disease, determined the strength of their bone tissue and, when deficient, left markers on their bones and teeth (Larsen 1999: 61; Brickley 2000: 183–198). Previous studies using bioarchaeological evidence to understand diet have been very successful, for example at Alphen aan den Rijn (Kuijper and Turner 1992). The value of an isotopic approach has been proven at Poundbury Camp, where a study concluded that the diet was dominated to a large extent by marine resources (Richards et al. 1998: 1247–52). Food remains recovered from urban contexts have revealed a very varied diet – plums, sweet/sour cherries, walnuts, celery, wheat, crabs, mussels, garden dormice, dill, fennel, black cumin, eels, pig, cattle, fowl, sheep/goats, anise, wine from southern Gaul, honey, as well as rye, oats and barley (Dobney et al. 1999: 17–18; Davies 1971: 131–2; O'Connor 1988: 116–122; Kenward et al. 1986: 262–3; Hall and Kenward 1995: 404–409; Rowsome 2000: 30 & 36).

The bioarchaeological evidence shows that a wide variety of foodstuffs were available; however, we do not know who had access to a healthy diet, which would have provided the vitamins and minerals needed to avoid metabolic diseases. The incidence of internal parasites may be connected to food acquisition; night soil may have been used as manure and, therefore, any internal parasite eggs in the manure would have entered the food chain, or would have been transferred to agricultural workers if basic hygiene protocols were not followed (Knight 1982: 90, 93).

Palaeopathological evidence

In most skeletal samples, the remains will have been affected by a variety of cultural and taphonomic processes, and are not always reflective of the population from which they are derived (Waldron 1994: 10–250). This is further complicated by the fact that we will never know individual fraility and risk of death, which will determine at what age the person could have become incorporated into the skeletal sample (Wood et al. 1992: 345). Furthermore, within any human skeletal sample, many individuals will not display any pathological changes on their skeleton – something that is known as the 'osteological paradox' (Wood et al. 1992: 353). The key issue of Wood et al.'s argument highlights the view that these individuals are regarded as healthy because there is no change on their skeleton, which may not actually reflect their true health status. 'Frailer' individuals would die before a bone response could develop (1992: 353), therefore masking the presence of a disease which may only be identifiable through aDNA analysis. Many of the 'frailer' individuals who had reached adulthood, would have been individuals who had suffered from stressful episodes in non-adulthood, which resulted in their poor growth and early death (Jantz and Owsley 1984; Saunders and Hoppa 1993; Humphrey 1998; 2000). This has been shown in a palaeopathological and clinical study, which proved that "poor early growth does appear to generally predict decreased adult health" (Clark et al. 1986: 152).

Table 3: Lack of an osseous response

Cemetery	Female	Probable female	Male	Probable Male
Cirencester	10/78 (13%)	5/15 (33%)	36/207 (16%)	3/9 (33%)
Poundbury Camp	4/226 (2%)	–	4/251 (2%)	–
Colchester	33/129 (26%)	8/17 (6%)	49/171 (29%)	3/6 (50%)
Ilchester	2/2 (100%)	5/13 (38%)	–	10/28 (36%)
Chichester	11/12 (92%)	–	14/19 (74%)	3/9 (50%)
London	5/36 (14%)	8/12 (67%)	14/96 (15%)	4/17 (24%)
York	32/42 (76%)	13/21 (76%)	149/311 (48%)	13/21 (62%)

Within the chosen sample of Table 3, the numbers of females in this category are low. This may be due to various factors such as:

1) A lack of urban cemeteries which have been completely defined and excavated;
2) The cultural separation of women from urban cemeteries or their burials in less visible spaces (Davison 2000: 234);
3) Inter-observer error in diagnosis (see Lovell 2000; Buikstra and Ubelaker 1994: 183–4);
4) The use of older methods.

Stress indicators

Selye has defined stress as an anthropological concept, as "the state manifested by a specific syndrome which consists of all the non-specifically induced changes within a biological system. Thus, stress has its own characteristic form and composition but no particular cause" (1957: 54, cited in Bush 1991: 14). In palaeopathology, stress is investigated by using a combination of three osseous changes – cribra orbitalia, periostitis and enamel hypoplastic defects (for complete aetiologies see Aufderheide and Rodriquez-Martin 1998; Larsen 1999: 29–61). The female prevalence can be used to interpret the palaeopathology seen in the infant sample. In this study, the number of females affected was lower than the males (see Table 4), but a chi-squared statistical test (only undertaken on the stress indicators, to test significance at 5% = 9.49, as this had sufficient data necessary for the test) showed that the females levels were as significant, thereby supporting the hypothesis that urban living may have been stressful and often detrimental to health, whatever the sex.

The act of migration from other parts of the Empire or from within Britain may have created stress; women were known to have travelled with the army as wives, such as Sulpicia Lepidina who lived at Vindolanda (Birley 1995: 20). Epigraphic analyses have also shown that women had moved to Britain; a gravestone from Netherby stated that Titullinia Pussitta had originally come from Raetia (Allason-Jones 1989: 64). Isotopic work at Poundbury Camp has shown that two females had probably spent most of their lives in a warmer climate (Richards et al. 1998: 1251).

Table 4: Stress indicators

Cemetery	Periostitis	Cribra Orbitalia	Enamel Hypoplastic Defects
Cirencester	Female 5/78 (6%) Pfemale 2/15 (13%) Male 15/220 (7%)	Female 1/78 (1%) Male 9/220 (4%)	Female 8/78 (10%) Pmale 1/9 (11%)
Poundbury Camp	Female 20/226 (8%) Male 29/251 (12%)	Female 81/292 (27.7%) Data from Stuart-Macadam (1991, 102) Male 1/251 (0.4%)	–
Colchester	Pfemale 2/17 (2%) Male 6/171 (4%) Pmale 1/6 (17%)	Female 7/129 (5%) Male 6/171 (4%)	Female 25/129 (19%) Pfemale 1/17 (1%) Male 30/171 (18%)
London	Female 5/36 (14%) Male 9/96 (9%) Pmale 1/17 (17%)	Female 1/36 (3%) Pfemale 1/12 (8%) Male 3/96 (3%) Pmale 1/17 (6%)	Female 7/36 (19%) Pfemale 5/12 (42%) Male 18/96 (19%) Pmale 2/17 (12%)

Key: Pmale = probable male. Pfemale = probable female.

Allason-Jones' examination of the repercussions of urbanism in Roman Britain used research generated by social geography to good effect in order to "get into the minds of some of the inhabitants of Roman Britain and imagine what they were going through" (2001: 4). In this paper, medical anthropological research has been used to demonstrate the links between a new living environment and the development of disease. It is accepted that modern urban areas have a great deal more 'stress' than the Romano-British; however, trends have been noted with migration to an urban area, and it is considered that these could have been present in Romano-British urban areas – migration frequently results in a change of socio-economic status, poor living conditions and consequently a higher exposure to disease (Ehrlich et al. 1973: 40–44). The nature of urbanism during this period may have had health repercussions, as urban areas have a higher risk of physical and mental morbidity (Harrison 1980: 61). Leatherman has shown that economic and social marginality leads to poor health by increasing exposure to 'insults' (1992: 883). Bogin has shown that migration may cause stress to the individual which would alter their cortisol levels, resulting in a significantly lowered immunity and a statistically significant increase in the frequency of illness, therefore beginning an increased cycle of morbidity (1999: 395).

The low prevalence of stress indicators in the female sample may alternatively show the enhanced immune system of women compared to men, as from birth females tolerate environmental stress better than men. During childhood they can better endure diseases, and are able to withstand infectious diseases and nutritional deficiencies better than males (Ortner 1998: 81; Overfield 1995: 165–170; Stinson 1985). This is due to an evolutionary adaptive mechanism, which increases female immune reactivity so that the hazards of pregnancy, particularly infection, could be coped with (Ortner 1998: 81). It is suggested that this is why there is a lower prevalence of dental enamel hypoplastic defects in the sample.

The females in the sample suffering from cribra orbitalia may represent women within the community who were pregnant, had just given birth, or had had a succession of narrowly spaced births. During pregnancy, maternal iron demands are ignored in preference for the foetus. If the women were iron-deficient before pregnancy, then the iron levels of the foetus will be affected and they will increase their anaemic status (Palkovich 1987: 530; Ryan 1997: 35–60). Females with this change would have sustained a very low intake of iron from their diet, and would only have developed iron-deficiency anaemia after two to three years. This time may have been reduced if they suffered from a heavy parasite load, a chronic infection and/or an inflammatory condition (Stuart-Macadam 1992: 157–90). This provides a connection to the infants with cribra orbitalia and other indicators of anaemia.

It is believed that the interpretation applied to the Cannington population can be used here – that the lesions were acquired in childhood due to hard life conditions and adaptation to the environment (Robeldo et al. 1995: 190–1). However, Stuart-Macadam suggests that adult lesions, although reflecting childhood levels of non-specific infections, do not provide a true picture of the past community's health (1991: 101). It must also be stated that Stuart-Macadam, amongst others, argues that people with low iron levels have lower parasite loads, and that it may be an adaptive response to urbanism (1992: 164–5).

Infectious disease (tuberculosis, non-specific infections and osteomyelitis)

Table 5: Evidence of infectious disease

Cemetery	Infectious disease	Osteomyelitis
London	Female 3/36 (8%) Pfemale 8/12 (67%)	Female 1/36
Cirencester	Female 1/78 (1%) Male 2/220 (1%)	Female 1/78
Colchester	Female 1/129 (1%) Male 1/171 (3%) Pmale 1/6 (17%)	Female 1/129 Male 1/171
Poundbury Camp	Female 4/226 (2%)	Male 1/251

Key: Pmale = probable male. Pfemale = probable female.

It can be seen from Table 5 that infectious disease prevalence was higher in females than in males. This supports Ortner's assertion that women will have higher rates of disease than men, as women will display the chronic and long-term effects of infection, due to their enhanced immune response. The women affected may have had the disease present at the time of conception, when the immune system is lowered in order to stop the foetus being rejected, enabling the disease to spread quicker and shortening the time before an osteological response was created (1998: 81 & 87–88; see earlier discussion on female immune response).

The female way of life may have played a role in the exposure to the agents of these diseases, particularly if women were responsible for the domestic environment, where cooking and sources of disease were closely associated. The low prevalence of infectious diseases, also seen in the sample, reflects individuals who were healthy enough to sustain the infection long enough to develop an osseous response. The high prevalence in London may be the result of the local environment, which elsewhere may not have been so polluted or unhygienic.

The ability of women to sustain a serious infection over a long period can be seen in those who have evidence of osteomyelitis (see Table 5). A woman from London developed a draining abscess on her tibia, caused by pus escaping from the inside of the bone. This abscess would have required care and assistance, because her ability to walk would have been compromised. She would have suffered from fevers, weight loss, her leg would have been massively swollen, and the abscess would have to be tended and kept clean in order to avoid the introduction of more infection (Oxford Concise Dictionary 2000: 472).

Tuberculosis has been identified at Poundbury Camp, in "two or three suspected cases" (Farwell and Molleson 1992: 190), and it is proposed that if a re-evaluation using modern clinical and palaeopathological criteria was applied to the samples (see Redfern 2002), then more cases would be identified (see Santos 1999; Lagier 1999; Rothschild and Rothschild 1999; Baker 1999; Roberts et al. 1998). A re-appraisal of these cases by the author demonstrates that at least one case has the distinct changes associated with tuberculosis (Lagier 1999: 288–290). The transmitter of tuberculosis (human or bovine), can only be identified using bacteriological or genetic methods (Vincent and Perez 1999: 139); therefore, the proposition that tuberculosis may have been transmitted between individuals by the bacilli present in their breath, sputum and excreta (Roberts and Manchester 1999: 137; Vincent and Perez 1999: 140) in the urban area cannot be dismissed (Roberts pers.com).

The evidence from Poundbury Camp needs to be re-assessed using aDNA to determine the strain of tuberculosis, as recent work has shown that human and bovine tuberculosis are separate strains – therefore the human strain did not evolve from bovine tuberculosis (Brosch et al. 2002: 3684–3689).

The connection between tuberculosis and urban environments is well attested (Ortner 1999: 255). Its identification in Romano-British urban areas is important, as it demonstrates that the urban areas had a high population density, unsanitary environment and available modes of transmission in the local environment (Ortner 1999: 255). This relates to the bioarchaeological evidence for the local living environment, which is seen as being unsanitary, with waste being disposed close to living areas. The transmission of the disease to large sections of the population would be facilitated by the communal places available in an urban settlement i.e. baths and markets.

The role of migrants as vectors of tuberculosis transmission in unsanitary urban areas is also an important consideration. Recent aDNA work has shown that tuberculosis was present in Iron Age Dorset, although the aDNA was unable to determine whether the transmitter was bovine or human (Mays and Taylor 2002 pers. comm.), therefore it could have been present / sustained within the Durotrigian community into the Roman period. The rural Romano-British cemetery of Tolpuddle Ball (Dorset) included a man with spinal changes indicative of tuberculosis, and a female with periosteal new bone formation on the visceral surface of her ribs, which is an indicator of tuberculosis (Roberts et al. 1988; Kelley and Micozzi 1984; McKinley 1999a: 167–8 and McKinley 1999b: 5–6). Therefore, it is possible that these individuals may have acted as vectors of disease in Dorchester; they may have been infected in town, or may reflect the community of tuberculosis in rural populations.

Metabolic diseases

Table 6: Evidence of metabolic disease

Cemetery	Female	Male
Poundbury Camp	31/226 (14%)	16/251 (6%)
Colchester	1/129 (1%)	0/220
London	3/36 (8%) Pfemale 1/12 (8%)	10/96 (10%)
York	Pfemale 1/21 (6%)	0/311

Key: Pfemale = probable female.

In Table 6, osseous changes reflective of metabolic diseases in the female sample was due to cribra orbitalia and adult vitamin D deficiency which causes femoral bowing, known as osteomalacia (Brickley 2000: 189). The number of females affected was far higher than in the male sample (see Table 6). Evidence for subadult rickets was found at Poundbury Camp, where a female had bowed tibiae and flattened os coxae (Farwell and Molleson 1993: 184). The role of preferential treatment of males generally within Roman society is well attested elsewhere in the Empire (Adkins and Adkins 1998: 339). However, information for Romano-British society suggests that this was not the case and, as Roman law was interpreted locally (Allason-Jones 1989: 15 & 19), a case could be made to suggest that women had equal access to food, due to the emancipated position of women in Iron Age society (Allason-Jones 1989: 17–29) and therefore, reasons for developing metabolic diseases could have been similar.

As shown in the table, there are clear inter-site differences in the number of females affected by metabolic diseases. The reasons behind this difference may be due to differences in the local environment, in access to food, in access to military health services, and in country of origin, as it is unknown how many females may have had poor metabolic health before their inclusion in British cemeteries.

Trauma

Trauma was recorded in most cemeteries. Many females were reported to have vertebral body fractures; however a precise diagnosis of these fractures was difficult, as underlying factors such as osteoporosis or tuberculosis can cause this trauma (Apley and Solomon 2000: 55–57; see also Merbs 1983: 32–35). Diagnosis was compromised by the lack of radiographic analyses and accurate descriptions, which are necessary in determining an accurate diagnosis (Resnick and Niwayama 1988: 1812–22); therefore these were excluded from the results. The trauma results of Table 7 were dominated by fractures.

The highest prevalence was recorded at Poundbury Camp, which had forty-four females with fractures (see also the study of trauma on this sample by Walker (1997); this is in contrast to York, where only one female had evidence of fracture. Following Judd's analysis of the causes of trauma-related fractures, it is considered that most of the fractures resulted from encounters with the environment or through accidental fall (2000: 64–5; see also Lovell 1997: 161).

Table 7: Evidence of fracture

Cemetery	Female	Male
London	6/36 (17%)	15/96 (15%)
Cirencester	7/78 (9%)	54/220 (25%)
Poundbury Camp	44/226 (18%)	71/251 (28%)
Colchester	7/129 (5%)	16/171 (9%)
Ilchester	Pfemale 2/13 (15%)	Pmale 1/28 (4%)
York	1/42 (2%)	14/311 (5%)

Key: Pmale = probable male. Pfemale = probable female

The healing and treatment of the fractures appears to have been very satisfactory, as only one example of a disability was reported from London (see Figure 6). The disability was caused by an un-united Monteggia fracture, where both the radius and ulna are fractured, (Jurmain 1999: 219). The failure for the radius and ulna to unite could have been the result of inadequate blood supply to the site; metabolic deficiencies of vitamin D and / or C as well as calcium; trapping of soft tissue between the elements; movement of the arm before the callus had set; or due to the unstable nature of the fracture (Lovell 1997: 147). The lack of union in the forearm would have compromised the use of the arm and hand, limiting the range of tasks that she would have been able to undertake.

The conscientiousness in treatment and reduction of the fractures demonstrates a great deal of care especially where women had broken their tibia and fibula or their femur, as these are serious fractures which can lead to disruption of the blood supply therefore interrupting the healing process (Ortner and Putschar 1985: 65). The lack of secondary infection demonstrates that despite the unsanitary nature of some of the living conditions represented in the bioarchaeological record, the women may have received medical treatment (see Baker 2001; Fleming 2000; Jackson 2000; James 2000; Huber and Anderson 1996), and were cared for in a clean local environment with access to a good diet, which would have assisted adequate healing (to combat the cycle between poor nutrition and infection, see Larsen 1999: 88). As Roberts notes, "skeletal remains from cemeteries do not represent individuals who lived cocooned in isolation from their environment" (1991: 238).

Table 8: Evidence of trauma

Cemetery	Female	Male
York	1/42 (2%) Pfemale 1/21 (6%)	2/311 (1%)
London	3/36 (8%) Pfemale 1/12 (8%)	4/96 (4%)
Colchester	1/129 (1%)	1/171 (1%)
Poundbury Camp	4/226 (2%)	6/251 (2%)

Key: Pfemale = probable female.

Table 8 shows that, at Colchester, three women had evidence of blunt force cranial trauma, which may have been the result of inter-personal violence, as two are situated on the occipital, indicating that the woman may have been struck from behind by an 'aggressor'. These fractures can also be easily caused by accidents; consequently I am in agreement with Merbs, who states that "even when damage is convincingly intentional, the actual intent may not be obvious" (1989: 187; see also Jurmain 1999: 230). It cannot be certain whether these fractures were the cause of death in these females, as no scanning electron microscopy analysis was employed to determine whether any healing had taken place before the death of the individual (Roberts 1997).

Primary evidence for surgery using Roman equipment was found at the railway site at York, where a woman had a drilled trepanation on her mastoid process (which is situated behind the ear) (Brothwell 1974). The trepanation may have been employed in order to relieve a middle ear infection (Brothwell 1974: 210; or alternatively see Martin 2000; Roberts and McKinley 2001). There was no evidence of healing or infection, which indicates that the individual did not live long after the operation (Brothwell 1974: 209–10; c.f. Roberts 1997: 132; Rösing and Nerlich 2000). This discovery is important, as it demonstrates the use of Roman medical equipment in Britain, as earlier British examples were made using a scraping technique – a safer method (Larsen 1999: 153; see Verano 2000), which was found on the other example of a trepanation from the Roman period in York (Warwick 1968; Roberts and McKinley 2001). The use of Roman medical equipment suggests that this may have been undertaken by a doctor in the military fort (see Baker 2001; Jackson 2000).

Infant health and its relationship to female health status

Infant health is an important aspect of palaeopathological study as it can be used as a gauge for the health status of the community (Saunders and Barrans 1999: 184; Goodman and Armelagos 1989: 239). The role of maternal health in infant survival is well documented within medical literature (www.vh.org). Schell's work on stress in urban centres (1997) is important in demonstrating these links, especially during the uterine period and where the mother may have been a recent migrant to the area. Schell concludes that the urban environment can create stressors against which culture cannot buffer, as it poses a challenge to survival (i.e. toxic accumulations of materials) and dictates who is exposed to the infectious agents (1997: 67–8). Parents who were living in unsanitary conditions and were exposed to unhygienic materials (i.e. by-products of fulling – the production of cloth and felt, which used urine during manufacture) would subject the infant to a high risk of peri-natal death (Saunders and Barrans 1999: 197).

A large proportion of the infant remains in Table 9 did not display any osseous change. This may have been because they were incompatible with life due to soft tissue defects (see Barnes 1994: 5). However, it is proposed that many may have died from the effects of acute diarrhoea. Today, this remains the main killer for small children in developing countries, accounting for thirty percent of infant deaths (Mata 1983: 15), and was the main cause of death for children under ten in antiquity (Holman 1998: 1).

Table 9: Infants without an osseous response

Cemetery	Data
London	19/36 (76%)
Ilchester	5/6 (83%)
Chichester	1/1 (100%)
Colchester	33/36 (92%)
Poundbury Camp	1/50 (2%)
Cirencester	19/30 (90%)
York	18/18 (100%)

Just as likely in rural as in urban locations, it is prevalent where sanitation and personal hygiene are low, where infants are exposed to contaminated water, to internal parasites and food sources carrying salmonella (Mata 1983: 4–6; Bradley-Sack 1983: 60), and where breast-feeding is not regularly practiced (Saunders and Hoppa 1993: 135), as breast-feeding reduces the risks of contamination from other food sources (Rao and Rajpathak 1992: 1536). Its quality will not be reduced even if the mother has a low health status (Gopalan and Puri 1992: 1080). The risks and agents of morbidity are out of control of the infant, despite having serious consequences for its chances of survival, especially if the mother had succumbed to an infection during pregnancy which could be passed to the foetus, or passed on later during breast-feeding, thereby dramatically reducing the infant's chances of survival (Hall and Peckham 1997: 17).

If we accept that some women with iron deficiency in the sample were new mothers, important implications for infant care can be made. If a mother is anaemic, she will have lower activity levels, attention span and motivation, which will impact upon the level of care given to the infant (Ryan 1997: 50).

Conclusions

The analysis of stress indicators, metabolic and infectious disease, in conjunction with a biocultural approach, strongly suggests that the effects seen on the individuals who were buried in urban cemeteries *may* reflect the urban environment in which they lived. However, until the results have been fully compared with those from rural cemeteries, urbanism itself cannot be proved to be the cause of such stress and disease.

The research has highlighted the differences between male and female health, especially with regards to metabolic and infectious disease and trauma. The focus upon female palaeopathology permits a greater understanding of subadult health, as well as providing links between osteological data and research into medical treatment and its access. The use of a biocultural approach has shown that the interpretation of palaeopathological data cannot be fully undertaken unless all facets of a culture are taken into account and combined to create an integrated and multifaceted analysis of past peoples. Therefore, a true understanding of Roman

Britain cannot be obtained unless the health of the people who helped to create it is integrated into the overall analysis of their archaeological record.

Department of Ancient History and Archaeology,
University of Birmingham.

Acknowledgements

I would like to thank Dr. Charlotte Roberts for all her help with my master's thesis and the writing of this paper; Dr. Simon Esmonde Cleary and Dr. Megan Brickley for their help in writing this paper, as well as the reviewers and editors for their comments and help on this paper; Bill White for his help collating the data from London; Dr. Andrew Millard for his help with the statistics, Mr Graham Norrie for making the slides, Lindsay Allason-Jones for allowing me to use her unpublished paper; Dr. Patricia Baker for her advice concerning army medical practices; Dr. Rebecca Gowland for her discussions of this topic and the Poundbury Camp skeletal material; Dr. Louise Humphrey and Robert Kruszynski at the Natural History Museum; Dr. Simon Mays for allowing me to use his research on tuberculosis; Peter Woodward and the Dorset Archaeological Committee; and Vincent for his line drawings and help with the editing.

Bibliography

Ancient sources
Vitruvius Pollio. (translated by M. H. Morga 1960). *Vitruvius: the ten books on architecture*. New York: Dover Publications.

Modern sources
Ackerknecht, E. H. 1977. Primitive Surgery. In M. H. Logan and E. E. Hunt (eds.) *Health and the Human Condition. Perspectives on Medical Anthropology*. Massachusetts: Duxbury Press. 164–180.
Adkins, L. and Adkins, R. A. 1998. *Handbook to Life in Ancient Rome*. New York: Oxford University Press.
Allason-Jones, L. 1989. *Women in Roman Britain*. London: British Museum Press.
Allason-Jones, L. 2001 unpublished. *Urban Angst in Roman Britain*. Paper presented at 'Roman Working Lives and Urbanization'. Conference held by the Research Centre for Roman Provincial Archaeology at the Department of Archaeology, The University of Durham. 14th July 2001.
Armelagos, G. J., Goodman, A., and Jacobs, K. H. 1977. The ecological perspective in disease. In M. H. Logan and E. E. Hunt (eds.) *Health and the Human Condition. Perspectives on Medical Anthropology*. Massachusetts: Duxbury Press. 71–88.
Apley, A. G. and Solomon, L. 2000. *Concise Systems of Orthopaedics and Fractures*. Second Edition. London: Arnold.
Aufderheide, A. C. and Rodríquez-Martin, C. 1998. *The Cambridge Encyclopedia of Human Paleopathology*. Cambridge: Cambridge University Press.
Baker, B. 1999. Early manifestations of tuberculosis in the skeleton. In G. Pálfi, O. Dutour, J. Deak, and I. Hutás (eds.) *Tuberculosis Past and Present*. Budapest: Golden Book Publisher Ltd. 301–307.
Baker, P. A. 2001. Medicine, Culture and Military Identity. In G. Davies, A. Gardner and K. Lockyear (eds.) *TRAC 2000. Proceedings of the Tenth Annual Theoretical Roman Archaeology Conference London 2000*. Oxford: Oxbow Books. 48–68.
Baker, P. A. and Carr, G. (eds.) 2002. *Practioners, Practices and Patients: New approaches to Medical Archaeology and Anthropology*. Oxford: Oxbow Books.

Barnes, E. 1994. *Developmental Defects of the Axial Skeleton in Paleopathology*. Colorado: University Press of Colorado.

Bédoyère, de la, G. 1992. *English Heritage Book of Roman Towns in Britain*. London: B. T. Batsford Ltd.

Bentley, D. and Pritchard, F. 1982. The Roman Cemetery at St Bartholomew's Hospital. *Transactions of the London and Middlesex Archaeological Society*, 33: 134–182.

Birley, A. 1995. *The People of Roman Britain*. London: B. T. Batsford Ltd.

Bogin, B. 1999 (second edition). *Patterns of Human Growth*. Cambridge Studies in Biological and Evolutionary Anthropology 23. Cambridge: Cambridge University Press.

Bradley-Sack, R. 1983. Bacterial and Parasitic Agents of Acute Diarrhea. In J. A. Bellanti, (ed.) *Acute Diarrhea. Its Nutritional Consequences in Children. Néstle Nutrition Workshop Series Volume 2*. New York: Raven Press. 53–65.

Brickley, M. 2000. The diagnosis of metabolic disease in archaeological bone. In M. Cox and S. Mays (eds.) *Human Osteology in Archaeology and Forensic Science*. London: Greenwich Medical Media Ltd. 183–198.

Brosch, R., Gordon, S. V., Marmiesse, M., Brodin, P., Buchrieser, C., Eiglmeier, K., Garnier, T., Gutierrez, C., Hewinson, G., Kremer, K., Parsons, L. M., Pym, A. S., Samper, S., van Soolingen, D. and Cole, S. 2002. A new evolutionary scenario for the Mycobacterium tuberculosis complex. *Proceedings of the National Academy of Sciences, USA*, 99(6): 3684–3689.

Brothwell, D. R. 1974. Osteological Evidence of the Use of a Surgical Modiolus in a Romano-British Population: An Aspect of Primitive Technology. *Journal of Archaeological Science*, 1: 209–211.

Brothwell, D. R. 1994. On the possibility of urban-rural contrasts in human population palaeobiology. In A. R. Hall, and H. K. Kenward (eds.) Urban-rural connexions: perspectives from environmental archaeology. *Symposia of the Association for Environmental Archaeology No. 12*. Oxford: Oxbow Books. 129–136.

Buikstra, J. E. and Ubelaker, D. H. (eds.) 1994. Standards for Data Collection from Human Skeletal Remains. *Proceedings of a Seminar at The Field Museum of Natural History Organized by Jonathan Haas*. Arkansas: Arkansas Archaeological Survey Research Series No. 44.

Bush, H. and Zvelebil, M. (eds.) 1991. Health in Past Societies: biocultural interpretations of human skeletal remains in archaeological contexts. Oxford: *British Archaeological Reports International Series*, 567.

Bush, H. 1991. Concepts of Health and Stress. In H. Bush and M. Zvelebil (eds.) *Health in Past Societies: biocultural interpretations of human skeletal remains in archaeological contexts*. Oxford: British Archaeological Reports International Series, 567. 11–21.

Clark, G. A., Hall, N. R., Armelagos, G. J., Borkan, G. A., Panjabi, M. M., and Wetzel, F. T. 1986. Poor Growth Prior to Early Childhood: Decreased Health and Life-Span in the Adult. *American Journal of Physical Anthropology*, 70: 145–160.

Davies, R. W. 1971. The Roman Military Diet. *Britannia*, 2: 122–142.

Davison, C. 2000. Gender Imbalance in Romano-British Cemetery Populations. In J. Pearce, M. Millett, & M. Struck (eds.) *Burial, Society and Context in the Roman World*. Oxford: Oxbow Books. 231–237.

Dobney, K, Hall, A. and Kenward, H. 1999. Its all garbage … A review of bioarchaeology in four English colonia towns. In H. Hurst (ed.) *The Coloniae of Roman Britain: New Studies and a review. Papers of the Conference held at Gloucester on 5–6 July, 1997. Journal of Roman Archaeology Supplementary Series. No. 36*. Portsmouth: Oxbow Books. 15–31.

Ehrlich, P. R., Ehrlich, A. H. and Holden, J. P. 1973. *Human Ecology. Problems and Solutions*. United States of America: W.H. Freeman and Company.

Eisenberg, L. 1991. Interpreting measures of community health during the Late Prehistoric period in Middle Tennessee: a biocultural approach. In H. Bush and M. Zvelebil (eds.) *Health in Past Societies: biocultural interpretations of human skeletal remains in archaeological contexts*. Oxford: British Archaeological Reports International Series, 567. 115–128.

Esmonde Cleary, S. 1992. Town and country in Roman Britain? In S. Bassett (ed.) *Death in Towns: urban responses to the dying and the dead, 100–1600*. Leicester: Leicester University Press. 28–41.

Evans, J. and O'Connor, T. 1999. *Environmental Archaeology Principles and Methods*. Stroud: Sutton Publishing Limited.

Everton, R. F. and Rogers, J. 1982. The Human Remains. In P. Leach (ed.) *Ilchester Volume 1. Excavations 1974–1975*. Bristol: Western Archaeological Trust Excavation Monograph No. 3. 263–265.

Farwell, D. E. and Molleson, T. L. 1993. *Excavations at Poundbury. 1966–80 Volume II: The Cemeteries*. Dorchester: Dorset Natural History and Archaeological Society Monograph Series Number 11.

Fleming, R. 2000. *Medicine and the Making of Roman Women. Gender, Nature and Authority from Celsus to Galen*. Oxford: Oxford University Press.

Freeth, C. 2000. Dental Health in British antiquity. In M. Cox and S. Mays (eds.) *Human Osteology in Archaeology and Forensic Science*. London: Greenwich Medical Media. 227–237.

Foden, R. D. 1993. A Report on the Human Skeletal Remains. A. Down and J. Magliton (eds.) *Chichester Excavations VIII*. Chichester: Chichester District Council. 89–94.

Gopalan, S and Puri, R. K. 1992. Breast Feeding and Infant Growth. *Indian Pediatrics*, 29: 1079–1086.

Goodman, A. H., Allen, L. H., Hernandez, G. P., Amador, A., Arriola, L. V., Chávez, A. and Pelto, G. H. 1987. Prevalence and Age at Development of Enamel Hypoplasias in Mexican Children. *American Journal of Physical Anthropology*, 72: 7–19.

Goodman, A. H. and Armelagos, G. J. 1989. Infant and childhood morbidity and mortality risks in archaeological populations. *World Archaeology*, 21(2): 225–243.

Goodman, A. H. and Rose, J. C. 1991. Dental Enamel Hypoplasias as Indicators of Nutritional Status. In M. C. Kelley and C. S. Larsen (eds.) *Advances in Dental Anthropology*. New York: Wiley-Liss. 279–293.

Goodman, A. H. 1993. On the Interpretation of Health From Skeletal Remains. *Current Anthropology*, 34(3): 281–288.

Goodman, A. H. and Song, R.-J. 1999. Sources of variation in estimate ages at formation of linear enamel hypoplasias. In R. D. Hoppa and C. M. Fitzgerald (ed.) *Human growth in the past: studies from bones and teeth*. Cambridge: Cambridge University Press. 210–240.

Hall, A. J. and Peckham, C. S. 1997. Infections in childhood and pregnancy as a cause of adult disease – methods and examples. *British Medical Bulletin,* 53(1): 10–23.

Hall, A. R. and Kenward, H. K. 1995. *Environmental Evidence from the Colonia*. The Archaeology of York. The Environment 14/6. York: Council for British Archaeology.

Harrison, G. A. 1980. Urbanization and Stress. In E. J. Clegg and J. P. Garlick (eds.) *Disease and Urbanization. Volume XX. Symposia of the Society for the Study of Human Biology*. London: Taylor and Francis Ltd. 55–72.

Holman, S. R. 1998. Infant feeding in Roman antiquity: prescription and risk. *Nutrition Today*. http://www.findarticles.com/cf_0/m0841/n3_v33/21181283/print.jhtml

Huber, B. R. and Anderson, R. 1996. Bonesetters and Curers in a Mexican Community: Conceptual Models, Status, and Gender. *Medical Anthropology*, 17: 23–38.

Hughes, C. C. 1977. Medical Care: ethnomedicine. In M. H. Logan and E. E. Hunt (eds.), *Health and the Human Condition. Perspectives on Medical Anthropology*. Massachusetts: Duxbury Press. 150–158.

Humphrey, L. T. 1998. Growth Patterns in the Modern Human Skeleton. *American Journal of Physical Anthropology*, 105: 57–72.

Jackson, R. 2000. *Doctors and Disease in the Roman Empire*. London: British Museum Press.

James, S. 2001. Soldiers and civilians: identity and interaction in Roman Britain. In S. James and M. Millett (eds.) *Britons and Romans: advancing an archaeological agenda*. CBA Research Report 125. York: Council for British Archaeology. 77–89.

Jantz, R. L. and Owsley, D. W. 1984. Long bone growth variation among Arikara skeletal populations. *American Journal of Physical Anthropology,* 63: 13–20.

Jenkins, A. V. C. 1997. Human Remains. In R. J. C., Smith, F., Healy, M. J., Allen, E. L., Morris, I. Barnes, and P. J. Woodward, (eds.) *Excavations Along the Route of the Dorchester By-pass, Dorset, 1986–8*. Wessex Archaeology Report No. 11. Dorchester: Henry Ling. 254–255.

Jones, D. M. 1980. *Excavations at Billingsgate Buildings 'Triangle', Lower Thames Street, 1974*. http://www.lamas.org.uk/abstracts/jones1980.html

Jones, R. F. J. 1993. Parasitiological Investigations. In D. E. Farwell and T. L. Molleson. *Excavations at Poundbury 1966–80, Volume II: The Cemeteries*. Dorchester: Dorset Natural History and Archaeological Society Monograph Series Number 11. 197–8.

Judd, M. A. 2000. *Trauma and Interpersonal Violence in Ancient Nubia during the Kerma Period (ca. 2500–1500 BC)*. University of Alberta: Canada. PhD Dissertation.

Jurmain, R. 1999. *Stories from the Skeleton. Behavioral Reconstruction in Human Osteology*. New York: Gordon and Breach Publishers.

Keily, F. 1988. *Skeleton Report. 13 Haydon Street*. Unpublished: Museum of London Archaeology Service.

Kelley, M. A. and Micozzi, M. S. 1984. Rib lesions in chronic pulmonary tuberculosis. *American Journal of Physical Anthropology*, 65: 381–386.

Kenward, H., Hall, A. R. and Jones, A. K. G. 1986. *Environmental Evidence from a Roman Well and Anglian Pits in the Legionary Fortress*. The Archaeology of York. The Past Environment of York 14/5. York, Council for British Archaeology.

Kenward, H. and Hall, A. 1997. Enhancing bioarchaeological interpretation using indicator groups: stable manure as a paradigm. *Journal of Archaeological Science*. 24: 663–673.

Kenward, H. 1999. Pubic Lice (*Pthirus pubis* L.) were present in Roman and Medieval Britain. *Antiquity*, 73: 911–15.

Knight, R. 1982. *Parasitic Disease in Man*. Edinburgh: Churchill Livingstone Medical Texts.

Kuijper, W. J. and Turner, H. 1992. Diet of a Roman centurion at Alphen aan den Rijn, The Netherlands, in the first century AD. *Review of Palaeobotany and Palynology*, 73: 187–204.

Lagier, R. 1999. Paleopathological diagnosis of skeletal tuberculosis. In G. Pálfi, O. Dutour, J. Deak, and I. Hutás (eds.) *Tuberculosis Past and Present*. Budapest: Golden Book Publisher Ltd. 285–290.

Larsen, C. S. 1999. *Bioarchaeology. Intepreting behaviour from the human skeleton*. Cambridge: Cambridge University Press.

Leatherman, T. L. 1992. Illness as Lifestyle Change. In R. Huss-Ashmore, J. Schall and M, Hediger (eds.) Health and Lifestyle Change. Philadelphia: *MASCA Research Papers in Science and Archaeology*, 9:13–22.

Lee, F. date unknown, unpublished. *The Human Skeletal Assemblage from Hooper Street, London*. Unpublished Report: Museum of London Archaeological Service Archive.

Lukacs, J. R., Nelson, G. C. and Walimbe, S. R. 2001. Enamel Hypoplasia and Childhood Stress in Prehistory: New Data from India and Southwest Asia. *Journal of Archaeological Science*, 28: 1159–1169.

Lovell, N. C. 1997. Trauma Analysis in Paleopathology. *Yearbook of Physical Anthropology*, 40: 139–170.

Lovell, N. C. 2000. Paleopathological Description and Diagnosis. In M. A. Katzenberg and S. R. Saunders (eds.) *Biological Anthropology of the Human Skeleton*. New York: Wiley-Liss Inc. 217–248.

Martin, G. 2000 unpublished. Why trepan? Answers from history and anthropology. In *International Colloquium on Cranial Trepanation in Human History, University of Birmingham 7th–9th April 2000*.

Mata, L. 1983. An Overview. In J. A. Bellanti (ed.) *Acute Diarrhea. Its Nutritional Consequences in Children*. Nestlé Nutrition Workshop Series Volume 2. New York: Raven Press. 3–22.

Manchester, K. 1992. The palaeopathology of urban infections. In S. Bassett (ed.) *Death in Towns: urban responses to the dying and the dead, 100–1600*. Leicester: Leicester University Press. 8–14.

Mays, S. and Taylor, G. M. (forthcoming). A first prehistoric case of tuberculosis from Britain.

McElroy, A. and Townsend, P. K. 1996. *Medical Anthropology in Ecological Perspective*. Boulder Colorado: Westview Press.

McGrath, J. W. 1992. Behavioral Change and the Evolution of Human Host-Pathogen Systems. In R. Huss-Ashmore, J. Schall, and M. Hediger (eds.) Health and Lifestyle Change. Philadelphia: *MASCA Research Papers in Science and Archaeology*, 9:13–22.

McKinley, J. 1999a. Human Bone from Tolpuddle Ball. In C. M. Hearne and V. Birbeck (eds.) *A35 Tolpuddle to Puddletown Bypass DBFO, Dorset, 1996–8*. Trowbridge: Trust for Wessex Archaeology. 150–172.

McKinley, J. 1999b. *A35 Tolpuddle Ball Cemetery (W2405.17) Human Bone Archive Report*. Unpublished: Dorchester County Museum.

McKinley, J. 2000. The Analysis of Cremated Bone. In M. Cox and S. Mays (eds.) *Human Osteology in Archaeology and Forensic Science*. London: Greenwich Medical Media Ltd. 403–421.

Merbs, C. F. 1983. Patterns of Activity-Induced Pathology in a Canadian Inuit Population. *Archaeological Survey of Canada Paper No. 119*. Ottowa: National Museums of Canada.

Merbs, C. F. 1989. Trauma. In M. Y. Isçan and K. A. R. Kennedy (eds.) *Reconstruction of Life from the Skeleton*. New York: Alan R. Liss. 161–189.

O'Connor, T. P. 1988. *Bones from the General Accident Site, Tanner Row*. The Archaeology of York. The Animal Bones. York Archaeological Trust 15/2. York: Council for British Archaeology.

Ortner, D. J. and Putschar, W. G. J. 1985. *Identification of Pathological Conditions in Human Skeletal Remains*. Smithsonian Contributions to Anthropology. Number 28. Washington D.C.: Smithsonian Institution Press.

Ortner, D. J. 1992. Skeletal Pathology. Probabilities, Possibilities and Impossibilities. In J. W. Verano and D. H. Ubelaker (eds.) *Disease and Demography in the Americas*. Washington DC: Smithsonian Institution Press. 5–13.

Ortner, D. J., Tuross, N. and Stix, A. I. 1992. New Approaches to the Study of Disease in Archaeological New World Populations. *Human Biology*, 64.3: 337–360.

Ortner, D. J. 1998. Male-female immune reactivity and its implications for interpreting evidence in human skeletal paleopathology. In A. L. Grauer and P. Stuart-Macadam (eds.) *Sex and Gender in Paleopathological Perspective*. Cambridge: Cambridge University Press. 79–92.

Ortner, D. J. 1999. Paleopathology: Implications for the history and evolution of tuberculosis. In G. M. Pálfi, O. Dutour, J. Deák and I. Hutás (eds.) *Tuberculosis Past and Present*. Budapest: Golden Book Publisher Ltd. 255–261.

Overfield, T. 1995. *Biologic Variation in Health and Illness. Race, Age, and Sex Differences. Second Edition*. New York: C.R.C. Press.

Palkovich, A. M. 1987. Endemic Disease Patterns in Paleopathology: Porotic Hyperstosis. *American Journal of Physical Anthropology*, 74: 527–537.

Perring, D. and Brigham, T. 2000. Londinium and its Hinterland: The Roman Period. In M. Kendall (ed.) *The archaeology of Greater London. An assessment of archaeological evidence for human presence in the area now covered by Greater London*. Suffolk: MoLAS Monograph, Museum of London. 120–170.

Pinter-Bellows, S. 1995. The Human Bone. In N. Crummy, P. Crummy and C. Crossans (eds.) *Colchester Archaeological Report 9: Excavations of Roman and later cemeteries, churches and monastic sites in Colchester, 1971–88*. Colchester: Colchester Archaeological Trust Ltd. 61–92.

Polunin, I. 1977. The Body as Indicator of Disease. In Blacking, J. (ed.), *The Anthropology of the Body*. London: Academic Press. 85–98.

Ramm, H. G. 1957. Roman Burials from Castle Yard, York. *Yorkshire Archaeological Journal*, 39: 400–413.

Rao, S. and Rajpathak, V. 1992. Breastfeeding and Weaning Practices in Relation to Nutritional Status of Infant. *Indian Pediatrics*, 29: 1533–1539.

Redfern, R. C. 2002 unpublished. *A re-evaluation of the Poundbury Camp human remains: a palaeopathological analysis*. Personal notes and data from PhD thesis 'A biocultural analysis of health in Dorset from the Iron Age to the post-Roman period'. University of Birmingham.

Resnick, G. A. and Niwayama, G. 1988. *Diagnosis of Bone and Joint Disorders. 3ʳᵈ Edition*. London: W. B. Saunders.

Rheinhard, K. J. 1992. Parasitology as an interpretative tool in archaeology. *American Antiquity*, 57.2: 231–245.

Richards, M. P., Hedges, R. E. M., Molleson, T. L. and Vogel, J. C. 1998. Stable Isotope Analysis Reveals Variations in Human Diet at the Poundbury Camp Cemetery Site. *Journal of Archaeological Science*, 25: 1427–1525.

Roberts, C. 1991. Trauma and treatment in the British Isles in the historic period: a design for a multidisciplinary research. In D. J. Ortner and A. C. Aufderheide (eds.) *Human Paleopathology: Current Syntheses and Future Options*. Washington: Smithsonian Institution Press. 225–40.

Roberts, C. 1997. Forensic anthropology 2: Positive identification of the individual; cause and manner of death. In J. R. Hunter, C. Roberts, and A. Martin (ed.) *Studies in Crime: An Introduction to Forensic Archaeology*. London: Routledge. 122–138.

Roberts, C. A., Boylston, A., Buckley, L. Chamberlain, A. C. and Murphy, E. M. 1998. Rib lesions and tuberculosis: the palaeopathological evidence. *Tubercle and Lung Disease*, 79(1): 55–60.

Roberts, C. A. and Manchester, K. 1999. *The Archaeology of Disease. Second Edition*. Ithaca: Cornell University Press.

Roberts, C. A. 2000. Did they take sugar? The use of skeletal evidence in the study of disability in past populations. In Hubert, J. (ed.), *Madness, Disability and Social Exclusion. The archaeology and anthropology of 'difference'*. London: Routledge. 46–59.

Roberts, C. A. and McKinley, J. 2001 unpublished. *Review of trepanations in British antiquity focusing on funerary context to explain their occurrence*.

Robeldo, B., Trancho, G. J. and Brothwell, D. 1995. Cribra Orbitalia: Health Indicator in the Late Roman Population of Cannington (Somerset, Great Britain). *Journal of Paleopathology*, 7(3): 185–193.

Rogers, J. 1997. Human Remains. In R. J. C., Smith, F., Healy, M. J., Allen, E. L., Morris, I. Barnes, and P. J. Woodward, (eds.) *Excavations Along the Route of the Dorchester By-pass, Dorset, 1986–8*. Wessex Archaeology Report No. 11. Dorchester: Henry Ling. 154–157.

Rothschild, B. and Rothschild, C. 1999. Evolution of osseous/radiologic signs of tuberculosis. In G. M. Pálfi, O. Dutour, J. Deák and I. Hutás (eds.) *Tuberculosis Past and Present*. Budapest: Golden Book Publisher Ltd. 293–298.

Rösing, F. and Nerlich, A. 2000 unpublished. The pathology of trepanation: indications, healing and dry bone appearance in modern cases. In *International Colloquium on Cranial Trepanation in Human History, University of Birmingham 7th–9th April 2000*.

Rowsome, P. 2000. *Heart of the City: Roman, medieval and modern London revealed by archaeology at 1 Poultry*. London: English Heritage, Museum of London Archaeology Service.

Ryan, A. S. 1997. Iron-Deficiency Anemia in Infant Development: Implications for Growth, Cognitive Development, Resistance to Infection, and Iron Supplementation. *Yearbook of Physical Anthropology*, 40: 25–62.

Salway, P. 1985. Geography and the growth of towns, with special reference to Britain. In F. Grew and B. Hobley (eds.) *Roman urban topography in Britain and the western Empire. Proceedings of the third conference on urban archaeology organized jointly by the CBA and the Department of Urban Archaeology of the Museum of London*. Research Report 59. The Council for British Archaeology. 67–73.

Santos, A. L. 1999. TB Files: new hospital data (1910–1936) on the Coimbra Identified Skeletal Collection. In G. M. Pálfi, O. Dutour, J. Deák and I. Hutás (eds.) *Tuberculosis Past and Present*. Budapest: Golden Book Publisher Ltd. 127–134.

Sargent, C. F. and Johnson, T. (eds.) 1996. *Medical anthropology. Contemporary theory and method*. London: Praeger.

Saunders, S. R. and Barrans, L. 1999. What can be done about the infant category in skeletal samples? In R. D. Hoppa and C. M. Fitzgerald (eds.) *Human growth in the past: studies from bones and teeth*. Cambridge: Cambridge University Press. 183–209.

Saunders, S. R. and Hoppa, R. D. 1993. Growth Deficit in Survivors and Non-Survivors: Biological Mortality Bias in Subadult Skeletal Samples. *Yearbook of Physical Anthropology*, 36: 127–151.

Schell, L. M. 1997. Culture as a Stressor: A Revised Model of Biocultural Interaction. *American Journal of Physical Anthropology*, 102: 67–77.

Scheuer, L. and Black, S. 2000. *Developmental Juvenile Osteology*. London: Academic Press.

Scobie, A. 1986. Slums, Sanitation, and Mortality in the Roman World. *Klio*, 68(2): 399–433.

Selye, H. 1957. *The Stress of Life*. London: Longmans Green and Co.

Stinson, S. 1985. Sex Differences in Environmental Sensitivity During Growth and Development. *Yearbook of Physical Anthropology*, 28: 123–147.

Storey, R. 1992. Preindustrial Urban Lifestyle and Health. In R. Huss-Ashmore, J. Schall and M, Hediger (eds.) Health and Lifestyle Change. Philadelphia: *MASCA Research Papers in Science and Archaeology*, 9: 33–42.

Stuart-Macadam, P. 1991. Anemia in Roman Britain: Poundbury Camp. In H. Bush and M. Zvelebil (eds.) *Health in Past Societies: biocultural interpretations of human skeletal remains in archaeological contexts*. Oxford: British Archaeological Reports International Series, 567: 101–113.

Stuart-Macadam, P. 1992. Anemia in Past Human Populations. In P. Stuart-Macadam and S. Kent (eds.) *Diet, Demography, and Disease. Changing Perspective on Anemia*. New York: Aldine de Gruyter. 151–170.

Verano, J. W. 2000 unpublished. Trepanation in prehistoric South America: geographic and temporal trends over 2000 years. In *International Colloquium on Cranial Trepanation in Human History, University of Birmingham 7ᵗʰ–9ᵗʰ April 2000*.

Vincent, V. and Perez, G. M. C. 1999. The agent of tuberculosis. In G. M. Pálfi, O. Dutour, J. Deák and I. Hutás (eds.) *Tuberculosis Past and Present*. Budapest: Golden Book Publisher Ltd. 139–143.

Waldron, T. 1983. *The Human Bones from 9 St Clare Street*. Unpublished: Museum of London Archaeological Service.

Waldron, T. 1984. *The Human Bones from West Tenter Street . Part 1: The Inhumations*. Unpublished: Museum of London Archaeological Service.

Waldron, T. 1985. *The Three Lords. Human Bone Report*. Unpublished: Museum of London Archaeological Service.

Waldron, T. 1989. The effects of urbanism on human health: the evidence from skeletal remains. In D. Serjeanston and T. Waldron (eds.) *Diet and Crafts in Towns. The evidence of animal remains from the Roman to the Post-Medieval periods*. Oxford: British Archaeological Reports British Series, 199: 55–73.

Waldron, T. 1994. *Counting the Dead. The Epidemiology of Skeletal Populations*. Chichester: Wiley-Liss.

Walker, P. L. 1997. Wife Beating, Boxing, and Broken Noses: Skeletal Evidence for the Cultural Patterning of Violence. In D. L. Martin and D. W. Frayer (eds.) *Troubled Times. Violence and Warfare in the Past. War and Society Volume 3*. India: Gordon and Breach Publishers. 145–180.

Warwick, R. A. 1968. Report on the Skeletal Remains. In L. P. Wenham (ed.) *The Romano-British Cemetery at Trentholme Drive, York*. London: Her Majesty's Stationary Office. Ministry of Public Buildings and Works Archaeological Reports. No 5. 129–145.

Wells, C. 1982. The Human Burials. In A. McWhirr, L. Viner and C. Wells (eds.) *Cirencester Excavations II. Romano-British Cemeteries at Cirencester*. Cirencester: Cirencester Excavation Committee. 135–202.

Weinberg, E. D. 1992. Iron Withholding in Prevention of Disease. In P. Stuart-Macadam and S. Kent (eds.) *Diet, Demography, and Disease. Changing Perspectives on Anemia*. New York: Aldine de Gruyter. 105–150.

White, B. 2000. The Human Remains. In A. McKinder (ed.) *A Romano-British cemetery on Watling Street. Excavations at 165 Great Dover Street, Southwark, London*. London: Museum of London Archaeological Service. 33–49 and 63–4.

Wood, J. W., Milner, G. R., Harpending, H. C. and Weiss, K. M. 1992. The osteological paradox: problems of inferring prehistoric health from skeletal samples. *Current Anthropology*, 33: 343–58.

Websites

http://www.vh.org.com
http://www.vh.org/Patients/IHB/Peds/Safety/DrinkingWater/DrinkingWater.html
http://www.vh.org/Providers/ClinRef/FPHandbook/Chapter18/03–18.html

Appendix of sites used in this study

London – St Bartholomew's Hospital (Bentley and Pritchard 1982), West Tenter Street (Waldron 1984), Watling Street (White 2000), Hooper Street (Lee date unknown), The Three Lords (Waldron 1985), St Clare's Street (Waldron 1983) and Haydon Street (Keily 1988).

Dorchester – Poundbury Camp (Farwell and Molleson 1993)

York – Castle Yard (Ramm 1957) and Trentholme Drive (Warwick 1968)

Colchester – Butt Road Site (Pinter-Bellows 1995)

Chichester – St Pancras Cemetery and Theological College (Foden 1993)

Ilchester – Little Spittle and Townsend Close (Everton and Rogers 1982), and

Cirencester – North and South of the Fosse Way (Wells 1982).